THE PRACTICE OF CHILD PROTECTION
AUSTRALIAN APPROACHES

THE PRACTICE OF CHILD PROTECTION
AUSTRALIAN APPROACHES

GILLIAN CALVERT, ADRIAN FORD
AND PATRICK PARKINSON, EDITORS

© 1992 by Gillian Calvert, Adrian Ford and
Patrick Parkinson (eds)

This book is copyright. Apart from any fair dealing for the purposes of study, research, criticism, review, or as otherwise permitted under the Copyright Act, no part may be reproduced by any process without written permission. Inquiries should be made to the publisher.

Typeset, printed & bound by
Southwood Press Pty Limited
80–92 Chapel Street, Marrickville, NSW

For the publisher
Hale & Iremonger Pty Limited
GPO Box 2552, Sydney, NSW

National Library of Australia Cataloguing-in-publication entry

The Practice of child protection: Australian approaches.

Bibliography.
Includes index.
ISBN 0 86806 492 0.
ISBN 0 86806 493 9 (pbk.).

1. Social case work with children — Australia. 2. Abused children — Services for — Australia. 3. Child abuse — Australia — Prevention. 4. Children — Legal status, laws, etc. — Australia. I. Calvert, Gillian. II. Ford, Adrian. III. Parkinson, Patrick.

362.7680994

Contents

	Contributors	7
	Introduction *Gillian Calvert, Adrian Ford and Patrick Parkinson*	11

ABORIGINAL ISSUES
1	Aboriginal Child Protection *Brian Butler*	14

PREVENTION
2	Using Mass Media Campaigns to Prevent Child Sexual Assault in New South Wales *Gillian Calvert*	23
3	Education and Child Protection *Catherine Laws*	41
4	Effective Work with Vulnerable Families: The Experience of the Alys Keys Family Care Demonstration Project, 1986-89 *Wendy O'Brien*	53

CHILDREN IN THE LEGAL SYSTEM
5	The Competence of Child Witnesses *Kay Bussey*	69
6	Legal Intervention in Parent-Child Conflicts: The Emergence of No-Fault 'Divorce' in Child Welfare Law *Patrick Parkinson*	86

TEAMWORK AND DECISION MAKING IN CHILD PROTECTION

7 Case Conferences and Decision Making in Child Protection 101
   Bruce Lord

8 Practice Insights as Revealed by Child Death Inquiries
   in Victoria and Overseas 122
   Penny Armytage and Carol Reeves

9 The Management of Polarisation in Munchausen by Proxy 141
   Helen Freeland and Sue Foley

10 The Abuse of Young Children in Day Care 154
   Suzette Booth and Andrew Horowitz

11 Group Sexual Abuse of Children 163
   Robyn Lamb, Rhonda Mangan, Gay Pincus and Bev Turner

CHILDREN'S RIGHTS, ADULTS' RESPONSIBILITIES

12 Rights and Advocacy: A Framework for Child
   Protection Services 174
   Greg Smith

   Bibliography 193
   Index 207

Contributors

PENNY ARMYTAGE currently holds the position of Director, Staff Development Branch, Community Services Victoria. She has ten years of experience in the child protection field in direct client services and in supervisory and management capacities in both the government and non-government sector. She obtained her Social Work degree from Phillip Institute of Technology in 1976.

SUZETTE BOOTH joined the Child Protection Unit, The Children's Hospital, Camperdown as staff paediatrician in 1987 and became Head of the Child Protection Unit in 1990. She had previous experience in child protection through her training and post-graduate years on a part-time basis while also working with developmentally handicapped children. Currently she is the New South Wales (NSW) Government's representative on the National Child Protection Council.

KAY BUSSEY gained her Ph.D in child psychology from the University of Queensland. In addition to having published numerous articles on children's social development she is the author with David Perry of *Social Development*. She has been a visiting scholar at Stanford University as well as the recipient of a Fulbright Fellowship and an Early Career Award from the Australian Psychological Society. Currently she is a senior lecturer in child psychology at Macquarie University.

BRIAN BUTLER is Chairman of the Secretariat of the National Aboriginal and Islander Child Care Agency (SNAICC).

GILLIAN CALVERT lectures in welfare policy and management in the School of Social Work at the University of NSW. Prior to this she was Executive Officer for the NSW Child Protection Council where she pioneered many reforms to NSW's child protection system. She has also worked as a family therapist. Her research interests are child abuse prevention and management of human service organisations. Currently she is a community member on the National Child Protection Council.

SUE FOLEY is a social worker who is Manager of the Child and Family Services Program at Care Force in Sydney. She has worked with child protection services since 1973 in hospitals, child health centres and the NSW Department of Community Services. She has a strong commitment to helping child welfare professionals serve the community, and children in particular, efficiently and effectively.

ADRIAN FORD is Director of Scarba Family Centre (Benevolent Society of NSW) which is a service working to promote change among families where there is abuse and neglect. Previously he was Deputy Head of the Child Protection Unit at The Children's Hospital, Camperdown. Adrian chaired the 1990 Australian Child Protection Conference Committee and is a community representative on the NSW Child Protection Council.

HELEN FREELAND has a social work background and child protection experience in two states of Australia where she has worked as a casework supervisor and senior manager. She is presently General Manager, Individual, Children and Family Services with the Department of Community Services, Tasmania, with responsibility for child protection services in the state.

ANDREW HOROWITZ has eight years experience in child protection work and is currently Deputy Head of the Child Protection Unit at The Children's Hospital, Camperdown, Sydney. Prior to this he worked for the NSW Department of Community Services.

ROBYN LAMB is Senior Social Worker at The Children's Hospital, Camperdown. She has worked with abused children and their families for the past ten years and has provided training to many professional staff in the area of child abuse. She was the Deputy Head of the Child Protection Unit at The Children's Hospital, Camperdown for a period of time. Currently she is developing a comprehensive treatment program including both individual and group work for sexually abused children.

CATHERINE LAWS has taught in several schools, working with students presenting with behaviour problems. She has also been principal of two schools, one in a residential unit, the other in a juvenile detention centre. Catherine was Senior Policy Officer (Child Protection) for the NSW Department of School Education and represented the department on the NSW Child Protection Council. She was responsible for issues relating to mandatory notification by teachers and to the introduction of a child protection curriculum throughout NSW.

BRUCE LORD is Social Worker-in-Charge at The Children's Hospital, Camperdown. His professional background is in children's welfare, protective services and hospital based social work with children and adolescents. He has extensive experience in case assessment and case planning particularly in relation to physical abuse and neglect. He holds a Master of Social Work degree from the University of New South Wales.

RHONDA MANGAN is a social worker who has worked in a number of child protection assessment and treatment settings over the last six years. She is currently employed as a Team Leader, Client Services at Scarba Family Centre (Benevolent Society of NSW) supervising a multi-disciplinary outreach team which focuses on the treatment of child abuse and neglect.

WENDY O'BRIEN is a social worker with twenty years experience in the public welfare area, covering the fields of child abuse prevention, family support, protective services, community services, foster care, mental health and corrective services.

PATRICK PARKINSON is a senior lecturer in Law at the University of Sydney where he lectures in family law and child protection. He is the author of a number of articles on child sexual abuse allegations in custody and access disputes, children's evidence, and the legal rights of adolescents. He is a member of the Legal Committee of the NSW Child Protection Council.

GAY PINCUS is Senior Social Worker in Paediatrics at Prince of Wales Children's Hospital. She has worked for twenty years with children and families in a variety of settings. More recently she worked for six years in the Child Protection Unit at The Children's Hospital, Camperdown. She has presented and published a number of papers on child protection.

CAROL REEVES is Manager, Family, Youth and Children's Services in the Southern Metropolitan region of Community Services Victoria. She has over 10 years of experience in the child protection field in direct service, supervisory and management capacities.

GREG SMITH is a social worker who has been involved in a range of roles with Community Services Victoria's child protection services. These have included streetwork, client advocacy within secure facilities, program development and management. Greg has also a Bachelor of Science (Hons) degree and worked for several years in the area of conservation.

BEV TURNER is a Registrar in Psychiatry. Prior to this she worked as a medical officer in the Child Protection Unit at The Children's Hospital, Camperdown for six years. She has been involved in educational programs and community training for medical and non-medical staff. On completion of her Registrar training she will specialise in Child and Family Psychiatry.

Introduction

This book takes the view that as professionals we continually need to examine ways that children can be protected from abuse and neglect, and that child protection is a responsibility both of professionals and of the wider community. The focus of the book is upon seeking ways to make children safe in the community. In this sense it has a practical concern. Other books deal well with issues of causality, diagnosis and the prevalence of child abuse and neglect, and can act as useful introductions to the work of child protection. Our aim in this book is not to duplicate those works, but to review our existing practices and to endeavour to share the insights of those involved in child protection work in Australia. Together, as professionals involved in this important work, we can seek to improve our responses in aiding children at risk of abuse and neglect.

The chapters in this volume are a collection of papers which were presented at the Australian Child Protection Conference held at Macquarie University, Sydney in April 1990. The conference was sponsored by the NSW Child Protection Council. This was the first national conference held in Australia since 1981 and brought together practitioners and academics of many disciplines, and other members of the community who were seeking solutions that took account of the Australian context. From this context, practices have emerged which are uniquely Australian but which could also inform child protection work overseas.

Developments in the past twenty years have placed child abuse and neglect on the social and public agenda in a way not previously seen.

Australia, like other countries, began to acknowledge the existence and extent of the physical abuse of children during the 1960s and 1970s and this culminated in the introduction of mandatory reporting laws in a number of Australian states. Along with this came the establishment of a few specialist workers and agencies to deal with the problem of child abuse and neglect. In the 1980s child sexual assault became the major focus of public attention resulting in significant legal changes, service development and procedural reform.

More recently in Australia there has been increased public awareness of the complexity of the problem of child abuse and neglect and the complexity of the responses it requires. Attention has focused on child sexual assault in group care and on the more unusual forms of child abuse such as Munchausen by Proxy. There has been an increased concern by the professional community to understand what prevents child abuse, and how best to respond to it when it does occur. The long term nature of the problem and its apparent intractability has led to a recognition that we have to search for sophisticated responses which involve a range of activities and support programmes across the community in order to protect children and to bring about change in their families. Many of the issues involved in this are taken up within this volume.

This volume emphasises the importance of the practitioner's view, in whatever is his or her discipline, and also the importance of the views of the recipients of the services. It includes the reflections of those teaching in Australian universities as well as drawing upon the practical experience and wisdom of those working in the field in a number of different States. It shares the ideas of those working in child protection, reflects on them and suggests lessons that can be learnt from their experiences. At the same time it challenges our current practices and priorities and explores new areas of practice.

The volume does not attempt to represent the breadth of work in all Australian states and territories. Rather it highlights many current issues of importance in Australia, and searches for new solutions, as well as exploring selected issues in greater depth. It attempts to convey the complexity of child protection practice in Australia and it explores ways that abuse can be prevented while respecting the rights of both children and their caregivers within families.

Aboriginal Issues

It is fitting that a book on Australian approaches to child protection should begin with a chapter on Aboriginal issues. Developing sound policies for the future involves a clear perception of past mistakes. In regard to the Aboriginal population, child welfare authorities have been guilty of more than mere 'mistakes'. As Brian Butler notes in his chapter, child welfare laws were abused in pursuit of political objectives which caused enormous suffering to aboriginal families. It is one of the most shameful chapters in Australian history. The deep scars which this policy left, still remain.

In recent years, there has been an increasing sensitivity to the needs of Aboriginal communities. Laws reflect a policy that Aboriginal children will be placed with Aboriginal families wherever possible; there has been an awareness that child protection authorities need to understand and respect the values of Aboriginal societies; and it is realised that there is an ever-present danger of imposing Western values inappropriately in the assessment of child protection cases.

Much remains to be done. Aboriginal people focus our attention on the broad issues of child welfare policy in a multicultural society. We have repented of the use of child welfare laws as instruments of deliberate cultural oppression. The question remains whether our policies and methods still inappropriately reflect the values and practices of the dominant culture.

1
Aboriginal Child Protection

Brian Butler[*]

In 1990, the Secretariat for National Aboriginal and Islander Child Care (SNAICC) with the assistance of the Brotherhood of St Laurence, launched a report entitled *Aboriginal Child Poverty* (Choo, 1990). It is important because it outlines the experiences of our children: what it is like to be Aboriginal, poor and growing up in Australian society. I mention it because I want to paint a picture for you that will set the context of this paper regarding the notion of child protection in our community. Child protection for us is not just a matter of identifying physical or emotional abuse or the neglect of an individual child; it is more a matter of the improvement of the conditions of life of all our people so that they are then better able to care for themselves and their children. In the course of seeking this overall improvement, we have to help individual children and their families to cope with their lives as they currently find them.

Child protection is a relatively new concept for Aboriginal people. In the days before the invasion and occupation of our island continent by the Europeans, we had no need for services such as the ones we currently provide. Then we were able to rear our children as our people had for thousands of years. We had our system of education and socialisation that was unique and particularly suited to the environment we lived in. Our children were generally healthy, fed on

---

[*] This paper was presented at the Australian Child Protection Conference in 1990. It was prepared by Nigel D'Souza, Executive Officer of SNAICC, in collaboration with member Aboriginal and Islander Child Care Agencies. It represents the views of SNAICC, based on ten years of its existence.

the abundance of indigenous foods and were spiritually linked with the land. Our system of kinship was based on the idea of collective responsibility of our clan or tribes. The responsibility for the upbringing of children was spread widely in the extended family rather than just with the natural parents. Whatever problems the tribe or family encountered were dealt with according to customs and laws based on precedents considerably older than British common law.

The world changed for my people when Europeans arrived in this land in 1788. Many other peoples had passed through or visited our shores without much change to our lifestyle before this, but British colonisation was both speedy and brutal. Since the invasion, our folklore has been dominated by stories of atrocities and injustices. Our tribes and their structures, except for those which had around them the walls of remote areas to protect them, were virtually destroyed. Our languages and culture were considered to be dangerous and subversive and were forbidden. Our men and women were put in chains and enslaved. Our children were taken away, making it even harder for us to pass on our language and cultural heritage to them. Tribes were herded together without regard for their relationships with each other.

It has been said that we did not have concepts of ownership. This of course is not true. Our concepts of ownership of land were collective and carried with them strong obligations to maintain and look after it. Each tribe had its precisely defined area on which others could not trespass without adhering to strict protocol. Our children were brought up to be the guardians of the land we had inherited from our ancestors. They were educated about their complex kinship structure which was tied up with rights, duties and obligations towards the land and the people. All this that had taken thousands of years to grow was rudely, violently and irrevocably interrupted in 1788. Our land was taken away for agriculture and mining. The invaders introduced foreign flora and fauna that further destroyed our traditional forms of subsistence. We were subjected to a deliberate policy to kill us off.

Today we stand before you battered and bruised but as a constant reminder to you about the sins of your forefathers. We are still here and we have not forgotten whose land this is, and neither will we let you forget the debt Australia owes to us, not just to compensate for the violence perpetrated against us, but also for the wealth you have taken out of this land that is part of our very being.

Over the years numerous departments and agencies assisted in the overall task of 'assimilating' us. There were those who made us accept Christianity and forget our own religion. There were others who took our children.

In this context you will not be surprised to know that for us, child protection began when we started to do something about the abuses against us and against our children. It is true that there were government departments that said they were taking our children from us because it was in their best interests and that they needed care and protection. Our children were also adopted out, their parents being coerced into letting go of them. Frequently they were just taken away and never returned. There were holiday programs that our children went on never to be returned. Thousands were taken away in so many different ways and with so many different reasons to justify the removals, that in the end, it did not matter what they were ostensibly taken away for. The fact was they were taken away without the consent of and indeed against the wishes of their families. The trauma and the scars are still with us.

This is the history of child protection in relation to Aboriginal children. Whilst the state has actively promoted abuses against our children, we have had to fight hard to keep our children or conceal them from the 'welfare'. In the 1970s, with the tide of the Australian public in sympathy with us, we persuaded and pressured governments into making changes to their methods. Laws relating to child welfare, in some cases, have been developed in consultation with Aboriginal people. In spite of the changes, though, Aboriginal children are disproportionately over-represented in the statistics of children in the care of the state in every state and territory of Australia. Today the causes for this continued removal of our children are far more complex. Despite changes to legislation and practices by state governments, most of our agencies, which now number nineteen around the country, report ever larger caseloads.

In the report, *Aboriginal Child Poverty* (Choo, 1990), Aboriginal children are shown to be materially and financially much poorer than non-Aboriginal children because the communities to which they belong are much worse off than their non-Aboriginal neighbours. The poverty that we experience includes:

- the loss of our children from our communities and families
- the resulting loss of identity, loss of spiritual and cultural heritage, loss of contact with the land
- the loss of dignity and self respect through oppression over the years
- lack of access to a reliable supply of good clean water, food and other essential services in many communities
- alcoholism and homelessness, contributing to the incidence of physical and sexual abuse of children

- the increasing incidence of sexually transmitted diseases among our people, and especially among our children
- the very poor health of our children, which affects their long term life chances
- the locking up of our children in institutions and prisons
- chronic homelessness, which affects the health and education of our children
- the negative effects of all these on access to employment and income, which keeps our children and communities in poverty.

This state of indigence that our people continue to endure is part of the racism that is deeply embedded in the very fabric of this society. Racism is destructive because it goes hand in hand with white society's denial of our Aboriginal identity. The programs implemented by Aboriginal education groups around the country will of course eventually begin to create changes in attitudes in younger generations if these programs continue to receive government support. Further, if we do not imbue in our children a healthy sense of Aboriginal identity, they will develop a low self esteem and tend to deny their own Aboriginality.

Given the poverty and the racism, the work we do in the area of child protection is really a 'band-aid' job. How are we expected to sort out the problems of an individual child and family when we know that they are the direct result of the conditions they live in every minute of the day? This is what we have to do nevertheless. The remarkable thing is that we do succeed in cases in assisting children to adjust and develop into 'normal' Aboriginal children: that is, normal in the sense that they are proud of their identity and strong enough to deal with the battering they will inevitably receive in their lives.

Child protection for us is firstly a matter of protecting our children from the negative and destructive influences of society, and from the intrusion of the 'welfare' and other authorities in their lives. Secondly, it is a case of protecting our families and our communities from the attacks we have experienced for the last 200 years. A strong community will mean strong families and children.

Thirdly, child protection for us is acting politically to change the things that continue to keep us economically, socially and politically dispossessed; beggars in our own land. Fourthly, it involves developing our services like the Aboriginal and Islander Child Care Agencies (AICCA) so that we can continue to learn how to deal with the problems our children have as they grow up. We already have almost fifteen years of experience in this field. Fifthly, it means educating non-Aboriginal people who work in the area of child protection, so that they can be sensitive to our needs and support us when and if we want this support. Sixthly, our form of child protection will work if government departments and their personnel recognise that our work is valid and here to stay.

Many of our children in former years were removed because of material neglect. I think that over the years we have convinced 'professionals' in welfare departments that it is better to keep children with their families in spite of their material poverty, as this will ensure they receive the love nobody else can give them, and will allow for the healthy development of their identity which is crucial to their survival as Aboriginal people.

There are children, however, who are abused and neglected. For these children we have to assess their situation very carefully. If the situation requires the removal of a child because of the gravity of the neglect or abuse, we will support the removal of the child. We assess each case on its own merits and we view the best interests of the child as bound inextricably with that of their extended family. Indeed, whenever we seek solutions we try to involve the extended family in the decisions about the child. This ensures we do the right thing in the eyes of the family. It also means they have a vested interest in the positive outcome of the decision made. There certainly is no point in doing something contrary to the wishes of the extended family. The question about the interests of the child being paramount is an important one. I believe that in our work, we do view the child's best interest as being tied up with the family and our community. This is not a way of disregarding the interests of the children concerned. We genuinely see the future survival of our people as being linked to our ability to rear our children as Aboriginal children. We must be able to educate them with our values and beliefs. A community does not just exist as a physical entity; it also exists through a common culture, language, customs and experience. These can only be provided by Aboriginal people to Aboriginal children. If we fail in this task we cease to exist as a people.

In many parts of Australia our agencies work with state and territory governments. In Victoria, Community Services Victoria has to involve the Victorian Aboriginal Child Care Agency in all Aboriginal cases. Although this is not always done, there are not many that slip through the net. In Alice Springs, the Central Australian Aboriginal Child Care Agency is a permanent member of the child protection team. In Townsville, the Aboriginal and Islander Child Care Agency is co-opted onto the Suspected Child Abuse and Neglect (SCAN) Team. These are some recent developments, but it is too early to judge the effectiveness of them. However, I think everyone agrees that co-operation assists the department in its work and the advice given by the Aboriginal and Islander Child Care Agencies is sound and produces results. There is no foolproof system and mistakes will occur. These days, however, I believe we are closer to arriving at a method and solution that cuts down the margin for error. Certainly there will not be a return to the days when we had no control over our own lives.

Almost fifteen years ago when the first AICCA was established, we began the formal work of the protection of our children. The early ideas and methods were based on practices that had contributed to the survival of our people to that time. Today our agencies are larger and more sophisticated but essentially the basic principles according to which we operate are the same. We continue to demand the return of our rights with regard to the care, custody and control of our own children and will do so until we have this basic right that any other Australian enjoys.

Our organisation also seeks the enactment of national legislation along the lines of the Indian Child Welfare Act in North America that will bring us closer to our goal. The government has done very little to strengthen the services for Aboriginal children. Funding for new AICCA type services or for the expansion of existing AICCAs has been frozen since 1986. At a time when our caseloads were increasing, this move astounded and angered us. In part it prompted us to work with the Brotherhood of St Laurence on a joint report, *Aboriginal Child Poverty* (Choo, 1990).

We also want an inquiry into the removal of Aboriginal children. For too long this issue has been kept under wraps, yet the effects of the removal policies have had devastating consequences for us and remain with us in a very real way today. One Aboriginal health service recently found that of 120 cases of patients with psychiatric disorders they surveyed, 60 per cent had been removed as children. Peter Read (1982) in his pamphlet *The Stolen Generations*, estimated that one in six Aboriginal children were removed. He has said he thinks almost 15,000 children were taken away in New South Wales alone!

All of this then in black and white is what our approach to child protection is. If it seems a little unorthodox, we make no excuses for it, for what is at stake after all is our most valuable resource, our children.

Prevention

Prevention of child abuse gains widespread support from child protection workers, partly because of the difficulties inherent in the detection, investigation and case management of child abuse. Given these difficulties it is frequently argued that prevention is a more attractive and worthwhile activity — worthwhile in that it will stem the tide of children who have been abused or neglected who present to welfare authorities. It is attractive also in that the day to day difficulties of dealing with a complex and at times contradictory system are placed at a distance. Often though the challenges of prevention work are overlooked both by those demanding accountability and for those standing outside this child protection activity. And it is the challenges of prevention work that the three chapters in this section take up.

The development of models and frameworks for understanding prevention is still in its infancy. Advancing the development of child abuse prevention models within a framework that is Australian is a task this section begins. The political, social and physical landscape offer unique opportunities and present unique threats to Australian child abuse prevention work. Critical questions remain such as how to develop a campaign that reflects national identity while still respecting the cultural diversity of Australia, how to combine resources to get the greatest benefit while understanding state differences, and how to have an Australia-wide focus while encouraging local initiatives?

Perhaps the greatest challenge facing Australian child abuse prevention work is the need for research to provide directions for future activity. There is almost no Australian based research to help practitioners understand which prevention activities are the most effective and efficient in stopping child abuse. Ideas about what might make a difference have largely been intuitive. As yet there is almost no systematic research to support or refine these commonsense ideas. Research from related disciplines and from other countries has been imported to provide some guidance, however these often have underlying assumptions and practices which make their findings unreliable for the Australian context. Two of the chapters directly address this problem by reporting on research designed to evaluate the impact of Australian prevention programs.

The third chapter raises some of the difficulties in researching prevention programs. Also taken up by the three chapters is the need for a co-ordinated approach to prevention, co-ordinated across departments as well as within programs. The strength that is gained from such team-work and co-operation is identified by all three chapters as critical to the successes achieved by their programs. The relationship between prevention activity and protection activity is highlighted by the inclusion in this group of chapters of one which reports on treatment programs. The others consider mass media campaigns and a child protective curriculum in schools.

2
Using Mass Media Campaigns to Prevent Child Sexual Assault in New South Wales

Gillian Calvert

Child abuse prevention is not a highly researched area of practice within child protection. A review of the literature in 1985 revealed that only a small number of articles on primary prevention have been published (Rosenberg and Reppucci, 1985, 576). While further work has been published since, there is still limited theoretical development of the prevention area. This probably reflects the paucity of research and development in the broader field of prevention and promotion which has had to 'borrow concepts and methods' from other fields, rather than representing a lack of interest from within the child abuse area (Rolf, 1985, 632).

One of the most popular of these borrowed concepts in the child abuse prevention area is Caplan's framework (Cohn, 1983) of primary, secondary and tertiary levels of prevention. Primary prevention refers to stopping abuse before it starts by targeting members of the community through broad based programs directed at populations of people. Secondary prevention programs are aimed at early intervention in high risk, vulnerable groups. Tertiary prevention targets those individuals, families or groups where abuse has occurred, and attempts to prevent its recurrence.

New South Wales chose to address all three levels of prevention through the four year comprehensive Child Sexual Assault Program (CSAP) which was directed at reducing the incidence of child sexual assault in NSW and improving the response of the child protection system to children who had been sexually assaulted. The CSAP involved legal reforms, a significant increase in services, a review of procedures, the implementation of an extensive statewide multi-disciplinary training program and the development of a primary prevention strategy including mass media campaigns. Considerable planning effort, involving all relevant arms of government, community based groups and the public was involved in developing the program (Calvert, 1991).

The primary prevention strategy of the CSAP had several components. The community based prevention programs, the 'I Know That Now' puppet show, and the 'Protective Behaviours Program' complemented the child protection curricula developed by the Department of Education and the Catholic Education Commission and implemented in schools throughout NSW. A video developed jointly with the Queensland Centre for the Prevention of Child Abuse was directed at educating adults in the community about the nature of child abuse. These face to face educational strategies were paralled by the three media campaigns under discussion which focused on raising public awareness. The media campaigns were specifically targeted at people over the age of sixteen years, as the use of mass media to reach children about child sexual assault was considered unsuitable.

The NSW media campaigns assumed that if the community's awareness is raised about the true nature and incidence of child sexual assault then a climate will be created which will encourage children to disclose abuse and receive a sympathetic response. This specific anti-abuse approach assumes that bases of the preventative efforts are increased understanding of the problem and where to get help (Rosenberg and Reppucci, 1985, 579). Breaking the silence will challenge offenders' power over children, and reveal the real nature of the relationship between men and women, and adults and children. Support for this view is found in the research on adults who were assaulted as children (Walby, 1985).

This paper describes the NSW mass media campaigns. It reports on the results of the market research conducted and identifies the factors contributing to the campaign's success. Based on these findings the possibilities and limitations of mass media campaigns in preventing child sexual assault are then discussed.

The Campaigns

The NSW state government Minister responsible for the NSW Child Protection Council launched the first statewide community education campaign on 1 October 1986. The campaign was designed to break the silence surrounding the subject of child sexual assault and 'give the public of New South Wales the facts' (NSW CPC, 1986). It included a 30-second television spot on the theme 'Child Sexual Assault, It's Often Closer to Home Than You Think' and a booklet called *Child Sexual Assault, How To Talk To Children* (NSW CPC, 1986).

The television message stated clearly that children face a far greater threat of sexual assault from relatives and family friends than they do from the then more widely publicised 'stranger danger'. It was given a Parental Guidance Recommendation rating which meant it could only be shown from 7.30 pm-5.00 am Sunday to Saturday or 10.00 am-4.00 pm Monday to Friday (school days only) viewing slots. The television commercial was broadcast for three weeks followed by a two-week break then shown again for two weeks.

The booklet tells parents and other adults what sort of information to give to children to help make them safer from sexual assault. The booklet also challenges some of the common myths about child sexual assault and counters these with facts. It contains a comprehensive list of services for child victims of sexual assault and their families throughout NSW (NSW CPC, 1988a).

In May 1987, the NSW state government Premier launched the Council's second statewide community education campaign on the theme 'Child Sexual Assault Offenders. No Excuses Never Ever'. This campaign theme was again publicised by a television commercial broadcast over four weeks with a two-week break followed by another two weeks of broadcasting. A booklet was also released. A radio commercial in English and in twenty community languages, stickers, multilingual wall and billboard posters which were displayed in towns and cities all over New South Wales were added media for conveying the central message. The second campaign continued the process begun by the 'Closer To Home' campaign of increasing community awareness about, and understanding of the crime of child sexual assault (NSW CPC, 1989).

While the first campaign broke the silence surrounding child sexual assault, the second raised some of the underlying issues. The booklet which complemented the radio and television material focused in some detail on the questions:

- who child sexual assault offenders are
- why they commit this crime
- how attitudes in society influence their behaviour
- how these attitudes arise in the first place (NSW CPC 1987)

The 'No Excuses' campaign also stressed the need for child sexual assault offenders to take responsibility for their actions and not to blame their child victim (CPC, 1989). Because the campaign focused on the behaviour of men, the television commercial targeted viewing times that would attract a male audience: for example, during sports programs.

On 19 June 1988 following a change in government, the Minister responsible for the NSW Child Protection Council launched the third phase of the mass media community education campaign. This campaign stressed the need for greater emphasis on providing support for families in which child sexual assault has occurred. 'Because it is so important the child is helped, families often need special support to help them accept the uncomfortable truth and act to protect the child' (NSW CPC, 1988).

Two new booklets were released as part of this campaign. *It's Often Closer to Home than you Think* explores the reactions that different members of a family may have to the disclosure of child sexual assault (NSW CPC, 1988a). The second booklet *Where to Get Help* contains a detailed directory of government and non-government services which can provide help to child victims and their families (NSW CPC, 1988a). A new poster and sticker were also released. The radio and television advertisements used in the first two campaigns were replayed as community service announcements.

Throughout all three campaigns the media, particularly radio, donated significant free air time for the advertisements. The donated air time was generally at times appropriate to the target audience and supplemented the paid air time secured by the NSW Child Protection Council.

To monitor the effects of the three mass media campaigns on child sexual assault, a series of market research studies was commissioned. The aim was

1. to provide a benchmark measure of community awareness of the problem of child sexual assault;
2. to assess the community's knowledge of certain facts and information concerning child sexual assault;
3. to measure community interest in getting help for victims;
4. to assess community attitudes to the problem of child sexual assault; and
5. to measure awareness of advertising and promotion about the problem (Elliot and Shanahan, 1986).

A benchmark study was conducted in September 1986, a month before the launch of the first campaign. A telephone questionnaire was administered to 400 randomly selected households in the Sydney metropolitan area drawn from the white pages of the telephone directory. The market research examined how much 'reach' was achieved, that is how many people saw the campaign. It also asked what they thought of it and attempted to track any changes in knowledge. Such changes may point to the degree of impact which the campaign had on people's attitudes to child sexual assault.

Two further studies, which tracked and monitored public reactions to the NSW Child Protection Council's community education campaigns in 1986 and 1987, provided valuable feedback. As well as demonstrating the measure of the campaign's effectiveness, the feedback highlighted areas which needed further emphasis and contributed to the development of the campaign (NSW CPC, 1989). Market research was not conducted following the third campaign as a change in government at the March 1988 election forced a realignment of the NSW Child Protection Council's funding priorities (Calvert, 1991).

Key Findings — the Campaign's Advertising Success

Recall of Information About Child Sexual Assault

Table 1 summarises the results for unaided recall of recent information on child sexual assault. Unaided recall means those respondents who spontaneously recalled recent information about child sexual assault. Recall with prompting means those respondents who did not spontaneously recall and who were asked if they could recall seeing the

Table 1: RECALL OF RECENT INFORMATION (UNAIDED)

	Benchmark %	Nov. '86 %	July '87 %
Yes	87	82	91
No/don't know	13	18	8
Base	407	404	400

Source: Elliot and Shanahan 1986, 1986a, 1987.

Chi square (df=1), 52.84, p<.0001; All chi squares were calculated on the raw figures.

campaign or some part of it. The main feature is the lower percentage of respondents who recalled information following the first campaign than in the benchmark study. The benchmark study occurred a month after the highly publicised Sixth International Congress on Child Abuse and Neglect, held in Sydney in August 1986. At about the same time, a particularly sensational case of neglect in one of Sydney's suburbs received extensive media attention. This probably contributed, in the Sydney area, to a greater than expected public awareness of child abuse issues, including child sexual assault. It may also account for the drop to 82 per cent in November 1986. The July 1987 figures following the second campaign are an increase over the November 1986 figure following the first campaign and probably reflect the uncontaminated impact of the media campaign.

Newspaper articles and general TV were mentioned most frequently as sources of information. (See Table 2.)

Table 2: SOURCES OF INFORMATION

	Benchmark %	Nov. '86 %	July '87 %
Newspaper article	69	60	65
General TV	63	68	63
General radio	12	10	18
Magazine	8	3	7
Word of mouth	6	3	3
Newspaper ad	4	6	5
Pamphlet	2	2	3
Radio ad	—	5	3
Poster	—	—	6
TV ad	—	28	23
Base	355	332	363

Source: Elliot and Shanahan 1986, 1986a, 1987
Totals do not add up to 100% because of availability of multiple response.

Recall of Television Commercial
Table 3 summarises responses to questions about recall of the commercials. With prompting 38 per cent of people recalled the television commercial in 1986. This increased dramatically to 64 per cent in July 1987. That is, nearly two out of every three respondents recalled the commercial on prompting in 1987. Approximately half

Table 3: RECALL OF TELEVISION COMMERCIAL

	Nov. '86 %	July '87 %
Yes	38	64
No	62	36
Base	404	404

Source: Elliot and Shanahan 1986a, 1987.
Chi square (df=1), 52.84, p<.0001.

the respondents recalled the byline or message of the commercial in the 1987 campaign 'Child Sexual Assault Offenders. No Excuses Never Ever'.

Believability of Television Commercials
As can be seen from Table 4 the vast majority of respondents in both surveys thought the commercial was believable or very believable. Only 6 per cent of respondents thought the commercial was unbelievable. Qualitative probing, that is further questioning by the interviewers revealed people liked the commercial because it brought the problem out into the open and made them aware of the issue of child sexual assault. For both surveys, half of the sample registered some dislike. Of those who did however, the most common dislikes were the lack of impact for the July 1987 commercial and the perception that the November 1986 commercial did not get the message through to children or get their attention. Even though the commercials were directed at adults not children, 18 per cent of respondents identified failure to get the message to children as a dislike for the November 1986 campaign. Respondents correctly identified the 1987 campaign as directed at adults.

Table 4: BELIEVABILITY OF COMMERCIALS' CONTENT

	Nov. '86 %	July '87 %
Very believable	35	36
Believable	53	50
Unbelievable	12	14
Base	154	254

Source: Elliot and Shanahan 1986a, 1987.
Chi square (df=2), 0.660, not significant.

Comprehension of the Two Television Commercials
The results in Table 5 show that most people easily understood both commercials. They found them straight to the point with a clear and simple message. Few found the commercials difficult to understand.

Who Understood the Message
Table 6 presents the responses to questions about who understood the television commercial's message. As can be seen there was very little change between the two surveys. Most people thought the television commercials would be understood by adults or both adults and children. Those who nominated children thought they would understand

because it was easy to follow, was a real life situation and because it told you where to get help. Those who thought it was directed at adults felt that young children would not understand and that it would not catch their interest. Those who thought the message was for both adults and children thought they would understand because it was easy to follow and a real life situation.

Table 5: TELEVISION COMMERCIAL COMPREHENSION LEVEL

	Nov. '86 %	July '87 %
Very easy	62	60
Fairly easy	26	30
Not easy	13	10
Base	154	254

Source: Elliot and Shanahan 1986a, 1987.
Chi square (df=2), 1.39, not significant.

Table 6: MESSAGE IN COMMERCIAL RECEIVED BY

	Nov. '86 %	July 87 %
Children	5	5
Adults	51	59
Both	39	30
Don't know	5	6
Base	154	254

Source: Elliot and Shanahan 1986a, 1987.
Chi square (df=3), 3.65, not significant.

Key Findings-Community Knowledge of Child Sexual Assault

Child Sexual Assault as a Problem
Table 7 shows that an overwhelming number of respondents identified child sexual assault as a problem. The salience or importance in the minds of the public of the issue is at a high level across all three surveys.

Frequency of the Problem
Approximately half of the respondents for all three surveys considered child sexual assault a 'very common' problem. See Table 8. A further one third thought it was 'common'. Over the three surveys the

proportion of people thinking the problem was very common has shown a trend towards increase and the proportion of people thinking the problem was not so common has seen a trend towards decrease although these are not statistically significant.

Table 7: CHILD SEXUAL ASSAULT AS A PROBLEM

	Benchmark %	Nov. '86 %	July '87 %
Yes	94	90	91
No/don't know	6	10	8
Base	407	407	400

Source: Elliot and Shanahan 1986, 1986a, 1987.
BM x Nov 86 Chi square (df=1), 3.94, not significant.
BM x July 87 Chi square (df=1), 1.16, not significant.
Nov 86 x July 87 Chi square (df=1), .06, not significant.

Table 8: FREQUENCY OF PROBLEM

	Benchmark %	Nov. '86 %	July '87 %
Common	75	78	84
Not common	25	22	16
Base	407	404	400

Source: Elliot and Shanahan 1986, 1986a, 1987.
BM x Nov 86 Chi square (df=1), .87, not significant.
BM x July 87 Chi square (df=1), .59, not significant.
Nov 86 x July 87 Chi square (df=1), 4.36, not significant.

What should be done?
There were some notable changes in perceptions of what should be done about the problem of child sexual assault over the three surveys. See Table 9. After a fall between the benchmark study and November 1986 survey 'education in schools' picked up markedly in 1987 as a measure of what should be done. There was a steady increase between the November 1986 and July 1987 survey in the number of people advocating capital punishment. 'More media coverage' dropped significantly between the November 1986 and July 1987 campaigns. This may be because the July 1987 campaign was more comprehensive than the November 1986 campaign, thus people's expectations for 'more media' were satisfied by the July 1987 campaign.

Table 9: WHAT SHOULD BE DONE?

	Benchmark %	Nov. '86 %	July '87 %
'Bring into Open/More Media'	36	39	31
'Education in Schools'	22	13	35
'Harder Jail Sentences'	20	20	24
'Parental Advice'	14	9	6
'Capital Punishment'	–	11	21
Better Authorities 'Counsellors'	–	10	7
'Encourage People to Report'	–	10	7
Base	382	364	365

Source: Elliot and Shanahan 1986, 1986a, 1987.
Totals do not add up to 100% because of availability of multiple responses.

Government Involvement

Table 10 shows a significant drop between the benchmark study and July 1987 in the number of respondents advocating government involvement. This may be because the government's involvement had been demonstrated by the campaigns and other parts of the CSAP thus satisfying respondents' demands for government involvement in the area. Alternatively it could indicate an increased realisation that government involvement may not always be successful or have an impact on the problem of child sexual assault. The call for harsher penalties, capital punishment and more education in schools suggests however that respondents were able to specify what type of government involvement they wanted. (See Table 9.) This may suggest respondents were wanting less involvement by politicians rather than less government involvement.

Offenders

A high proportion of people across all three survey periods thought offenders were usually someone known to the child. (See Table 11.) There was a significant increase in the number of people electing 'someone known to the child' from the benchmark survey to the November 1986 and the July 1987 survey. The high number of respondents in the benchmark study who thought offenders were known to the child is interesting given most child sexual assault education to date had focused on 'stranger danger'.

Table 10: GOVERNMENT INVOLVEMENT

	Benchmark %	Nov. '86 %	July '87 %
Yes	92	90	85
No/don't know	8	10	15
Base	382	364	365

Source: Elliot and Shanahan 1986, 1986a, 1987.
BM x Nov 86 Chi square (df=1), .52, not significant.
BM x July 87 Chi square (df=1), 8.19 p<.004.
Nov 86 x July 87 Chi square (df=1), 4.01 not significant.

Table 11: OFFENDERS

	Benchmark %	Nov. '86 %	July '87 %
Strangers	5	1	3
Known to child	77	79	85
Equally	13	16	10
Don't know	5	4	2
Base	407	404	400

Source: Elliot and Shanahan 1986, 1986a, 1987.
BM x Nov 86 Chi square (df=2), 13.4, p<.004.
BM x July 87 Chi square (df=2), 10.03, p<.018.
Nov 87 x July 87 Chi square (df=2), 13.27, p<.004.

Criminal Offence
Most respondents considered child sexual assault is always a criminal offence. Table 12 shows these figures remained fairly stable over the three survey periods.

Action Taken if Child Sexual Assault Suspected
Table 13 summarises the responses to the question what action should be taken if child sexual assault is suspected. The dominant response across all three surveys was 'report to police'. There was a trend towards increase in this alternative between the November 1986 and the July 1987 survey. There was also a trend towards increase in the number of people who claimed they would 'go to a social worker' and a drop in those who would 'report it to the authorities' between the three surveys. It would seem that over the three surveys respondents were able to be more specific about who they would report an allegation to.

The number of respondents who would 'talk to the offender' increased over the three surveys. This trend caused concern for those with responsibility for intervening in child sexual assault cases. While it could be seen as people being willing to confront the issue themselves, it is an action which could expose the child to increased harm.

Table 12: CRIMINAL OFFENCE

	Benchmark %	Nov. '86 %	July '87 %
Always	81	81	82
Sometimes	13	11	9
Never/don't know	6	8	9
Base	407	404	400

Source: Elliot and Shanahan, 1986, 1986a, 1987.

BM x Nov 86 Chi square (df=2), 1.97, not significant.
BM x July 87 Chi square (df=2), 5.59, not significant.
Nov 86 x July 87 Chi square (df=2), 1.01, not significant.

Table 13: ACTION TAKEN IF ASSAULT SUSPECTED

	Sept. '86 %	Nov. '86 %	July '87 %
Report to police	50	48	61
Report to authorities	44	25	16
Talk to parents	9	10	12
Go to social worker	9	20	27
Check facts	7	14	18
Talk to offenders	5	2	7
Base	407	404	400

Source: Elliot and Shanahan, 1986, 1986a, 1987.
Totals do not add up to 100% because of availability of multiple responses.

Achieving Market Reach and Giving People Greater Knowledge

One out of every three respondents recalled the November 1986 television commercial with prompting. Nearly two out of every three respondents recalled the July 1987 commercial with prompting. Given the competition from other messages and stimuli in the audience environment, this is an exceptionally pleasing result. Almost all who recalled the television commercials generally found them believable and over half of the respondents did not identify a dislike about either of the two television commercials. The majority correctly identified who the commercials were directed at. Most respondents found the commercials easy to comprehend. The television commercials were not seen by respondents to raise children's fears and anxieties.

Clearly the campaigns, as represented by the television commercials, were successful in achieving a large share of the market or its reach. The results also show some change in the community's knowledge about child sexual assault. Respondents were able to identify more accurately the incidence of child sexual assault and who commits these offences. They were also more specific about who they would report an offence to, suggesting greater knowledge of services available to victims. To the extent it achieved improved knowledge about child sexual assault it would appear the campaigns were successful.

The demand for government involvement dropped over the three surveys — this may reflect the respondents' satisfaction with the level of government involvement or a desire for a change in the type of government involvement rather than a wish for the government to withdraw from the area. Capital punishment as a response to asking what should be done about child sexual assault increased over the three surveys. This may reflect the campaign's message that child sexual assault is a crime, in particular the 'Child sexual Assault Offenders. No Excuses Never Ever' campaign. At the same time, a greater number of respondents wanted education in schools.

A number of possible reasons for the campaign's success in achieving its market reach can be put forward. No one part of the campaign was given sole responsibility for carrying the message but was assisted by a range of other strategies, for example, the community based prevention programs, the school based education programs, legal reforms, training programs, service development, and by the previous campaigns. When the advertising asserted, for example, 'child sexual assault is a crime' (NSW CPC, 1987), it was backed up by earlier media coverage on the introduction of law reforms designed to make it easier for children to report and the introduction of tougher sentences.

The campaigns in turn provided support for the other parts of the CSAP. The July 1987 survey showed an increase in the number of respondents wanting child protection education introduced into schools. This gave impetus to the development and implementation of a curriculum in the school system and was used in justifying the introduction of the curriculum. Such 'piggybacking' maintained child sexual assault as a salient issue in the minds of the community and the media. Thus they were not one-off events in isolation, but part of a deliberate effort sustained over a number of years to raise awareness about child sexual assault.

Similarly the messages of the three campaigns built on each other. Raising awareness about the problem preceded messages about why child sexual assault happens, what can be done in response to a disclosure and how to prevent it. Consequently 'the messages were changed over time as the target audience moved to higher stages of awareness, knowledge and motivation' (Kotler and Roberto, 1989, 202). This broad brush and co-ordinated approach complemented a similar strategy adopted with the entire CSAP.

A further factor contributing to the campaign's success was the simultaneous use of a number of communication channels. Television commercials were put on at the same time as radio commercials, which were played at the same time as billboards appeared. Posters and free booklets were distributed to all relevant community and government agencies. This reflected the synchronisation in all aspects of planning and implementation of the CSAP and the mass media campaigns.

The campaigns focused on one form of abuse at a time, thus avoiding the problem of collapsing quite separate phenomena (emotional abuse, physical assault, verbal abuse, neglect) under the one general category of 'child abuse'. Thus the campaigns could be quite specific about the information produced as they were grounded in knowledge about the causes of that particular assault, and could raise awareness about some underlying issues such as the importance of the relationship between gender and power in understanding why child sexual assault occurs. Interventions aimed at changing attitudes are more successful if 'grounded in an approach that stresses the function and acquisition of attitudes' (Chassin, *et al* 1986, 615). By focussing on child *sexual* assault, the NSW Child Protection Council was relieved of the burden of developing a broad, all encompassing campaign. The danger in such a narrow emphasis of course was that in being so specific, essential connections with other forms of child abuse may not have been made.

The use of media launches with the campaign had a dual effect. They clearly indicated government endorsement as the campaigns were launched by either the Minister or Premier. This not only maintained the issues' salience but importantly made the message acceptable. Endorsement is a common marketing strategy to achieve greater sales. The launches secured additional publicity and increased exposure. By alerting people to the fact that these commercials would be played, they may have attracted more notice when they were played.

The use of mass media campaigns was a particularly appropriate way to give a message to the community that it was okay to talk about child sexual assault. The campaigns themselves broke the taboo about talking openly about child sexual assault which in turn may have encouraged people to adopt that behaviour. Permission to talk about a taboo subject was given by showing 'the government' talking about it. This also involved people in the issue — an important factor in any attempt to increase awareness of an issue. This process mirrors the discount hierarchy used in the Protective Behaviours Program (Flandreau West, 1989). The first step is to acknowledge the existence of a problem, secondly to understand the extent, next to believe there is a solution and finally to believe you can take action which will contribute to a solution.

At a more local and organisational level, the prior liaison and consultation that occurred added to the campaign's success. This continued through to the actual design of the campaign with the involvement of all government agencies and key community groups in the actual development of the three campaigns, in particular those agencies who were involved in other prevention activities of the CSAP. The scripts of the television and radio commercials, the content of all the booklets and the design of the posters were all subject to scrutiny by these key agencies.

The consultation involved in developing the Report of the NSW Child Sexual Assault Taskforce and the media interest in the adoption and implementation of the recommendations prepared the audience market for the campaigns. The community response to the idea of using the mass media was overwhelming. For example, 97 percent of people who responded to the Taskforce supported the idea of a community education, mass media campaign (NSW Government, 1984). At the same time the mass media campaign was often used by politicians as an example of what the government was doing to prevent child sexual assault. This demand from both the community and the politicians created a market for the mass media campaigns (Fine 1981, 63).

The use of jargon free, simple language with a 'catchy' byline also assisted in recall of the messages and in the campaign's success. 'It was easy to pronounce, recognise and remember' (Kotler and Roberto, 1989, 153). The booklets were simple to read and distinctive in design and use of colour. A particular shade of blue was adopted to enhance the corporate image of the NSW Child Protection Council and its publicity. The booklets aimed to strike a balance between providing information for the people to feel their interest had been satisfied, but not providing so much information that people were overwhelmed.

Small booklets were used so that people could put them in their bags and it would not be obvious that they were carrying this information around.

Efficient and widespread distribution channels may be a further reason for the success of the campaign. Most key agencies had copies of the booklets and posters within a week of the launch of each campaign. Memembers of the community could therefore gain access to them almost immediately from a number of different settings. People could avoid the connotations of being sick, deviant or criminal for collecting the booklets because so many different outlets were used, (eg direct mail, community centres, police stations, community health centres, legal centres and state welfare centres).

Finally the relationship built up with the advertising agency and production team was probably critical in ensuring the campaign's success. The opportunity to build up a relationship of trust and to establish patterns of communication between the same group of people over the three years meant 'the wheel' was not continually reinvented. The advertising agency staff shifted their perceptions on the issue of child sexual assault and we expanded our knowledge about mass media campaigns. A further incentive for the advertising agency to treat such a small account well was the international award won by the television commercial following the November 1986 campaign. The July 1987 television commercial also won an international award. So even though it was an extremely small account in financial terms it brought the agency some status and exposure in their industry.

Limitations to the Campaign
The major limitation of the campaign was the reported inability to reach people who spoke a language other than English. Even though the booklets were translated into thirteen community languages, the radio commercials translated into twenty community languages and broadcast over the ethnic radio station and the posters were multilingual, members of those communities reported in various follow-up consultative settings that the campaigns were insufficient to impact in any real way.

Although this evidence is anecdotal it does perhaps highlight the importance of the relationship between any community education campaign and the other related activities. The limited training, minimal increase in service delivery for ethnic groups and the lack of face to face contact could be seen as factors which minimised the campaign's success with these communities. Further feedback from some groups highlighted the necessity for material to be developed specifically for each of the communities as the problem is perceived differently by each community.

This limitation is perhaps illustrated by the relatively greater success with the Aboriginal communities where the NSW Child Protection Council funded the Aboriginal Medical Service to set up a counselling service, conduct training and develop its own booklets and posters specifically for the Aboriginal community on child sexual assault. As a consequence of this, some Aboriginal workers have reported the issue appears to have achieved some awareness in the Aboriginal community.

Preventing Child Sexual Assault
Achieving significant market reach and giving people greater knowledge however will not by themselves prevent or protect children from assault. It is probably unrealistic to ask any campaign, run on a small budget for three years, to do that. Furthermore it is unlikely that mass media campaigns by themselves change attitudes or behaviour. The resistance on the part of many communities to talking openly about child sexual assault and the range of defences used to resist these messages means mass media campaigns will only have an impact on attitudes and behaviour if they are run over long time periods and are supported by a range of other activities. Advertising by itself will not change attitudes. However as the NSW experience shows, advertising used with other reforms probably has some potential to help increase knowledge and awareness about a problem. Given this finding, it is important to use the mass media campaigns to strengthen child sexual assault as a salient issue in the minds of the community. The NSW campaigns may well have succeeded in slowing down the slippage of child sexual assault on the social and political agenda and probably achieved as much as was possible, given its dependence on ongoing financial commitment from the government.

This is not to deny the impact of mass media campaigns as forming one part of a long term strategy aimed at preventing child abuse. Rather they serve to remind us that the powerful underlying forces which create the climate in which children are abused must be acknowledged, otherwise we make a rod for our own backs and set up unrealistic expectations of such campaigns or programs.

Furthermore prevention strategies obviously require a sustained effort and commitment to resources if they are to be successful. Unfortunately there is rarely any quick measure of success, and they are not popular programs in a climate of shrinking resources and where there is an increased requirement to demonstrate success.

In this context programs based on protecting children seem

somewhat more achievable than programs aimed at preventing child abuse, particularly as programs based on protecting children can also be preventative. If, for example, a climate can be created that encourages children to report the abuse through 'No Go, Tell' strategies and the subsequent intervention is more successful at stopping the abuse and healing the effects through improved training, legal reforms and increased services, then more children will have been protected. In this sense protecting children seems more achievable than preventing child abuse.

Protection programs also usually have some measure of success which can be reported on within the life of that government. Press releases listing the number of services developed, the number of training programs run and describing the legal reforms put in place, improve the government's image. Thus protecting children is more saleable to the Government and to other funding sources, is proactive and has some sense of still being preventative. It is also extremely important for children who disclose they are being abused.

However, relying on protection strategies with no attempt at preventing child abuse is ultimately to apply band-aids only. Looking down the next millenium of child abuse with no attempt at preventing it seems not only profoundly depressing but a false human economy. Preventing child abuse, as the research indicates, probably results in fewer children in care, and in juvenile detention centres, fewer people in the adult prisons and in the mental health system (Finkelhor, 1986). So it is essential, even if difficult to establish, to support long term prevention strategies as having a high priority in child protection programs. And it must be done in conjunction with protection strategies, not instead of them. It is not a question of shifting the meagre current child protection resources over to provide funds for prevention programs. Additional and adequate funding must be provided. Unless these things are achieved, the prevention campaigns will be like pouring water on sand: gone as soon as it is poured.

3
Education and Child Protection

Catherine Laws

The Context for Child Protection Education
The way an issue is defined by the policy makers in government and the community often determines the types of responses and strategies that will be used to address that issue (Hogwood and Gunn, 1984). In New South Wales child sexual assault was placed by key commentators in a context which addressed the nature of the relationship between adults and children (Calvert, 1991). Central to the definition was the unequal power relationships between adults and children and the abuse of that power by some adults for their own sexual gratification. Initially it was defined in the *Report of the NSW Child Sexual Assault Task Force* (NSW Government, 1985). This definition became a driving force for the types of prevention and intervention responses developed by government departments.

The *Report of the NSW Child Sexual Assault Task Force* outlined a number of strategies to assist the community in addressing the problem of child sexual assault. These strategies included a major community education campaign under the auspices of the newly established coordinating body of the NSW Child Protection Council, training for workers and the establishment of both community based and departmental prevention programs (Calvert, 1991).

As part of the action recommended by the report, teachers in both government and non government schools were made mandatory notifiers of child sexual assault by legislation in July 1987. This action had the support of the Department of School Education and the NSW

Teachers' Federation. Other professions were scheduled to be made mandatory notifiers, but up until now teachers and doctors are the only professional groups which have been made mandatory notifiers by legislation.

While many of these strategies, addressed in the Child Sexual Assault Program, assisted children who had been sexually assaulted, these were short term strategies. As there was a basic emphasis on the nature of relationships in child sexual assault, there was a need to look at long term prevention, on how the community might move to consider parent-child and adult-child relationships where power is not abused. As with many other social issues, education was seen as an effective way of introducing long term prevention programs (NSW Government, 1985).

In this sense prevention was seen in its broadest terms. Prevention at this level sought to establish a climate where assault does not occur and people are involved in positive, non-violent relationships. Such primary prevention goals were seen to be achieved best through educational programs in schools.

Along with primary prevention strategies, secondary prevention education strategies also needed to be implemented. These strategies focused on protection skills and were considered necessary to target those children who were 'at risk'. This was particularly difficult in cases of child sexual assault, given the limited information about the population of children likely to be assaulted and under what circumstances. Research (Goldman and Goldman, 1986) indicated that child sexual assault occurred in all socio-economic and professional groups and across school ages. Consequently, it was difficult to target specific groups in the population for intervention.

Tertiary prevention programs, aimed at assisting children who had been assaulted and who needed protective skills to prevent further assaults, were also considered. Once again, this type of response, on the part of relevant authorities, was considered difficult given the secrecy surrounding child sexual assault and the relatively small number of children who disclosed that they were being sexually assaulted (Goldman and Goldman, 1986).

Given the constraints on targeting specific groups for secondary and tertiary intervention, the NSW Department of School Education prepared protective skills' material for use with all children as well as addressing primary prevention through teaching all children about developing and maintaining positive relationships both as children and as adults. Preventive education in the area of child sexual assault is complex; nevertheless through the Department of School Education's membership on the NSW Child Protection Council and its committees on policy, training and community education, the issues in preventive education were explored.

Issues in Child Protection Education

When teachers were made mandatory notifiers of child sexual assault, an extensive in-service program was undertaken to give them information about child sexual assault and notification procedures (Lamond, 1989). During this training, many teachers raised their concern for the long-term prevention of child sexual assault and the need to include prevention measures in the school curriculum strategies. There were of course some teachers and members of the community who, while concerned about the issue, did not feel that the responsibility for long term prevention belonged only to schools. The mass media campaigns of the NSW Child Protection Council further raised awareness of the issue and the importance of education for long term prevention. These campaigns generally elicited the support of teachers for having a prevention program in schools.

The topic of protective skills presented many problems for those developing and implementing an appropriate teaching curriculum. There is always the concern that children may be given the message that they alone are responsible for protecting themselves from assaults. It was considered that children should never be placed in the position of taking responsibility for an adult's behaviour, yet in many situations it is the children alone who must take action with an abusive adult to protect themselves. A balance needs to be sought between empowering children to take action, and at the same time clearly giving a message that it is the adult's wrong behaviour that is the issue and that children should never be blamed if they were unable to stop an assault. It was considered paramount to address the myth that children cause assaults or that their sexuality contributes in any way to the irresponsible behaviour of adults towards them.

Another dilemma involved the educational concern that teaching children about child sexual assault may frighten them or have a negative impact on children's positive relationships with adults. In providing preventive education for all children, there was a concern expressed that those children who had not been assaulted would be unnecessarily frightened by preventive education or that these children would develop a fear of adults. In developing the content of education programs to protect children, care needed to be taken that children were not frightened by the issue and that the positive relationships they had with adults were not damaged but rather enhanced.

There was also concern for those children who had been, or were being, assaulted. This concern centred on ensuring that these children did not feel that they were to blame for the assault. In communicating a message that children need to be responsible for protecting themselves, those children who are assaulted might then believe that they must in some way be at fault because they were, or are, unable to protect themselves. This was a particularly sensitive issue requiring specific educational strategies to ensure that children did not believe that they were to blame if they were unable to use their protective skills and prevent an assault.

In addition to teaching protective skills, the aspect of teaching about developing and maintaining positive relationships also was canvassed widely. This aspect provides for longer term prevention. Teaching children about such issues as identifying their feelings, helping them to build self-esteem, to develop interpersonal communication skills, to identify and clarify values, and giving them the skills to develop and maintain positive relationships is central to assisting them to participate in positive, non-abusive relationships and to have these types of relationships with their own children as adults.

It was strongly believed that both protective skills and relationship skills were necessary components of an effective prevention program. These aspects also need to be presented to children in a way that takes account of their developmental stages and which is consistent with how children develop understanding.

While there are safety aspects in child protection education, teaching children about protection from child sexual assault is different from teaching them about how to cross the road safely. While basic protective skills such as saying 'no', trying to get away, and telling a trusted person about sexual assault are strategies which can be taught to children in a similar way to other safety rules, there are significant issues in the area of child sexual assault which cannot be addressed in the same way.

The emotional pressures on children not to tell about child sexual assault, the belief often held by children that assaults are somehow their fault, the trust that children are encouraged to have in adults and to follow an adult's directions are more complex issues. They require an approach where children examine their feelings and their values and develop a belief that they have a right to be safe and not to be assaulted. Such education requires a process of values' clarification where students are encouraged to explore their beliefs and values in relation to child abuse.

Preventive education also needs to be presented over time and not given in a 'one-shot', short term program run over a few days. The skills for identifying 'safe' and 'unsafe' feelings and situations are developmental. The types of skills that would be taught to a five year old are different from those that a seventeen year old would require. The situations differ and the ways the situations are interpreted and acted upon differ. Consequently, preventive education needs to be sequential and presented in a way which takes into account the different learning styles, as well as the ages and developmental stages of children.

It is also important to consider how prevention programs are taught in schools. The context in which this type of education is placed is critical in assisting children to make sense of protection education in a positive way. In New South Wales, child protective education is part of the schools' policy on student welfare. Through this policy, schools place a broad range of child protection issues, such as notification of suspected child sexual assault and support for children who have been sexually assaulted in the educational context. The student welfare area also addresses issues of education about drugs, and HIV/AIDS, as well as programs and practices such as development of leadership skills.

The issue of parental and community involvement in child protection education is crucial. The area of child protection would be considered by some to be controversial and a *Child Protection: Parent and Community Participation Manual* (NSW Department of Education, 1989) was prepared for schools to use with the community. This included the development of a video to assist principals in discussing the curriculum materials with parents.

At all stages of the development of the materials, representatives from parent organisations were involved. This included the early piloting of the materials where meetings were organised with parents of students in the pilot schools to assist parents to become aware of the issues, address any concerns they might have, gain approval for the materials to be trialled with their children and fully explain the content and context of the materials. Parents have a right and need to know what their children will be learning at school and feel comfortable with this. It was considered unproductive to embark on a project which involves such sensitive issues where there are many differing values, beliefs and legitimate concerns if the type of content involved is not supported and reinforced in the home.

Educators and welfare experts, for example, believed that child sexual assault education should include the specific names for genitalia. It was argued that this would give children the appropriate language to communicate effectively with an adult should an assault occur. NSW government schools have a tradition of consulting parents and giving parents the authority to approve their children participating in lessons on what might be described as controversial issues. While teaching children words such as 'vulva' and 'penis' was not considered controversial by many members of the community, some parents wish this type of education to be their own responsibility. This view is respected and the child protection curriculum materials use the terms 'private parts of the body' unless parents have given approval for the precise terms for the genitalia to be used with their children.

When developing the curriculum materials, community members also expressed concern about the process of teaching children to protect themselves and the possibility that they would not then obey parents in other matters. This is an understandable concern which needs to be addressed with parents and community members. Preventive education does not teach children to disobey or be bad mannered to adults. The emphasis needs to be on the children discussing with adults in their immediate community network if they are feeling unsafe or uncomfortable as well as communicating their feelings in an assertive way. While children need to be taught protective skills for threatening situations, this is not to be confused with complying with the legitimate instructions of parents and other adults. While children are taught about their right to be safe in child protection lessons, they are also taught about their responsibilities to others and the importance of caring for and nurturing others. Through the development of problem solving and decision making skills, children need to be taught to differentiate between situations where they assert their rights to be safe and protected, and situations where they must follow the reasonable instructions of adults.

Child Protection Curriculum Materials

The issues discussed above were taken into account when developing the child protection curriculum materials. The materials were developed over three years and were developed by the NSW Department of School Education (1989). They were:

Child Protection: Preventing Child Sexual Assault, Kindergarten to Year 6;
Child Protection: Preventing Child Sexual Assault, Years 7 to 12;
Child Protection: Preventing Child Sexual Assault, Students with an Intellectual Disability;
Child Protection: Preventing Child Sexual Assault, Early Childhood Curriculum Ideas;
Child Protection: Staff Development Support Document;
Child Protection: Parents and Community Information Manual.

There are two main curriculum documents *Child Protection: Preventing Child Sexual Assault, Kindergarten to Year 6* (NSW Department of Education, 1989) and *Child Protection: Preventing Child Sexual Assault,*

Years 7 to 12 (NSW Department of Education, 1989). The content of the curriculum materials is divided into two strands — 'Protecting Oneself' and 'Nature of Relationships' reflecting the belief that both protective skills and relationship skills are necessary components of an effective prevention program.

The 'Protecting Oneself' strand recognises that children have an immediate need to learn ways that will help them to protect themselves if an older or bigger person sexually threatens or assaults them. Children and adolescents learn that they have personal and legal rights which can be exercised to help them prevent sexual assault. While children learn that they should never be given the sole responsibilty for preventing sexual assault, there are many ways that they can be empowered to help protect themselves from assault. Children learn that sexual assault occurs and includes a range of sexually exploitative behaviour. The type of understanding developed in the curriculum materials varies according to the age of students. For example, in kindergarten, students may understand different types of touch which makes them feel uncomfortable or unsafe. A student in Year nine will develop more sophisticated understandings of sexually exploitative behaviour.

The 'Nature of Relationships' strand provides a long term perspective which recognises that social change is needed to reduce the incidence of child sexual assault. By assisting students to develop and maintain positive relationships, the incidence of child sexual assault can be reduced. Sgroi (1982, 13) writes that child sexual assault most often involves a

> known adult who is in a legitimate power position over a child and who exploits accepted societal patterns of dominance and authority to engage the child in sexual activity. It is impossible to overemphasise the significance of this exploitation and the misuse of accepted power relationships when assessing the impact of sexual abuse on the child.

Students examine power in relationships and the use and abuse of such power. They are encouraged to develop a sense of their own power, that is, a sense of their capability to act and effect change in their lives. The teaching/learning activities in the curriculum help students to become confident, capable of thinking for themselves and of making judgements and decisions.

This strand also focuses on the development and maintenance of self-esteem, communication skills, identifying and expressing feelings, values, decision making, sexuality, assertiveness and the skills for developing and maintaining positive relationships. The enhancement of self-esteem is a particularly important component of the prevention program both from the point of view of potential offenders as well as victims.

The importance of men and women learning caring and nurturing skills as an essential step in the prevention of child sexual assault is reinforced by Finkelhor (1982, 101) who writes that 'as they take more and more responsibility for the care of children, men will come to identify more closely with children's well-being'. Respect for the rights of others, and the acceptance of responsibilities by those who are in positions of power increases the likelihood that students will develop and maintain positive relationships, both as children and as adults. This development and change in the nature of relationships is crucial to supporting the aim of decreasing the incidence of child sexual assault in our society.

The model suggested for organising teaching/learning activities in the child protection curriculum materials for students in kindergarten to year twelve is the I.O.D.E. (Intake, Organisation, Demonstration, Expression) model (Fraenkel, 1980). This model identifies a sequence of learning where *intake* involves gathering information about the topic to be explored using the senses; *organising* this information so that it can be used; *demonstrating* that the information has been understood or displaying skills; and creating an original *expression* of the information or skill in a new context.

In this framework several strategies are used including the following:

Unfinished stories: open ended stories are presented to students and students are asked 'What could this child do?'. It is important in child sexual assault education that the third person is used eg, 'this child' and not 'what could you do?'. This ensures that children are not asked to imagine themselves in threatening situations. Children develop possible strategies and actions for the child in the potentially threatening situation and discuss the implications of those strategies or actions. In child sexual assault education, teachers indicate responsible strategies which would not further endanger the child in the unfinished story.

Values inquiry: involves values clarification, analysis, and judging. Clarification requires students to identify ideas, concepts or beliefs which they consider important or worthwhile. Students reflect on the way their values influence attitudes and behaviour.

Analysis: requires students to explore the values of others, the values implicit in a described situation, and the possible reasons people have for adhering to those values.

Values Judging: requires students to choose between conflicting values and to decide on an appropriate course of action. This is important in child sexual assault as many victims have been told by offenders that if they tell, no-one will believe them, or others will hate them or that the child will get into trouble.

Roleplay or behaviour rehearsal: is used to have children rehearse safe practices. It should be noted that under no circumstances are students to be asked to role play an assault situation.

Brainstorming: involves the expression and recording of students' responses to a question or proposition. Brainstorming allows each student to make a contribution, brings sensitive issues into a more open forum and allows the teacher to assess the level of students' understanding of issues.

Questioning: inquiry, discovery and problem solving all depend on questioning by students and teachers. Questions can aim at acquiring information, organising data, seeking explanations, obtaining conclusions or creative thinking. Teachers need to avoid questions that are too specific or directive which may lead to a personal or anecdotal response inappropriate for classroom discussion. The teacher's skill in redirecting such responses is very important. The teacher can then address the issues individually with the students after the lesson is over.

A curriculum document, *Child Protection: Students with an Intellectual Disability*, was also prepared (NSW Department of Education, 1989). It was considered that this group was particularly vulnerable. Offenders may target children with an intellectual disability because of the low probability of their resistance, the fact that extreme vulnerability and powerlessness are in themselves motivating factors to potential offenders, and the low probability of a child who has been sexually assaulted reporting the offence.

Factors which may contribute to the powerlessness of children with an intellectual disability include their lack of opportunities to learn self-care skills which make them dependent on others for basic care; lack of assertiveness to stop inappropriate touching and to initiate action if their safety is threatened; lack of communication skills that would enable them to identify and report instances of assault and to interact socially with others in an appropriate manner; and lack of knowledge of sexual relationships which allows adolescents to discern consensual activity and assault.

The teaching/learning activities for students with an intellectual disability are based on a skills approach (Schiefelbusch 1981) which includes such strategies as activity analysis, task analysis, prompting, reinforcement and generalisation. This approach breaks down the tasks into their component parts. Using specific techniques such as reinforcing correct behaviour and modelling appropriate responses, the component parts are taught in sequence and build up to the whole action. This builds up into the desired behaviour. The units are suitable for students with varying degrees of intellectual disability and can be adapted for use with students with other special needs.

A document, *Child Protection: Early Childhood Curriculum Ideas* (NSW Department of Education, 1989) was also developed for students aged four to six years. There are key lessons, including identifying feelings and networking, and a number of lessons developing protective skills and positive relationship skills with young children.

Implementation and Evaluation
To work effectively with parents and children in this area, it is crucial that teachers receive appropriate staff development opportunities in the area of child protection. Awareness of child protection issues was raised in NSW government schools through an extensive in-service program when teachers were made mandatory notifiers of child sexual assault in 1987 (Lamond, 1989). During this training, teachers expressed concern about the general issue of child sexual assault and a desire to implement longer term preventive strategies. In order to assist teachers further with the implementation of the child protection curriculum materials a *Child Protection: Staff Development Package* (NSW Department of Education, 1989) was developed. This package followed a concerns-based adoption model for curriculum implementation (Hall, Wallace & Dossett, 1973) as this was considered to be the most appropriate model for curriculum implementation in this sensitive area.

This model proposes raising awareness of the issues, giving knowledge about the issues, developing ways to address individual concerns and school concerns, implementing the program and finally reorganising the problem as a result of an evaluation of the implementation. As child protection involves many sensitive issues, addressing concerns of teachers and the school is a critical step in the model.

A model of implementation was adopted which involved training key teachers in schools and developing a network of support for schools wishing to implement the materials. The initial training involved two teachers from ten schools in each of the ten education regions in the state. This was achieved over a four month period. There was a focus on these teachers both coordinating the implementation of the materials in their own school and later assisting other schools to implement the materials. Each of the ten education regions had a student welfare consultant who then coordinated the use of the trained teachers and presented further training. By the end of 1990 over two hundred schools were implementing the curriculum materials.

In general, there has been overwhelming support by parents resulting in parents and teachers working together for the protection of children. Another important aspect of working closely with parents in implementing child protection curriculum materials is that this was almost a second-phase community awareness program which complemented the mass media campaign implemented by the NSW Child Protection Council. Through meetings and discussions at school, parents and teachers had an opportunity to find out more about child protection issues and this supported preventive education programs being implemented at the broader community level.

One of the critical areas in child protection education is the evaluation of the effectiveness of strategies used both with children and used to assist teachers to implement the curriculum. The training program for teachers was evaluated very positively by the participants.

There is currently no formal structure in place for evaluating the effectiveness of the curriculum materials on a broad basis. In the child protection education area in Australia little long term research has been done in relation to the effectiveness of such education. While teacher evaluation of the program occurs constantly at a classroom level, one of the difficulties in evaluation is selecting measures which indicate an effective outcome at a broader level.

Evaluating the effectiveness of the shorter term strategies for secondary and tertiary protective skills can at first seem relatively simple. If the protective strategies of, for example, 'saying no, going and telling' is effective then more children will tell about an assault and, consequently, notifications of suspected child sexual assault will increase. On the other hand such strategies may be judged to be effective if children were able to avoid an assault and consequently have nothing to tell. In this situation, notifications would be expected to decrease.

At another level, effectiveness might not be measured by the number of disclosures but by the effects of an assault. An indicator of a successful education program might be that even when children are assaulted, they have an understanding of the issues and do not blame themselves, and those around them provide appropriate support. Success might be measured by the type of consequences a disclosure has for a child that is, the type of response by adults and the type and extent of support for a child might be a better indicator of success than simple disclosure and notification statistics.

It is, perhaps, in this context of the quality of response to reports of child sexual assault that the effectiveness of a program can best be measured. The quality of response, including the response to disclosure, notification, quality of intervention, investigation, counselling and the legal system will be the most telling measures of the effectiveness of a child protection program.

Ongoing Issues
The rights of children to a safe, secure and caring environment is not questioned within the community. The way that such a childhood is achieved is often hotly debated. In developing child protection education materials the broadest possible community input needs to be secured. The values and beliefs of different groups within the community will influence the type of materials developed. These values and beliefs range from those who believe that young children need to know all about the risks in the community and the potential harm to them; to those who believe that children are permanently affected by even knowing that risks might exist. These extremes are represented on many issues and there will be ongoing debate on the issue of child protective education. The child's welfare must always be paramount and, while all views will be discussed and lobbied for, it is important that the perspective of a 'reasonable person' is maintained.

Preventive education programs in schools are only one response required to the sexual assault of children. Child protective education cannot stand alone, as can none of the other parts of the child protection system. There must be a commitment to a quality response from all parts of the system — welfare, police, counselling and legal — if a community is serious about finding solutions to the problem of child sexual assault. Some vigilance is required to ensure that all aspects of a preventive response for a community is heading in a consistent direction and making sense of the issue in the same way.

Funding for different social programs is competitive and training a network of interested and committed people is critical in ensuring the implementation of preventive strategies even when funding has been redirected to other causes. Unless an initiative has been implemented to a stage where the direct implementers of that initiative, in this case teachers, have been trained and are motivated then the initiative is at risk of no longer being supported when policy priorities change. Difficult issues for the community, such as child sexual assault, need to be evaluated regularly and placed on the community's agenda for long term effective prevention to occur.

4
Effective Work with Vulnerable Families: The Experience of the Alys Key Family Care Demonstration Project, 1986-89

Wendy O'Brien

In October 1985, the Children's Protection Society relinquished its contract to provide the Victorian protection service to Community Services Victoria. For 90 years the Children's Protection Society had held the mandate to receive reports of child abuse and neglect, to make investigations and to take action to protect children within Victoria. This had been sufficient time for the society to have accumulated evidence of the generational cycle of child abuse and to have become aware that the rescue model approach, that is removing children from 'maltreating families', did not in itself ensure that these children became effective parents in the next generation. The Society was therefore keen to establish a service that could effectively assist families where children were being abused and neglected, without removing the children from the parents' care.

Before establishing the new service, a literature search was made to identify service models that demonstrated that positive changes had occurred with maltreating families. An extensive evaluation of child abuse and neglect demonstration projects in the USA had been undertaken by Cohn (1977) highlighting a number of features in service design and operating principles that were correlated with success. The features that seemed particularly relevant to creating our new service were the following:

Service Design
1. Specialist resources, ie social workers or other trained helping professionals, concentrated on intake, assessment, case review and coordination.
2. Individual programs and interventions were tailored to suit the needs of individual families. Many different strategies were seen to be effective. However, the more successful outcomes were obtained where families used a variety of service components, eg group work combined with family counselling, child care and family aide work.
3. Long term intervention (defined as in excess of six months), was required for many families.
4. Services that could respond at the time of crisis for families were seen to be more effective than those whose caseloads or work practices reduced their capacity to respond at times of crisis.
5. Services involved whole families, that is both parents and the children, rather than specific family members.
6. Programs contained both centre based and home based activities.
7. Programs included lay counselling (ie, family aide support), volunteers, self-help, group work, and a parent training focus emphasising parent-child interactions.
8. Services that worked towards reducing families' social isolation, increasing their use of community resources and the alleviation of their environmental stresses, were more successful than those that focused only on issues in the families' relationships.

Operating Principles
1. Emphasis was placed on quality staff selection, ongoing training, staff development, supervision and support.
2. Services were well integrated in the service network, maintaining appropriate referral between services.
3. Services providing a multi-faceted approach were well co-ordinated with links between service components so that an integrated approach was delivered to families.

The Alys Key Family Care Service
In its implementation, Alys Key Family Care has attempted to incorporate the findings of the literature search in its service model design and in its operation. In addition to the literature search, the

Society consulted with existing service providers in three areas of metropolitan Melbourne about its proposed service. These areas were the north east, inner and western suburbs, all of which had consistently registered high incidences of reported child abuse/neglect. In response to this consultation, the Heidelberg, Diamond Valley and Eltham municipalities of the north east region were chosen as the catchment area for the new service.

A formative research study (Martin and Pitman 1986) was commissioned and its recommendations were also incorporated in the service. As the service was essentially new and untried, the Society believed it essential to evaluate it and share the findings with other agencies and practitioners in the field. A full time research officer was one of the first staff appointed.

Target Population
Alys Key Family Care gives priority to families who would otherwise lose the care of their children. Many of these experience problems in every area of family functioning. Parenting problems are pronounced and parent-child interactions are often characterised by unpredictable explosive outbursts, or by an emotionally unavailable parent, who pushes away or does not respond to the child's needs. The children often show behavioural disturbances and/or developmental delay. The families have few supportive relationships amongst friends, neighbours or relatives, and whilst they are often well known to other community services, they are more likely to be known as users of the system than as families who make constructive use of community resources.

It was not surprising that when our research officer traced the history of the 62 families involved during the first two years of the service, she discovered that 42 had had prior contact with protective services. Child maltreatment, in all its forms, had been identified strongly by the community within our client group of families (McIntosh, 1988).

The socio-economic profile of the client population of Alys Key Family Care was detailed in the final research and evaluation report (McIntosh, 1989). What emerged was that the 'high risk' families, that is those who were likely to lose the care of their children because of identified child maltreatment, were more socio-economically disadvantaged than families involved with the agency for other reasons. Overall the socio-economic profile of all the families was much lower than that of the general population in the three municipalities serviced. For example, 90 per cent of all mothers were in receipt of some form of pension or benefit (n=68) and 47 per cent of all fathers were in receipt of a pension or benefit (n=32). Fewer than half the families (47 per cent) had fathers associated with the family unit, and not all of those contributed consistently to the income of the family unit. More than half of the families lived in Ministry of Housing rented accommodation: 70 per cent in the case of high risk families. Only six per cent of mothers and fathers from the high risk group had completed schooling to year eleven level.

Family Groupings

For research and practice purposes, groupings were devised to differentiate between 'high risk', 'medium risk' and 'low risk' families at the point of intake. This was based on the definition of family functioning and problems in family functioning as outlined by Geismer (1980). Geismer considered nine areas in developing a descriptive profile of family functioning (which the service initially adopted as an assessment tool). These were: family relationships and family unity; behaviour and adjustment of individual family members; care and training of children; social activities of the family; economic practices; home and household practices; health conditions and practices; use of community resources, and relationship with the agency. A pre-coded schedule devised by Geismer was used to score and chart each family's level of family functioning throughout their involvement with Alys Keys Family Care.

- Group 1 (High risk): Families with severe and chronic problems in family functioning where the children are likely to go into state care without significant intervention and change. (Such families had already been identified in the community because of child maltreatment, and protective services assessment indicated likely removal of children if the protective issues were not resolved.)
- Group 2 (Medium risk): Families with one or more severe problems in family functioning but where the family is not likely to lose the care of their children. (In these families, protective issues had been identified; however, referrers believed the removal of children was not indicated at that time.)
- Group 3 (Low risk): Families that basically function well, but because of some particular crisis, require short term, task focused intervention. (In these families, protective issues had been viewed by referrers as transient.)

These family groupings facilitated screening of families at intake, where every effort was made to accept referrals of high risk families (Group 1) while low risk families (Group 3) were referred to more generalist services.

Aims
Alys Key Family Care has four clear program goals:

1. To retain children within the care of their families without being subjected to severe abuse or neglect.
2. To enhance parenting skills and empower parents to nurture and care for their own children.
3. To improve children's physical, emotional, social and intellectual development.
4. To improve overall family functioning, both within the family as well as the family's links with their community.

As the service was initially established as a demonstration project for three years, the research officer spent time with casework staff transposing these goals into measurable objectives, and specifying indicators which would show whether or not the agency was achieving change with its families (McIntosh, 1986).

Service Model: The Importance of Team Work
Dale & Davies (1985), Dale, Waters, et al (1986) have highlighted the importance of teamwork and the use of family therapy concepts in effective work with maltreating families. Dale & Davies (1985) and Molin & Herskowitz (1986) also have highlighted how the helpers can mirror the relationships in dysfunctional families, and can collude with the families so that change does not occur. The Alys Key Family Care service design is based on the premise that family patterns of parenting are resistant to change, particularly in high risk families, and that sole workers are quickly placed in a powerless position against entrenched family systems.

The service model incorporates a team approach to whole families rather than individual family members. Depending on the particular needs of the family, a team of a family counsellor, family support worker and children's services worker, can be established to work with the family. In addition, a variety of group programs are available at the centre and volunteer 'special friends' can be linked with selected children. Fortnightly, family team meetings to review, plan and evaluate the ongoing work with families, are a key feature of the model and are essential in maintaining cohesive team work.

In addition to service delivery being based on a team model, the staff are also grouped in teams: the family counsellor, the family support worker, the child care and the parent education teams. This structure has allowed for mutual support, encouragement and cohesiveness to develop.

Organisation Structure:

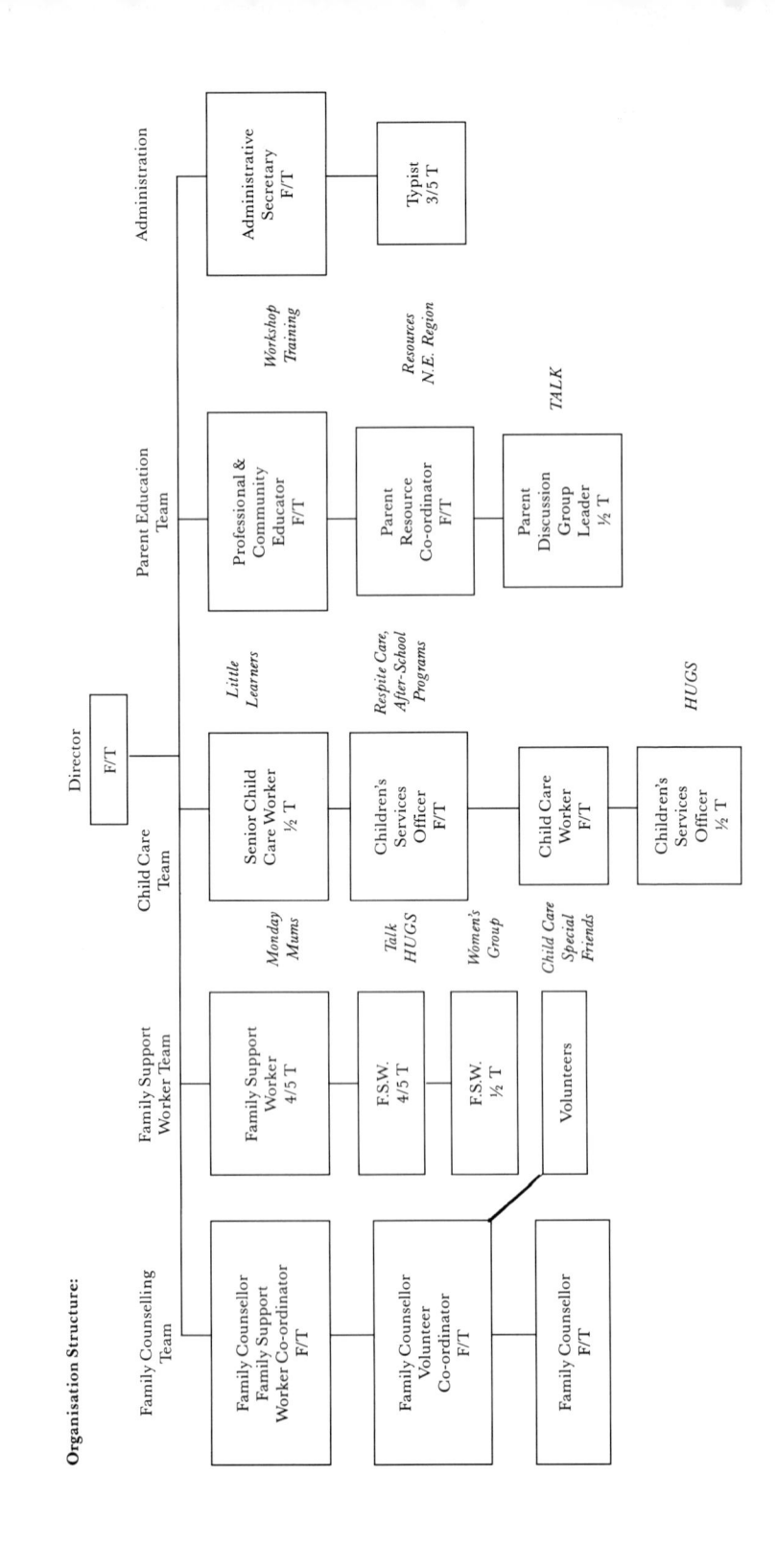

```
                                                    Director
                                                      F/T
                                                        |
  ┌──────────────┬──────────────┬──────────────┬──────────────────────┬──────────────────┐
Family         Family         Child Care     Parent Education                         Administration
Counselling    Support        Team           Team
Team           Worker Team
  │              │              │              │                                          │
┌─────────┐  ┌─────────┐   ┌─────────┐    ┌──────────────┐                        ┌──────────────┐
│ Family  │  │ Family  │   │ Senior  │    │ Professional │                        │Administrative│
│Counsellor│ │ Support │   │Child Care│   │ & Community  │                        │  Secretary   │
│  Family │  │ Worker  │   │ Worker  │    │   Educator   │                        │     F/T      │
│ Support │  │  4/5 T  │   │  ½ T    │    │     F/T      │                        └──────┬───────┘
│ Worker  │  └────┬────┘   └────┬────┘    └──────┬───────┘                               │
│Co-ordinator│        Monday     Little            Workshop                        ┌─────────┐
│   F/T   │        Mums        Learners           Training                         │ Typist  │
└────┬────┘   ┌─────────┐   ┌─────────┐    ┌──────────────┐                        │  3/5 T  │
     │        │  F.S.W. │   │Children's│   │   Parent     │                        └─────────┘
┌─────────┐   │  4/5 T  │   │ Services │   │  Resource    │
│ Family  │   └────┬────┘   │ Officer │    │ Co-ordinator │
│Counsellor│       Talk     │   F/T   │    │     F/T      │
│Volunteer │       HUGS     └────┬────┘    └──────┬───────┘
│Co-ordinator│  ┌─────────┐  Respite Care,              Resources
│   F/T    │   │  F.S.W. │  After-School               N.E. Region
└────┬─────┘   │   ½ T   │  Programs
     │         └────┬────┘   ┌─────────┐   ┌──────────────┐
     │          Women's      │Child Care│   │   Parent     │
     │          Group        │ Worker  │    │ Discussion   │
┌─────────┐                  │   F/T   │    │   Group      │
│Volunteers│                 └────┬────┘    │   Leader     │
└─────────┘                 Child Care      │    ½ T       │
     │                      Special         └──────────────┘
     │                      Friends                TALK
┌─────────┐                 ┌─────────┐
│ Family  │                 │Children's│
│Counsellor│                │ Services │
│   F/T   │                 │ Officer │
└─────────┘                 │   ½ T   │
                            └─────────┘
                              HUGS
```

Specific Roles

The Family Counsellor
After accepting a referral, the allocated family counsellor is introduced to the family and has the task of assessing with the family the problems that exist, what needs to be changed and how the service can assist in that process. The counsellor's aim is to engage the family fully in the process of change: agreement is reached between the family and the agency about mutual goals, and a working contract specifies how these goals are to be achieved. A full team is introduced to work on the strategies for achieving the goals, once a working contract is negotiated.

In ongoing work, the role of the family counsellor includes directing the team and providing whatever counselling is indicated, eg marital counselling, family therapy or individual work, advocating on behalf of the family, negotiating with other service providers and crisis intervention work. The family counsellor raises protective concerns with parents and ensures that these are fully addressed so that the children can safely remain at home. The family counsellor is responsible for organising six-monthly reviews with the family in relation to their progress and the relevance of each team member's work.

The Family Support Worker (Family Aide)
This worker provides practical modelling and guidance in establishing household routines, in budgeting, shopping, cooking and in other household chores. She provides emotional support and offers suggestions on child management, often being present in the home when problems arise between parents and children. She encourages parents to try more positive approaches, and links them in with other community resources. The support workers frequently provide nurturing, encouraging, prompting and, at times, push the parents to take control over their own lives and their children.

The Children's Services Worker
When the service first commenced, it was hoped the children's services worker would be able to assist the parents to understand better the needs of their children, and encourage parents and children to play and join in activities together. Quickly we learnt that this did not succeed with our high risk families. The parents were simply too overwhelmed and preoccupied with their own problems to even recognise their children as other people with needs to be met by them, when so many of their own needs remained unmet.

Consequently, we modified our approach and now offer a variety of group and individual sessions to the children at the outset. All too often the children are developmentally delayed or they exhibit behaviour problems, so that direct work with them is necessary immediately. Only when some of the parents' worries have subsided, and they can appreciate their children's needs, do we now attempt to bring the parents and children together in activities.

The Group Programs

TALK (Talk and Action for Living with Kids) provides a time for parents to share the difficulties of living with children and to learn different ways of coping as a parent. Building positive relationships with children is emphasised as is the development of the parents' self-esteem.

HUGS (Happiness, Understanding, Giving and Sharing) is a special group for parents and pre-school children where every activity invites positive interaction between parents and children, and new ways of managing children are suggested. This group is especially appropriate for parents who have little concept of relating to their children, or where there is difficulty expressing affection and caring.

LITTLE LEARNERS allows the child care team to work intensively with pre-schoolers who are slow in achieving their development.

RESPITE CARE is a weekly program for children aged one to five, with the essential purpose of 'giving mum a break', but with the added motive of providing the children with extra stimulation, enjoyment and friendship within a safe nurturing environment. The group runs every Wednesday morning for two and a half hours. The children are collected from their homes and cared for by child care staff and regular volunteers.

MONDAY MUMS ON THURSDAY is a support group for those women involved with Alys Key Family Care who are socially isolated, insecure and ill-equipped with even basic social skills. The group provides an opportunity for them to mix and socialise in a safe and familiar place and to grow with a sense of belonging.

AFTER SCHOOL GROUPS enable school age children to come to the centre for activities. Two of the groups cater for a mix of children from a number of families, but most are for sibling groups. Whilst the initial idea behind these groups was providing additional stimulation and opportunity for enjoyment for the children, they are now more focused around children's individual needs and are therapeutic in nature.

PUSH (Personal Understanding and Self Help) caters for parents who have progressed through other groups, such as TALK, but who need greater strengthening to cope independently. It offers a personal growth program aimed at enhancing self-esteem, learning assertive behaviour and problem solving skills.

STUDENTS' GROUP caters for many of the parents with minimal literacy skills, and is run by a literacy teacher from the Preston TAFE college.

The Research
The research officer produced three major reports at the end of each of the first three years (McIntosh, 1987, McIntosh, 1988 and McIntosh, 1989).

The aims of the research were threefold:

1. To explore, describe, monitor and evaluate the Alys Key Family Care service in its three years' operation as a demonstration project.
2. To clarify the sorts of programs and types of interventions that were effective with high risk families.
3. To modify and fine tune the service model and programs to meet families' needs.

The evaluation framework included collecting data on client characteristics at intake, monitoring all case inputs, assessing case outcomes using the Geismer pre-coded schedule of family functioning (Geismer, 1980), information being recorded on case file summary sheets, and also using client-structured feedback interviews. In addition, all group programs were reviewed and staff and local service providers were asked to review the effectiveness of the service.

Key Findings from the Research
During the years 1986-89, 264 children from 102 families were involved in the program. Of the 264 children, 129 were identified as children at high risk of being removed from their natural families because of potential or actual maltreatment and 46 already had some form of statutory status, that is, they were either state wards or under supervision orders at intake.

Total children in program 1986-89	264
Children considered at high risk	129
Children removed from parents' care	9
Overall percentage retention of children in parents' care	96%
Percentage retention of high risk children in parents' care	93%

Only nine children were removed from families during the families' involvement with the centre. Given that the service has a strong policy of immediately raising concerns directly with parents and of involving protective services, where risk to the children remains, the retention of 93 per cent of high risk children within their parents' care, is seen as very successful.

Endorsement of the Service Model
The final research and evaluation report (McIntosh, 1989) provided comprehensive evidence for the endorsement of the service model developed by Alys Key Family Care. There was evidence that the service was successful in enabling children to remain in their parents' care without being subjected to further abuse. A comparative cost study indicated the financial benefits of providing the service. Progress and outcome data from the Geismer pre-coded schedule of family functioning showed gains, particularly in the areas of reducing the family's social isolation, enhancing the mothers' individual functioning, and in improving the family's economic practices and use of community resources. The Little Learners group facilitated development of all the children involved in the group, and parenting skills and confidence was enhanced through parents' involvement in the TALK and HUGS programs.

Further, it has been our experience that effective work with high risk families incorporates the following key aspects:

1. A combination of services: (a) using teamwork, including a mix of professional and lay workers; (b) group work, with family members being introduced to appropriate groups: for example a low key informal social support group for an isolated mother who lacks confidence, rather than a more challenging group addressing parenting or personal growth.
2. The service initially must reach out to families putting considerable energy into the engagement and assessment phase of work.
3. Clear working agreements are important in setting out goals of work, and the family's and agency's commitment, expectations of and obligations to each other.
4. It is crucial to address all aspects of family functioning, both within the family and outside the family in working with high risk families.

Characteristics of Successful Workers
In the past five years, I have come to believe strongly that effective workers with high risk families have both the capacity to empathise with parents and join with their hurting child within, as well as have the capacity to be forthright and open about what is not acceptable

behaviour from the parents and to act strongly to protect the children at all times. I have seen highly skilled workers attempt therapeutic work with high risk families, where children have been further abused, because these workers themselves could not confront the protective issues in a clear and non-negotiable way. Some gains may have been made in individual functioning, but children were still hurt.

Effective Engagement of High Risk Families
Effective work begins when a family is properly engaged in a change process. We have found it useful to define four levels of engagement; if you can reach and maintain a level 4 engagement with a family, then positive change happens.

Level 1. Agreement of family to meet family counsellor.
Level 2. Meetings between family and service continue on a regular, planned basis, without 'missed' appointments or withdrawal by either family members or agency workers.
Level 3. Agreement is reached between family and family counsellor about family problems that need to be addressed.
Level 4. Agreement is reached between family and agency about mutual goals and a working contract spells out the strategies for achieving these goals. Expectations for both family and agency in working contracts are explicit.

Getting to level 2 can be greatly enhanced by having a very clear referral process, whereby the referrer introduces you to the family, all protective concerns are clearly tabled at the first meeting, a working relationship is established with the family and the family are clear about worker's role and aims.

Proceeding beyond level 2 to a level 4 engagement with high risk families requires:

- outreach
- persistence
- clear setting of expectations
- constant reiterating of purpose of involvement and clarification of the working agreement
- dependability
- empowerment
- providing information, enabling choices
- helping family members gain a sense of belonging, to feel appreciated and understood
- helping the family find order out of chaos

- acknowledgment of resistance, anger, fear
- providing hope
- anticipating difficulties

Protection before Treatment
One of the key principles that underpins effective work with families where children have been maltreated is that . . .

Protection Precedes Treatment
The team of workers at the Rochdale NSPCC in England in particular Dale, Davies and Morrison, (1986) have written widely on this principle. Other authors Jones & Alexander (1987) and Crittenden (1988) have independently reached similar conclusions. In Victoria, this is increasingly becoming an accepted principle in the child protection field.

The experience at Alys Key Family Care also endorses this principle, and yet it is easy for workers to work with parents because they are motivated to change behaviour in other areas without acknowledging responsibility for the abuse/neglect. It is important for workers to address the child maltreatment issues directly at the outset and to test whether the parents do accept responsibility by openly acknowledging their role as perpetrator or bystander in the abuse or neglect, and by being prepared to change the situation. If the parents do not accept this responsibility, minimal change occurs, and the children remain at risk. In these cases, the service and its workers tend to assume the greater responsibility for monitoring the children: considerable time and energy is expended by workers, rather than by the parents in ensuring the children's safe development. This is not a constructive use of the service and clear guidelines are needed for handling these families.

Effective Team Work
A team approach was chosen because it was felt that families with multiple problems required workers with a variety of skills to address the range of problems. The team could sustain a coordinated, goal oriented direction, whereas a sole worker could be easily overwhelmed by the magnitude and recurrence of problems.

An exploratory study (McIntosh, 1989) researched the team process within the agency by selecting two samples of ten high risk families, one group consisting of families who had noticeably improved in their family functioning during involvement with the Centre (as plotted on the Geismer index of family functioning), and the other group consisting of families where there had been no improvement in family functioning. These two samples were carefully matched in their

Geismer (1980) family functioning profiles at intake, and also in regard to major variables, such as number of single parent families, previous statutory involvement, numbers of children, existence of substance abuse by parents, marital breakdown and domestic violence. All twelve workers involved with the families in the study were individually interviewed about the way the various teams had operated in semi-structured interviews.

The teams from the improved sample, on average, reported greater clarity than the teams which worked with the unimproved sample in both immediate and long term goals. They also reported greater satisfaction with the number of team meetings and the ways these meetings were organised and said they were more likely to feel free to share feelings and opinions about their work in team meetings.

They rated the family's acceptance of protective issues and family's willingness to change higher. The teams from the improved sample also stated that any protective issues had been dealt with in the best possible way although they admitted there had been times when these issues could have been better dealt with by the team. They felt that for 60 per cent of the time, the families accepted responsibility for change, whereas in the unimproved sample, this was thought to only occur 20 per cent of the time.

This study by MacIntosh (1989) highlighted clear correlations between case outcome and team functioning, but this, of course, does not imply causality. Although small scale, it has produced some evidence of possible parallel processes occurring in 'poor' functioning teams and 'unimproved' families. It also provides some further evidence of the critical importance of dealing effectively with protective issues in maltreating families. It is tempting to suggest from this study that if teamwork is chosen as the core approach to working with maltreating families, then to be effective, management needs to ensure that teams achieve unity and co-ordination.

Conclusion

Alys Key Family Care emphasises teamwork as part of its service model, together with the innovative group programs that it offers. The research has demonstrated the worth of the service in meeting its stated objectives in working with high risk families and in demonstrating real cost benefits to government. Much has been learnt about the nature of the service and strategies that work with families who have previously been seen as 'too multi-problem' and 'too resistant to change'. It is our hope that others in the welfare field will learn from our exciting beginnings at Alys Key Family Care.

Children in the Legal System

The legal system plays a vital role in the protection of children. The law provides a framework in which child protection work can take place, and allows for coercive intervention wherever this is necessary to protect a child, whether through care and protection proceedings or through the prosecution of suspected offenders. It endeavours to safeguard the rights of both the children and adults, by ensuring that legal sanctions are only invoked where there is appropriate proof of the matters alleged. It also protects children and families from the despotic benevolence of which child welfare authorities have sometimes been guilty.

In recent years, however, the legal system has been widely perceived as failing to protect children. Most attention has been focused upon the criminal justice system, in cases where child sexual assault has been alleged. Rules of evidence and procedure which in another age were seen as essential, to protect a suspect's rights, have been attacked as violating the rights of victims, especially young children. Courts have not been accustomed to dealing with such young (and crucial) witnesses; still less have they been used to taking such evidence seriously. The new awareness of child sexual assault, from child welfare professionals and the wider community, has led to demands for changes in the law and in the attitudes of legal personnel. Such calls for change have often been met with resistance. Common law protections which have evolved over centuries are not lightly to be abandoned, and the legal profession has needed to be convinced that changes to law and procedure serve the interests of justice.

Structural changes, however, are only part of the answer. Just as important perhaps is the fostering of respect and co-operation between lawyers and other professionals, and the sharing of different perspectives and insights. The means by which a paediatrician or social worker diagnoses child abuse cannot always satisfy the lawyer for whom proof is not the same as diagnosis. The demands of the criminal justice system and the therapeutic needs of a child or family may also be at variance.

The following two chapters endeavour to encourage this interdisciplinary understanding. The first chapter reports on psychological research concerning the reliability of children as witnesses, and discusses the steps which may be necessary to facilitate children's participation in the criminal justice system. The second examines a quite different issue at the interface of law and child welfare — the use of legal proceedings in cases where the relationship between parents and a child (or young person) has broken down. Such breakdowns are one aspect of the crisis of homeless youth in Australian society. The question is raised whether, in these cases, the law really has a useful role.

5
The Competence of Child Witnesses

Kay Bussey

The conclusion of this paper is not new. It was reached in 1940, fifty years ago, by Wigmore (1940) in his volumes *On Evidence*. I will, however, argue the grounds for this conclusion on the basis of contemporary theorizing and research. First, Wigmore's conclusion:

> A rational view of the peculiarities of child nature, and of the daily course of justice in our courts, must lead to the conclusion that the effort to measure a priori the degrees of trustworthiness in children's statements, and to distinguish the point at which they cease to be totally incredible and acquire suddenly some degree of credibility, is futile and unprofitable . . . Recognising, on the one hand, the childish disposition to weave romances and to treat imagination for verity, and on the other the rooted ingenuousness of children and their tendency to speak straightforwardly what is in their minds, it must be concluded that the sensible way is to put the child upon the stand and let the story come out for what it may seem to be worth (Wigmore 1940, Section 509).

In recent times, a great deal of attention has been devoted by the media (both print and electronic), discussion groups, conferences and legislators, to children's capacity to serve as witnesses to their own sexual abuse in criminal proceedings.

The paucity of methodologically sound research has contributed to the controversy associated with the competence of young children to serve as witnesses in criminal court proceedings. At one end of the spectrum there are highly emotive assertions by some child advocates and at the other end there are the often unsubstantiated assertions made by the defence counsel's expert witnesses about children's competence as witnesses.

It is not surprising therefore that both lay persons and professionals working in the field find it difficult to make sense of the conflicting viewpoints advanced. This paper will by no means provide a beacon to navigate the reader clearly through the ragged edges of knowledge about the competence of child witnesses. For some issues we may see through the fog; however, for most issues associated with this area of enquiry it will be some time before the fog totally clears. Until that time, it is essential that incisive questions are asked and sound methodology is employed if research is to help. Although the findings from research conducted by developmental psychologists have not produced definitive results that have led to uniform changes in the laws relating to child abuse victims, it is certainly true that the information gained from such studies has informed legal decision making (Melton, 1984, Reppucci, 1990). It is my purpose in this paper to show how one area of developmental psychology research, the study of children's lying and truth-telling, can inform legal decision making in relation to the competence of child victims of sexual abuse to testify about their alleged abuse.

Children's Competency to Testify

One of the major problems facing professionals trying to substantiate cases of child sexual abuse is that often there is no witness to the abuse and no supporting medical evidence. Hence, it is the child's word against the word of the adult abuser.

The abuse can come to the attention of adults by means of either the child's disclosure or by its being suspected by adults. Whichever way the suspected abuse comes to the attention of the authorities, it is the child's account of the abuse that is crucial in deciding if sexual abuse has or has not occurred. Hence, the competence of child witnesses to testify in criminal court cases about their own alleged sexual abuse has been the topic of numerous government and professional organization enquiries, for example, the *Report of the NSW Child Sexual Assault Taskforce* (NSW Government, 1985). The competence of the child witness is just one of a number of evidentiary issues that these enquiries have dealt with.

Developmental psychologists' concern about children's competence to provide courtroom testimony is a direct result of the increasing numbers of child victims of sexual abuse called upon to testify in criminal courts. These adult oriented venues rarely cater to the special needs of children (Bussey & Steward, 1985) and instead, children's competence to provide reliable testimony is frequently questioned. Both their ability to report witnessed events accurately and their capability for honesty are doubted. Children incur challenges to the veracity of their testimony that are rarely directed at adults' testimony. As a consequence, children's lying and truthfulness have become topics of renewed interest to developmental psychologists.

Some researchers seem to think that it is necessary to demonstrate that young children never or rarely lie about abuse in order to have their testimony taken seriously. However, this requirement demands a level of honesty that is not expected of adults. There is little doubt that adult witnesses do sometimes lie. It is the role of the jury, sometimes with instruction from the judge, to adjudicate the truthfulness of testimony.

To expect children always to be truthful even about such important issues as abuse, although desirable, seems unreasonable in view of the many faces of adult deception. Depending on the situation, children, like adults, will be truthful in some situations but not in others.

Other researchers argue that children's suggestibility renders them unreliable witnesses. It is worth noting, however, that there are ambiguous situations in which adults are vulnerable to suggestion too. The concern about children seems to stem from the belief that young children are particularly compliant to adults' demands since their understanding of lying and truthfulness is limited (Melton, 1985). From this viewpoint, children could be persuaded to report abuse when it has not occurred, or not to report it when it has occurred. Most recent research has focused on the former scenario. In the studies I report here, the focus is on the latter scenario.

An important reason for this focus derives from anecdotal and clinical reports that children do not disclose sexual abuse because they are bribed to keep it secret or are threatened about disclosure, or after disclosure they sometimes recant the allegations of abuse. Hence, in this research we consider children's propensity to report an adult's transgression when requested not to.

The theoretical basis of this research derives from social cognitive theory (Bandura, 1986). In this theory different factors govern what individuals can do and what they will do or do in fact do. The 'can' question relates mainly to children's memory capabilities, ability to differentiate fantasy from reality, suggestibility, and ability to recount the abuse — if very young, maybe through enactment rather than words. The difficulty in researching these issues relating to children's competency to testify in the context of the legal system has contributed to the continuing controversy associated with the topic. The field has been plagued with anecdotal accounts of children's competence or lack of competence because of the impossibility of conducting controlled experiments in the legal context. Recently, researchers have resorted to analogue studies and have capitalized on naturally occurring stressful events that children experience to elucidate the processes associated with the reliability of children's eyewitness reporting. That research has focused on children's memory for eyewitnessed events and the degree to which children are vulnerable to suggestibility, particularly if they are asked leading questions (see Ceci, Toglia & Ross, 1987). In particular, Goodman and her colleagues have focused their research on children's suggestibility in simulated investigations of child abuse (eg Goodman, Hirschman & Rudy, 1987). This research has been highly innovative and provided investigators in the field with important information. Goodman has countered reports earlier this century by Binet (1900), for example, that children are highly suggestible. Her research is more ecologically valid than previous research and requires children to remember personally meaningful events. Employing this methodology she has demonstrated that children as young as three to four years are resistant to leading questions about abuse. On the basis of a series of studies from Goodman's laboratories in which they '. . . have been trying to produce false reports of abuse, particularly sexual abuse', the conclusion is drawn that 'if children are as suggestible as former research might lead us to believe, this should not be a difficult task. We find, however, that it is!' (Goodman, Hirschman, & Rudy, 1987, 2).

Goodman's studies have provided invaluable information about children's eyewitness capabilities particularly when they are involved in the event. The finding that children can remember more about central elements of an event and that they are less vulnerable to suggestion and leading questions about such events, indicates that victim-witnesses have the potential of being far more reliable than their non-participant witness counterparts. An important recent study (Steward, 1989) further reveals that children in the three to five years age range can accurately recall details of a genital examination conducted in a medical clinic even six months after the examination. However, to conclude on the basis of these studies that children never fabricate abuse even when highly suggestive questioning is used needs more cautious consideration. In most of Goodman's studies there has been no reason to lie. When asked to recall events associated with having an injection or undergoing a stressful medical procedure, why would a child be motivated to distort events intentionally?

In other situations, however, although a child might be quite capable of reporting abuse, or a crime that they have witnessed committed by an adult, an important determinant of whether or not they report it depends on what they expect will happen as a result of reporting that information (Bandura, 1986, 1991). For example, some children might freely disclose abuse to a caring counsellor, but might be reluctant to report it in a court of law either out of fear of retaliation from the accused (Cashmore & Bussey, 1990) or from embarrassment (Saywitz, Goodman, Nicholas, & Moan, 1989). Thus although children may be able to tell the truth about a particular event, whether or not they will tell the truth depends on their expectations of the outcome for truth-telling.

Under what conditions can adults influence children to distort the truth? From social cognitive theory it is argued that for older children, beyond seven years of age, and adults who are more aware of the consequences of their behaviour and verbal statements, decision-making associated with lying and truthfulness is likely to be a complex process. For example, fear of disclosure for whatever reason may be coupled with knowing that it is important to tell the truth. For younger children, however, such conflicting options may not be as readily accessible. So, for older children, if the expected outcome for truth-telling is severe censure, they might decide to lie intentionally about the event they are asked to report on. Do these same considerations influence young children's decisions about truth-telling? Before describing this research, it is necessary to consider some issues about children's lying and truthfulness.

Children's Understanding of Lying and Truthfulness

From the perspective of Piaget's work, whether or not children are even capable of telling a lie is an issue. This is because lying involves deception, and young children, according to Piaget (1932/1965), are not capable of intentional deception. Instead, he wrote, 'for the little child, who really feels no inner obstacle to the practice of lying, and who at six years old still lies more or less as he romances or as he plays, the two types of conduct are on the same plane' (136).

Contemporary researchers, however, have pointed out that several aspects of Piaget's methods work against an adequate assessment of younger children (eg Peterson, Peterson, & Seeto, 1983, Wimmer, Gruber, & Perner, 1984, 1985). By modifying Piaget's methods so that they are more concrete and more easily understood by young children, researchers have found that children are capable of differentiating between lying and truthfulness several years earlier than Piaget thought possible. In a recent study (Bussey, 1989, 1992) children were presented with everyday lies that their peers had reported telling. Children were tested across three age groups: four, seven and ten years of age. The seven and ten year olds were completely accurate in their identification of lies and truthful statements and the four year olds obtained an 88 per cent accuracy score. Other studies (Haugaard & Crosby, 1989) have also shown that when children as young as four years of age are provided with situations relevant to their everyday experiences, they are able to differentiate statements that are truthful from those that are lies. These findings are particularly important for the courts where as a legacy from Piaget it is often suggested that children are unable to make this differentiation until many years later.

While it still remains that younger children are more likely to subscribe to an over-inclusive definition of 'a lie' in comparison to older children and adults in that even an unintentional false statement is designated a lie, they are quite capable of differentiating a lie from a truthful statement particularly when the statement has a specific behavioural referent (Bussey, 1992). But the court requires more than the child's being able to differentiate a lie from a truthful statement. It is necessary that children understand the importance of telling the truth and not lying. Recent research (Bussey, 1992) demonstrated that even four year olds gave more negative ratings for lying than for truthful statements. In sum, from this research it seems clear that children from as young as four years of age can differentiate a lie from a truthful statement and understand the importance of telling the truth and that it is wrong to lie. But does this affect their actual lying and truthfulness? This is an important concern since for younger children the relationship between knowledge and behaviour is less strong than it is for adults (Perry & Bussey, 1984).

Children's Actual Lying and Truthfulness
Lewis, Stanger and Sullivan (1989) investigated various aspects of children's actual lying. Three year olds were instructed not to peek at a toy, placed behind them. The majority (88 per cent) of these young children did peek during a five minute observation period. Of those who did peek, an equal number admitted their transgression (38 per cent) as denied it (38 per cent). It is tempting, without comparative data from older children and adults, to be concerned at the high percentage of children who 'lied' in this situation. However, 62 per cent of the children who peeked either owned up to their transgression or simply did not respond (the 'don't know' response — a response that is characteristic of young children) when asked if they peeked. Thus, the majority of the children in this study did not try to deny their transgression by providing a false statement to the tester. Even for those who did deny their transgression, whether their false statement was a lie is a moot point. For a statement to qualify as a lie (Bok, 1978,

Piaget, 1932/1965) the speaker must intend to deceive by inducing a false belief in the listener. Although the children who denied their transgression in this study provided a false statement, it is not possible to determine from these data if their false statement was motivated by intentional deception. Children may have provided the false statement as a way of avoiding punishment for committing the transgression without necessarily attempting to manipulate the beliefs of another deviously. If children realize that a behaviour or act is naughty, one way of avoiding punishment is to deny having performed the transgression (Stouthamer-Loeber, 1987). This type of learning is clearly within the capabilities of three year olds, but whether intentional deception is within their capabilities is debatable (Wimmer, Hogrefe & Sodian, 1988).

Although not supported by some researchers (Chandler, Fritz and Hala, 1989), the major part of research shows that it is not until four to four and a half years of age that children understand the concept of false belief and are therefore capable of intentional deception (Gopnik & Astington, 1988, Sodian, 1989). Hence, the young children in Lewis et al's (1989) study may have provided a false statement to avoid punishment (Stouthamer-Loeber, 1987) without necessarily attempting to be intentionally deceptive. Thus it is possible that as in other domains of development, children engage in a particular practice (deceptive-like statements) before they have the cognitive capabilities for understanding that practice (intentional deception). It would seem that an understanding of the concept of false belief is a necessary prerequisite for intentional deception. Once an understanding of this concept is acquired, how does it affect children's truthful disclosure or deception?

To attempt to answer such a question, it is necessary to consider the differences in deceptive-like patterns between children who understand the concept of false belief and those who do not. Children of three and five years were tested (Bussey, 1990) in a similar setting to the three year olds in Lewis et al's (1989) study. A similar percentage of the three year old children denied their transgression. However, of the five year olds who transgressed (50 per cent), most lied about their transgression (98 per cent). All the five year olds had mastered the concept of false belief, whereas virtually none of the three year olds had. The important finding was that, having transgressed, older children were more likely to lie than their younger counterparts. Not only had the five year olds mastered the concept of false belief but most of them also anticipated getting into trouble for admitting their transgression. In contrast, the majority of the three year olds had not mastered the concept of false belief nor did they anticipate punishment for admitting their transgression to the same extent as the five year olds.

To explore further the influence of children's expectations for lying and truth-telling we attempted to influence children's expectations by providing them with different motivations for lying. This enabled us to study adults' influence on children's propensity to lie. In this study, however, children were required to report on a transgression they witnessed rather than their own transgression (Bussey, Lee, & Rickard, 1990).

In most court cases involving sexual abuse, the child witness provides testimony against an adult male. Some writers have suggested that in such instances the child witness may have been instructed by the accused not to report the incident, and this may undermine the child's ability to report the truth. Therefore, this study investigated whether or not children would lie about a transgression committed by an adult male who broke a 'prized' glass and then hid the broken pieces to cover up his 'misdeed'. The adult appealed to the child in a number of different ways not to tell the female interviewer about what had happened. These conditions provided the motivations of gain, avoidance, concern for others, and for fun, which were established as the most significant motivations for lying in a previous study (Bussey, 1988). That study also established retaliation as a motivation for lying. It was not included in this study, since retaliation only emerged as a significant motivation for lying from about eight years of age onwards.

Children of three and five years of age participated in the study. Each child was brought individually by the female interviewer to a mobile laboratory and introduced to the adult male whose task was to teach the child the balance scale task. Both adults had spent at least four sessions interacting with the children in their own classrooms. To parallel actual court cases, the male always committed the transgression and the female conducted the interviews. Each child was individually tested with the manipulations embedded in the teaching of the balance scale task. In the absence of the female interviewer, the male, midway through the teaching session, 'accidentally' broke the female interviewer's favourite drinking glass while pausing for a drink of water. He signalled his distress to the child and sought to dissuade her/him from disclosing what he had done by stating one of five appeals, which reflected the four major motivations for lying and a simple 'don't tell' statement.

Using a plausible pretext the adult male left the room when the female interviewer returned to assess the child's progress at the balance scale task. A series of questions about how much the child liked the game, how much he/she liked the adult male and whether he had touched her/him on the hand, nose or anywhere else were interspersed through the assessment. As well, the child was asked whether anything else had happened while she was away. The female interviewer then paused to get herself a drink of water but could not locate her special glass. For those children who did not spontaneously report what had transpired in her absence several questions were posed to encourage disclosure. Finally, those children who would not disclose were asked directly whether or not the adult male had touched the glass. After disclosure, children were asked to rate how easy or difficult it had been for them to disclose.

In this situation, across all conditions, approximately 75 per cent of the three year olds reported the witnessed event while only 55 per cent of the five year olds did. Apart from the greater propensity of three year olds to disclose the adult's transgression, the different types of appeal used to dissuade the child from disclosing impacted differentially on the three and the five year olds. Specifically, the three year olds were more likely to report the adult's transgression when the appeal was reward, concern, trick, or when they were simply asked not to tell, than when they were asked not to tell in a very stern manner. Few of the three year olds instructed in such a manner disclosed the adult's transgression.

The stern condition also reduced disclosure by the five year olds compared to the other conditions of reward, concern, and trick. Children from this age group were less likely to report the incident if simply instructed not to tell than the three year olds. Further, the three year olds were more likely to disclose the transgression spontaneously, whereas the five year olds were more likely to disclose the transgression only after direct questioning about the incident.

There was no difference among children by condition or age as to whether or not they liked the adult male, the game, or if they were touched. However, for the children who disclosed what happened there was a significant age effect for the difficulty associated with that disclosure. The five year olds found it harder to disclose the incident than the three year olds. Many five year olds did not disclose, and those who did found it difficult to do so. This implies that for older children who have become more aware of the consequences of disclosure, the task becomes more difficult.

In sum, when simply instructed not to tell, the three year olds were more likely to tell than the five year olds. The stern condition produced the most significant reduction in the three year olds' reporting of the transgression. Other appeals for not disclosing had more impact on the five year olds. The greater disclosure of three year olds than five year olds was confirmed in another recent study in which mothers requested their children not to report their accidental breaking of a Barbie doll (Bottoms, Goodman, Schwartz-Kenney, Sachsenmaier, & Thomas, 1990).

Even though the three year olds were more reluctant to report the adult's transgression when sternly requested not to, their level of disclosure was greater than that of the five year olds. A reason for this might simply be that they find it more difficult than the older children to generate an alternative to what actually happened. Hence, in a follow up study employing a similar methodology, children were presented with a plausible false story to tell the other adult (Bussey & Lee, 1990). This enabled a test of the impact of 'coaching' on children's accounts. Preliminary results indicate that a greater number of five year olds than three year olds succumbed to the coaching and hence did not report the transgression.

The results of the studies reported here and other studies from this research program point to the increasing use of deception by those who have the skills to behave deceptively. With increasing age, capacity for deception increases as leakage through non-verbal behaviours and verbal means diminishes. One of the basic tenets of social cognitive theory is that individuals do not say or do all they know. The expectations of what will happen for behaving in a certain way or making certain statements is the crucial determinant of what individuals will do. Hence, five year old children who have learned that they often get into trouble for admitting their own transgression, or one they have witnessed, are less likely to be truthful about such events than three year olds who have not learned such a negative outcome for truthfulness.

The results of this research program to date suggest that an important factor governing children's lying and truthfulness is the result they anticipate for either chosen course of action. The more censure children anticipate for truth-telling, such as threat from an adult, the less likely they are to tell the truth. Children may have more to fear for truth-telling than adults, especially in sexual abuse cases where they might be threatened with dire consequences for disclosure. It could be argued that special provisions need to be provided to promote truth-telling in children, particularly for children testifying about sexual abuse episodes where it is possible that they may have been threatened about disclosing the abuse. This issue is examined next.

Implications for the Courtroom
There is variability about the age at which children are considered

competent to testify both across and within countries. In the USA, where most of the research on children's competence has been conducted, Federal Rule of Evidence 601 states that no one can be declared incompetent on the basis of his or her age. However, it has been noted that Federal Rule of Evidence 403 may be used by defence attorneys to challenge the competency of young children to testify (Haugaard & Crosby, 1989). This rule states: 'Although relevant, evidence may be excluded if its probative value is substantially outweighed by the danger of unfair prejudice, confusion of the issues, or misleading the jury . . .'. Despite this, in the majority of states in the USA children are rarely disqualified as incompetent to testify because of their age. Rather, the competency of children to testify is established on a case by case determination (Melton, 1981), a procedure similar to that used in Australia.

The competence examination or the 'voir dire' is usually conducted by the presiding judge or magistrate. The primary focus is on children's understanding of the truth and obligation to tell the truth. A typical set of questions is as follows:

> What is your name? How old are you? Where do you live? Do you go to school? Do you go to Sunday School? Do you know what happens to anyone telling a lie? Do you know why you are here today? Would you tell a true story or a wrong story today? Suppose you told a wrong story, do you know what would happen? Do you know what an oath is? Did you ever hear of God? (Note, 1953, 362)

Here is an example from the examination of a boy who was determined competent to testify: 'The boy . . . said among other things that he knew the difference between the truth and a lie; that if he told a lie a bad man would get him, and that he was going to tell the truth. When further asked what they would do with him in court if he told a lie, he replied they would put him in jail.' (*Wheeler v. United States*, 159 U.S. 523, 1895, cited in Melton 1981, p.74) It can be seen from this excerpt that primary emphasis is placed 'on the child's ability to differentiate truth from falsehood, to comprehend the duty to tell the truth, and to understand the consequences of not fulfilling this duty' (Melton, 1981, 74). It is obvious that in the competency exam the court's focus is on the child's understanding of the moral principles of lying and truth telling, rather than on children's ability to apply such principles. While it is possible for a child to tell the truth and pass a competence exam, it is also possible for a child to pass a competence exam and not to tell the truth. Other than to provide additional information to the jury about a child witness's capabilities that might help in their assessment of the child's credibility as a witness, it is difficult to justify the value of the voir dire examination. Of course this is in agreement with Wigmore's conclusion as stated at the outset of this paper; it is also in agreement with the views of one of the most distinguished of contemporary scholars in this field, Gary Melton. Melton writes about the voir dire that, 'the court's time is wasted by a ritual that has very dubious value' (Melton, 1987, 193). There is no evidence that such a test is a valid assessment of the likelihood that the child will tell the truth.

Even if the voir dire is abolished, doubts about the veracity of testimony presented by children remain. In the USA and some states in Australia, the judge may warn the jury about reaching a guilty decision about the defendant on the basis of the uncorroborated evidence of a child witness. Thus, although the child may provide testimony to the court, the judge may direct the jury about the weight they should place on the child's testimony. Hence, at this point, the child's capacity for truthfulness is challenged, again. The media, adults, and teachers have also challenged the truthfulness of children. Why is this so? Why are children regarded as inherently less truthful than adults? As I have shown earlier in this paper children do know the difference between a lie and a truthful statement, and the importance of truthfulness and the wrongfulness of lying. Further, research has shown that three year olds for example are more honest than five year olds (Bottoms, et al 1990; Bussey, 1990; Steward, Bussey, Goodman, & Saywitz, in press). But yet concerns about the capability of young children to provide truthful testimony remain. Perhaps the reason for this belief is related to young children's inability to lie successfully rather than to their lack of truthfulness. Young children are more likely to be caught out when they lie than their older counterparts (Bussey, 1990, De Paulo & Jordan, 1982, Vasek, 1986). For example, a young child, when asked if he peeked at the Walt Disney toy behind him, replied: 'No, I just sat here and thinked maybe it's Mickey Mouse and Donald Duck'. Because the lies of young children are more readily detectable than older children and adults, and because younger children are more likely than their older counterparts to tell trick lies for fun where part of the fun stems from the truth being discovered (eg 'there's a spider on your back'), young children have earned the unfortunate reputation that they readily distort the truth (Bussey, 1988). As a result, in the more serious context of the court, the credibility of child witnesses is doubted.

If an understanding of lying and truth-telling does not guarantee truth-telling, what factors determine whether a child witness will provide truthful testimony? Is it at a certain age that individuals can be relied upon to tell the truth, or are some individuals more likely than others to be truthful, or is the situation the major determinant of an individual's truthfulness? No one cause alone is responsible for an individual's truthfulness. Having acquired knowledge about lying and truthfulness does not guarantee truth telling, just as telling the truth does not necessarily inform about knowledge of truthfulness.

The research previously described has shown that three year olds are more likely to be blatantly honest than their five year old counterparts. Children who have acquired the cognitive skills for intentional deception are more likely to lie especially when they anticipate punishment for truth-telling. During the middle childhood years, children become more skilled at lying. Although they know that lying is wrong, they increasingly expect to be believed when they lie. So what determines whether an individual will lie or not?

Children who have not mastered the concept of false belief, usually three year olds and below, would not be expected to produce intentionally deceptive false statements. If they do produce false statements their goal is probably more to avoid punishment than to induce a false belief in their listener. Most children lacking an understanding of the concept of false belief would expect to be caught out. It is posited that such non-adept liars are easily detected. It is expected that the more children anticipate being punished for truthfulness, the more likely they are to lie even when they know it is wrong to do so. On the other hand, if children are encouraged to be truthful and are sufficiently reassured about non-threatening consequences, there is no reason to believe that they will not tell the truth.

Ultimately, there is no way to guarantee that individuals will be truthful. Adults have a greater capacity for being deceitful and getting away with it, justifying their deceit (disengagement) and concealing it through providing minimal leakage cues. Competency examinations can do little to guarantee truthfulness from any age group, nor is there any evidence that expert witnesses are able to judge the veracity or mendacity of a witness's testimony.

Still, it remains, stemming largely from the legacy of Piaget, that children are often viewed by the media and judiciary as more prone to lying than adults. There is counter evidence, however, attesting that children are not convincing liars: they are not very skilled at masking their deception and so their underlying affect leaks out (De Paulo and Jordan 1982). In the studies that I have reported here the lies of three year olds were readily detected by adult 'judges' and similarly, although to a lesser extent, so too were the lies of the five year olds.

In conclusion, on the basis of the studies presented here and other studies from my research program it is argued that it is important to allow children to testify in cases in which they are the sole witness. It is difficult to conclude, from this research, how children would be any more capable than adults to lead the jury intentionally and successfully to a false understanding of a witnessed event. Competence testing of young children seems to add little to the determination of whether a child should testify or not.

The remaining question, however, of special provisions for child witnesses in adult-oriented criminal courts is a vexed one. It is not clear from existing research whether or which special provisions are warranted. Since the relationship between adults and children is different from the relationship between adults and other adults, threats and bribes delivered by adults can pose particular difficulties for young children. These effects may be exaggerated in the courtroom when children face the accused. Children under five years of age and older children under stress find it difficult to synthesize multiple pieces of information (Perry & Bussey, 1984). The salience of the accused who has threatened the child for truth-telling may undermine the child's capacity for truthfulness.

Courtroom Modifications for Child Witnesses

At this stage we do not know if children's truth-telling is affected by the presence or absence of the accused. We are currently testing this proposition in our research. If the results indicate that this is a significant factor, then it would seem to be important for the child not to be in the line of vision of the accused or for the child to be instructed to avert their gaze away from the accused. Several procedures have been proposed: for example, the use of video technology, the use of a one-way vision screen where the child, judge and counsel are blocked off from the rest of the court. The latter option might be preferable as this enables the jury to gain a realistic appraisal of how children provide their evidence, unencumbered by doubts about prompting that may be occurring out of vision of the cameras.

Although some of these alternative procedures are gaining wide support from lay people and the media, their basis in methodologically sound research is far from established. Legislators have introduced a barrage of new legislation in this country as well as many other Western countries to enable the use of such procedures. Essentially these procedures are designed to eliminate face to face confrontation with the defendant and/or diminish the courtroom audience. The purpose of these procedures, however, is dubious. 'For example, testimony via closed circuit television or videotaped deposition may deprive the jury of some cues to the witness's demeanour and thereby infringe upon the defendant's right to a jury trial' (Melton, 1987, 195).

Further, 'the jury may infer guilt from the procedure of putting the defendant and the child witness in different rooms. If the defendant were not guilty and dangerous, why would such a procedure be undertaken? If "child-courtrooms" (Libai, 1969) in fact foster such a conclusion, the defendant's right to due process would be violated by de facto negation of the presumption of innocence' (Melton, 1987, 195). In fact, in the USA, 'the Supreme Court has made clear that mandatory application of aberrant procedures to testimony by child witnesses is unlikely to pass constitutional scrutiny (see *Globe Newspaper Co. v. Superior Court* 1982)' (Melton 1987, 195). This view was recently upheld by the Supreme Court of the USA (*Maryland v. Craig* 1990). It was decided that children could deliver their testimony via one-way closed circuit television, but only if it could be shown that the child would suffer severe emotional distress as a result of testifying in the courtroom.

In this context it is important to restate Melton's opinion on the use of such procedures. He writes:

> The most basic problem with the statutory reforms is that neither need nor efficacy has been demonstrated. First, as a matter of strategy, if children can testify under standard procedures, it is foolish to open doors to appeal by introduction of aberrant procedures. Even if the special procedures are marginally less stressful, children may be kept in psychological limbo much longer than necessary by appeals and even a new trial.
>
> Second, both clinical experience and social and psychological theory indicate that testimony, even under standard procedures, is often a positive experience for child victims. Consider the following . . .
>
> 'The experience of testifying in court can have a therapeutic effect for the child victim. The child can learn that social institutions take children seriously. Some children report feeling empowered by their participation in the process. Some have complained, when the offender pled guilty, that they did not have an opportunity to be heard in court.' (Berliner & Barbieri, 1984, 135)
>
> [T]he court proceeding can have beneficial outcomes for the child. Children, like adults, often have strong feelings regarding their victimization and want the offender to be punished for his wrongdoing. Court proceedings are the only way that the victim can legally seek retribution against the perpetrator. Older children in particular often have a strong sense of social responsibility and will choose to proceed with prosecution even though it may be stressful in the belief that they are helping to protect other children

from being victimized. In many instances, court proceedings also serve to enhance the child's sense of personal vindication. Others are treating the child's victimization as a serious matter; and are tangibly expressing their trust and faith in the child's story. (Rogers, 1982, 150) (Melton, 1987, 196).

It is important to realize that most information about children's reactions to their courtroom experience relies on these kinds of anecdotal reports. Although this is changing there is still a need to investigate children's reactions to their participation in the legal system to determine if testimony in the courtroom is traumatic for children and what aspect of it is most traumatic (eg facing the defendant, judge, or jury; talking about the abuse). Despite the possible trauma of speaking before the accused, to 'say it to the face of (the defendant)' may be necessary on psychological as well as legal grounds. There is no doubt that this is a more difficult task for those who have been threatened by the accused for truth-telling, but on the other hand it may be easier to maintain a false allegation if the accused is not confronted. Bearing these issues in mind, psychologists and child protection workers might be far better directed to divert their attention firstly to better preparation of child witnesses under existing conditions, and secondly paying greater attention to reducing sexual abuse in the community — understanding its causes, rather than trying to redesign the legal system and reorganise the courtroom to accommodate it.

Alternatives to Changing Courtroom Procedures
In terms of preparation, children can be provided with basic information about the legal system and, most important, taught how to cope with cross examination. Earlier suggestions about children's court preparation (Bussey & Steward, 1985) can now be expanded. In particular, teaching children to answer the type of questions they might receive in cross examination, including negative appraisals of their competence, until they themselves are confident about facing such questions, is the basis of such a training program. The procedures ideally would be instituted initially through computer assisted interviewing. This procedure would gradually give way to interviewing procedures that more closely approximate cross examination in the court room. The computer assisted interview has been used successfully in the USA to interview children by both clinicians and law enforcement personnel (Steward, 1989).

Conclusion

There is little evidence to suggest that the incidence of child sexual abuse is reducing. Successful prosecution of the perpetrators of child sexual abuse may be one important factor in reducing this crime. It is therefore essential that children be allowed to testify about their abuse in courts. They must be empowered for that experience and not be dismissed from testifying through competency examinations or expert appraisals of their honesty or otherwise. If anyone can lie successfully in court and get away with it, it is probably the more skilled adult liar, rather than the novice younger liar. Ultimately, however, reducing the abuse should be the major goal of organizations and governments charged with the awesome task of protecting children.

Acknowledgments

The research described here was funded by a grant from the Australian Research Council. I gratefully acknowledge Kerry Lee, Karen Rickard, and Fiona Robertson for assistance in data collection and Elizabeth Grimbeek for her contribution to this research.

6

Legal Intervention in Parent-Child Conflicts: The Emergence of No Fault 'Divorce' in Child Welfare Law

Patrick Parkinson

Parent-child conflicts do not self-evidently raise issues of child protection. However, as a matter of social work practice, parent-child conflicts may raise concerns about the welfare of a particular young person. The conflicts themselves may be indicative of serious underlying problems, including abuse and neglect, or, if left unresolved may lead to the young person leaving home. In Australia, the figures for youth homelessness are alarming (Burdekin, 1989). Thus child welfare agencies have put resources into parent-child mediation and family counselling in order to prevent a total breakdown in the parent-child relationship which may lead to the young person being in need of care. These family conflicts have also been a traditional ground for state intervention, although they have not been described as such. Juvenile courts have long had jurisdiction over the 'uncontrollable child', and children in moral danger.

It is to address the causes rather than the symptoms of adolescent problems, that in Victoria, the Australian Capital Territory, (ACT) New South Wales (NSW), and in New Zealand, a radical new approach to the problem of legal intervention in parent-child conflicts has been attempted. In these jurisdictions, under the relevant child welfare law, a serious breakdown in the relationship between parents and an adolescent child, is a ground for care proceedings or other state intervention. In Victoria, it is open to the child or young person to apply to the children's court. These provisions either replace, or stand alongside, other grounds for intervention which are often termed 'status offences'.

The experience of these jurisdictions suggests, however, that the most important contribution which children's courts can play is by acting as a reception point where adolescents and parents in crisis may access services which make court proceedings unnecessary. The 'no fault' provisions in Australia and New Zealand thus raise questions about the limits of law, and the role of courts in dealing with family conflicts.

Setting the Context: The Debate about Status Offences
The origins of the Australian and New Zealand legislation lie in the debate which flourished in the 1970s about status offences, particularly in the USA but also in Australia and elsewhere. Ever since the early years of the juvenile court movement, courts motivated by a concern for children's welfare have intervened to prevent adolescents from engaging in behaviour which is deemed harmful to them. Unruly child statutes emerged in English speaking countries in the nineteenth century, (Platt, 1969, Garlock, 1979) and became firmly entrenched in the twentieth (Ferdinand, 1991). The juvenile court acted as surrogate parent, reinforcing parental authority and if necessary, taking over the parental role (Leaper, 1974, Mahoney, 1977). The grounds for court intervention were often extensive, ranging from quite specific forms of proscribed behaviour to quite general grounds for intervention based on the young person's disobedience or on the basis that he or she was beyond parental control.

Such offences have come to be known as 'status offences'. A status offence may be defined as a ground for coercive state intervention in the life of a juvenile which would not be a ground for intervention if that person were an adult. Running away, playing truant, being uncontrollable and being exposed to moral danger are all examples of status offences. The language might vary from jurisdiction to jurisdiction, but the central concept is the same. It is perceived that courts have a necessary role to play in dealing with the non-criminal misbehaviour of adolescents, and that sometimes it is in the young person's best interests to be taken into state care where he or she is beyond parental control.

Status offences have been much criticised, most strongly in the USA,

(Teitelbaum and Gough, 1977, Allison, 1978, Sacks and Sacks, 1980, Katz and Teitelbaum, 1977) but also in Australia (Leaper, 1974, Gamble, 1985) and elsewhere (Morris, Giller et al 1980, 130ff, Le Poole, 1977). They have been attacked on the grounds of vagueness and a failure to meet the strict requirements for a legal process (Stiller and Elder, 1975), gender bias, (Chesney-Lind, 1982, Hancock and Chesney-Lind 1985),[1] and on many other grounds (Andrews and Cohn 1974). One particular criticism which received a lot of attention in the literature in the 1970s was that status offences labelled young people. Another major ground of criticism centred upon the manner in which child welfare agencies, who had responsibility for both offenders and other children in need of care, often failed to distinguish between offenders and non-offenders in terms of accommodation and treatment. Both the depraved and the deprived were treated alike. Frequently, to be taken into care in one's best interests could be a serious punishment indeed.

Much of this has now changed. No longer is it common for status offenders to be incarcerated. In none of the Australian jurisdictions are adolescents routinely placed in secure facilities because they are deemed uncontrollable, although there is a regrettable tendency for this to happen on a temporary basis where young people are removed by the police from the streets on one or another of the statutory grounds for intervention.[2] Furthermore, clear distinctions have been made in the legislation between young criminal offenders and status offenders. Changes have been made to the language of the courts. No longer are young people labelled as 'uncontrollable.'

For all of these improvements, however, the basic concept of children's court jurisdiction for adolescents who may be uncontrolled or in situations of harm outside the home remains in the majority of Australian jurisdictions and in other English speaking countries. Much may have been done to develop alternative approaches, (Handler and Zatz, 1982, Allinson, 1977, Hickey, 1977) but there has been a strong defence of having a residual court jurisdiction where the problems cannot be resolved by other means (Martin and Snyder, 1976, Arthur, 1977, Gregory, 1978). For a system which has been so vigorously criticised, it has proved remarkably tenacious.[3]

It was to move away from status offences that Victoria initially, and later the ACT, NSW and New Zealand, adopted procedures based upon the breakdown of the family relationship.

Victoria: 'Irreconcilable Differences'
In Victoria, the *Community Welfare Services Act 1978* amended s.34 of the *Social Welfare Act 1970* which had allowed a parent to bring a child

before the court for an order that he or she was 'uncontrollable'. This was replaced by a provision that a parent may initiate an application to the children's court where he or she believes that there is a 'substantial and presently irreconcilable difference between himself and the child to such an extent that his care and custody of the child are likely to be seriously disrupted.' Any child who believes that such a difference exists may also apply. Section 34 applies to children under fifteen, while s.104 is in identical terms, but refers to young people over fifteen and under seventeen. These sections were not brought into force until 1982.

The model for the Victorian legislation of 1978 was provided by a Royal Commission on Family and Child Law in British Columbia which reported in 1975. (British Columbia, 1975). This Commission recommended that the legislative provision concerning 'unmanageable' children be replaced by one which established the court's jurisdiction to intervene wherever there were 'irreconcilable differences between the parent and the child which cannot be resolved unless the court makes an order.' It further recommended that in addition to the child welfare authorities, either parent or child should be able to apply to the court. It considered that in such cases, the most appropriate order might be a supervision order in which conditions could be imposed on the parent and the child, and services ordered to the family. Temporary guardianship might also be used but they recommended that permanent guardianship should only be ordered in exceptional circumstances. The recommendation was not adopted in British Columbia, but it provided the basic model for Victoria. (Norgard, 1976, Parkinson, 1990).

The *Community Welfare Services Act 1978* did not remove entirely a ground for care based on an absence of proper parental control. The *Community Welfare Services Act 1970* (as amended) retained as a ground for intervention in s.31(1)(b) that the guardians or caretakers of the child or young person 'do not exercise adequate supervision and control'. Official figures for the number who were wards of the state indicate that this ground vied with 'irreconcilable differences' as a ground for wardship. In 1984-85 there were 110 admissions on the ground of irreconcilable differences and 38 on the ground of inadequate supervision. In 1985-86, there were 82 admissions because of irreconcilable differences and 110 for inadequate supervision.

One of the most controversial aspects of the legislation in Victoria has been that it allows young people to apply as well as parents. Approximately one quarter of all applications are made by children, and three quarters by parents. According to figures provided by the Children's Court Advisory Service, in 1987, 65 applications were lodged in Melbourne's children's court. Thirteen were lodged by children, 39 by parents and in thirteen it was not known who lodged the application. In 1988, sixteen applications were made, four by children, twelve by parents.

Since that legislation was passed, Victoria's child welfare laws have been substantially rewritten by the *Children and Young Persons Act 1989*. However, the 'irreconcilable difference' provision remains largely unaltered. The new legislation adopts a twenty-one day 'cooling off period' in which counselling may take place before the matter is resolved by children's court proceedings. The new legislation no longer includes 'inadequate supervision' as an alternative ground for care proceedings however.

The Australian Capital Territory: 'Serious Incompatibility'
In 1986 the ACT passed legislation in not dissimilar terms to that in Victoria. The ACT legislation followed a report of the Australian Law Reform Commission (ALRC, 1981). The *Children's Services Ordinance 1986* makes it a ground for care that there is 'serious incompatibility between the child and one of his or her parents'. In the ACT the important feature of the child welfare structure is the position of the Youth Advocate, who is a senior member of the Territory's child welfare system. Care proceedings cannot be initiated without the involvement of the Youth Advocate, who therefore acts as a filter to prevent unwarranted state intervention. Unlike the *Children and Young Persons Act 1989* (Vic.), there is no mandatory counselling in the ACT but s.80 provides that all other alternatives must be tried first. In practice, attempts at conciliation are a prerequisite for the youth advocate's intervention.

New South Wales: 'Irretrievable Breakdown'
A similar approach was also adopted in NSW. In 1987, the NSW legislature passed the *Children (Care and Protection) Act* after many years of debate about reforming the child protection laws. Section 10 makes it a ground for care that there is a 'substantial and presently irretrievable breakdown in the relationship between the child and one or more of the child's parents'. This Act was brought into force in 1988. Only parents and the department may initiate an application to the court, (s.57). The Children's Court Rules 1988, provide that where an irretrievable breakdown application has been made, then the court must adjourn the proceedings to allow a reasonable opportunity to resolve the matter by conciliation. In the main, this function is performed by community justice centres.

Children's court proceedings may be avoided if the child is admitted to state care voluntarily. The Act provides that a child may be admitted to care for up to three months, renewable for a further three months. As originally enacted, the Act allowed young people of fourteen years and above to give their own consent to care, irrespective of parental involvement. Following a change of government, this 'age of discretion' was increased to sixteen years.

New Zealand: 'Serious Differences'
The Australian model was also adopted in New Zealand. The *Children, Young Persons and Their Families Act 1989* was passed after much debate in New Zealand about having a multicultural perspective in child welfare. Section 14 includes in its definitions of a child being in need of care that there are 'serious differences existing between the child and his parents or other caretakers, to such an extent that the physical, or mental or emotional well-being of the child or young person is being seriously impaired.'

The New Zealand legislation does differ from the others generally in that the *Children, Young Persons and Their Families Act 1989* has a very strong emphasis throughout on alternative dispute resolution. Whenever there is ground for state intervention whether on account of parental abuse or neglect or otherwise, the initial response of the authorities is to call a family group conference which includes not only immediate members of the family but the extended family. This family group conference has decision making powers. If the police, social workers and family members can reach an agreement then no court proceedings will be initiated, and the decision of the conference will be implemented by the department. Only where this conference fails to produce an acceptable outcome, will court proceedings become a possibility. (Atkin, 1990).

Counselling Services and the Use of the Legislation
The operation of the legislation in Victoria indicates the great value of alternative dispute resolution as the primary means of dealing with parent-child conflicts. Statistics on the number of applications made on this ground show a steady decline since 1985. Official figures published by Community Services Victoria indicated in 1985 that there were 230 applications in the Melbourne children's court, while in 1987, 65 applications were lodged, and in 1988, only sixteen. The decline is reflected in the official figures for admission to state wardship. In 1984-85 there were 110 admissions to wardship on the ground of irreconcilable difference. By 1987-88 the number had declined to 33.

The reason for this decline appears to be largely the success of the

Children's Court Advisory Service which is a branch of Community Services Victoria. In 1986 they established protocols with the Melbourne children's court to ensure that applicants were referred to the advisory service for advice and counselling before the case went to court. Figures provided by the Service indicate a 91 per cent diversion rate away from the courts through telephone counselling and face to face interviews. Thus in 1988 while sixteen cases did proceed to court, 177 others did not. Clearly the availability of counselling, and the provision of alternatives to court proceedings, made a very significant difference to the use of the legislation.

Evaluating the Procedure
In many respects, the legislation in the three Australian jurisdictions and in New Zealand offers an innovative approach to the problem of parent-child conflicts. Going hand in hand with available counselling services for families experiencing a breakdown in parent-adolescent relationships, it offers a solution of last resort in cases where the only possible answer appears to be a temporary or permanent removal from the home. In this respect, the court fulfils a role akin to that in a custody dispute. On behalf of the child, the court may use its authority to sanction the placement of a child with foster parents, or in another out of home placement. For parents, the procedure provides access for them to state resources in terms of alternative placements for an adolescent whom they are unable to cope with or control. In so doing, the law recognises that such breakdowns may occur without having to attribute blame either to the parent or the child.

The 'no fault' provisions have attracted considerable attention in the media in Australia, especially in Victoria which allows young people to apply. Although the number of applications by young people is comparatively small, and three quarters of all the applications are made by parents, the legislation has been criticised as allowing for 'children's divorce'.[4] In NSW also, the 'irretrievable breakdown' provision has excited some controversy, with social workers being accused of aiding children to leave home through such applications.

In many respects these criticisms reflect a misunderstanding of the procedure. The first misunderstanding here is to regard it as a kind of 'divorce'. One understands why this term has arisen, because of the similarity in the terminology used with divorce statutes. Nonetheless, it is different from divorce in the sense that there is no necessity for the matter to involve a permanent separation. There are a range of dispositions available to the court of which admission to wardship is the most extreme. Furthermore, there is, in all the social welfare departments concerned, an emphasis on endeavouring to restore the teenager to the family if possible (Community Services Victoria 1986). The second misunderstanding is to say that it undermines parents' rights. The criticism which is often made is that by expressing the problem between the parent and the child in 'no fault' terms, the law fails to reinforce appropriate parental authority.[5] The misunderstanding here is that it fails to see the situation from the social work perspective. From this perspective, the presenting problem is one of a breakdown in relationships in which there is an unresolved conflict which may lead imminently to the child either leaving home or being told to leave. In these cases, something needs to be done to prevent the crisis in the young person's life becoming even more serious.

The legal provisions have their greatest application as an early intervention strategy where a family comes to the attention of child welfare authorities at the point when breakdown is about to occur. It is useful primarily therefore before a child leaves home on a more or less permanent basis. (Cf Orten and Soll, 1980). It has been estimated that there are some 25,000 'street kids' in Australia (*Burdekin Report* 1989). The reasons why young people leave home are, of course, many. (Young, 1987, Palenski and Launer, 1987, Young, Mathews et al 1983, Shane, 1989). As the Burdekin Report put it, in many cases these are not young people who have left home, but young people for whom home has left them. There is a very strong link between youth homelessness and child abuse and neglect, especially the sexual abuse of young adolescents and pre-adolescents.

Once a young person has left home on a more or less permanent basis, the nature of social work intervention must necessarily change. Young people often become hardened to the street culture, and will not necessarily cope well with traditional out of home placements such as foster care and children's homes. Social work provision will need to take on other forms, such as providing youth workers for the street population and funding short and medium term accommodation in youth refuges and independent living facilities. To this population, children's courts exercising their civil jurisdiction, and social workers offering family conciliation counselling, have only limited relevance. Nonetheless, at the early stages of breakdown and youth detachment, social work intervention with the family may avert a complete breakdown, or at least prevent the young person joining the population of young homeless.

The central question which needs to be asked however, is: what is the role of the court in this early intervention process? It is of the essence of the various 'no fault' procedures that the court is seen as having a useful role. In child welfare law generally the court has two important functions. The first is to adjudicate on the evidence. It must be proven that abuse or neglect has occurred. In this respect, the court has a vital function as an independent scrutineer of the facts to ensure that state intervention is justified. The second role of the court is to adjudicate on disposition. Once a finding has been made that a child is in need of care, then the second stage is to consider what order, if any should be made. The pattern in Australian child welfare law at present is one of the least intrusive disposition. The court must consider all the options in an ascending order of intrusiveness, and only if there is no other alternative is the child admitted to wardship.

In applications based on a breakdown in the parent-child relationship however, the court has no adjudicative function in the first sense. This is because the facts lie not in objective evidence of abuse or neglect which may be examined by an independent arbiter, but in the expressions of belief and intention of the parties. If a parent says that he or she has 'had enough' or if a child refuses to return home, there is little a magistrate can do to gainsay it. Indeed, the very nature of the hearing reinforces the redundancy of the magistrate. For whereas in a family counselling session the parties may very well express their positions and desires ambiguously and with a door open for reconciliation, in a court application one party must allege an irreconcilable difference or irretrievable breakdown. The nature of the process means there can be only one outcome. The allegation is its own proof.

Does the court have a greater role in terms of disposition? Possibly. Admission to state wardship at least places the department under a legal duty to provide suitable accommodation for the young person. But no order of the court creates resources which are not there otherwise. It does not create any more foster placements, nor any more medium or long term youth housing. The obvious question to ask is whether the courts could not be bypassed totally, so that the disposition is a matter between the family and the department or a non-government agency, or perhaps between the young person and the department with or without parental approval.

Indeed, it is possible that there may actually be disadvantages to court proceedings, for the problem with legal involvement in parent-child conflicts is that courts are ill-adapted to deal with the sensitive ecology of human relationships. The first disadvantage is that with the possibility of a 'divorce' option in view either the parents or the children may harden into litigative mode, so that 'irreconcilable differences' are not the cause of an application to the court, but a product of it. A second disadvantage arises from the fact that the conflict is removed from its location in the home and family, to an external setting in which it undergoes a process of redefinition and possibly of distortion. What is a complex problem of family relationships, of interactions which have happened over months or years is redefined to conform to the terms of the relevant legislative provision. A problem is articulated by the family members to a lawyer who in turn conveys it to a magistrate. Yet the problem which has taken months and years to develop cannot be told in a few minutes; to do so is not merely to redefine the problem but to distort it, and the danger is that what is only a subjective reality at a certain point of time is treated as an objective fact. The nature of the declaration of 'irreconcilable differences' may be such as to make them so, and may decrease the prospects for a future reconciliation. Legal judgments and court findings have an air of finality about them which is inappropriate for many cases of parent-child conflict.

Courts are also bureaucracies: forms need to be filled in, lawyers spoken to, and parties need to fit their case into a court schedule. A final problem with court involvement in parent-child conflicts is that it can create false impressions for the parties concerned. Court cases can be won and lost, and legal rights vindicated. Where an application is contested by a parent who wants the child to remain at home, the parents may be chasing an illusion. Whatever the law may be it is a matter of reality that a court cannot enforce its order to a young person to go home against his or her determined opposition. In this sense, the parents can never win. If the young person refuses to go home, the court will not be able to enforce the parents' rights to custody. If the young person is willing to return home, there will be no court case.

The question remains therefore, whether there is any need for a court adjudication of the breakdown. The Institute of Judicial Administration/American Bar Association Joint Commission on Juvenile Justice Standards thought otherwise. In its *Standards Relating to Noncriminal Misbehavior* (1982) the commission considered that a juvenile's non-criminal misbehaviour should not provide a ground for juvenile court jurisdiction. Rather, it recommended that provisions be enacted giving to police the power to take a young person into custody for a limited period to facilitate his or her return home or until some alternative placement can be arranged. Until parents can be notified, or other arrangements made, the young person should be taken to a temporary non-secure residential facility. Counselling services should be made available to the family on a voluntary basis and an alternative residential placement may also be arranged by agreement. Only if the parent and child cannot agree does the court play a role. The young person, or someone acting on his or her behalf, would make an application to the court to approve or disapprove an alternative residential placement. In these *Standards*, the role of the court is different from that in the Australian and New Zealand legislation. Rather than needing to adjudicate on the presence or otherwise of irreconcilable differences, the court's role is to be limited to approving or disapproving the particular alternative placement put forward by the young person. It should approve that placement unless the placement would imperil the juvenile, in which case an alternative placement should be found. In this way the court plays merely a supervisory role in ensuring that the living arrangement is such that the young person's basic needs are met.

The proposals proved highly controversial, but some variations on the theme at least are to be found in a number of American States.[6] Washington State, for example, has provisions which reflect the spirit of the Standards but with a much greater emphasis on the reinforcement of proper parental authority. The *Family Reconciliation Act* provides that where the parent or child cannot agree on an alternative residential placement either of them (or failing such application, the child welfare department) may seek a court order. The court may order an alternative placement with a view to resolving the family conflict and restoring the child to the home.[7] One of the conditions of such an order is that the petition is not 'based only upon a dislike of reasonable rules or reasonable discipline established by the parent.'[8] A review must take place within three months and the placement may not last beyond another 180 days after the review.[9] Amendments in 1990 provide that in the alternative, or following the failure of the out of home placement to resolve the family conflict, the child may be deemed to be an 'at risk youth'. This allows the court to make a range of supervisory orders or to order the young person to stay at home or at an alternative place approved by the parent. Failure to comply with such an order may result in the young person's detention.[10]

It would be a bold step to abandon court proceedings entirely, or to maintain merely a residual jurisdiction to approve or disapprove alternative residential placements as recommended in the *Juvenile Justice Standards*. The Fogarty Report (1989) recommended the retention of the 'irreconcilable differences' jurisdiction since it provided a useful service in a small number of cases. Certainly, there are arguments for retention.

At the present time, the experience of the three Australian jurisdictions suggests that court proceedings are playing the following roles:

1. They are being used when the child welfare authority considers that a voluntary agreement will not last. While out of home placements may be arranged if the parents agree without the need for

court approval, the court application is seen by some authorities as a necessary safeguard in certain cases to prevent deleterious results if a parent withdraws consent.
2. They are being used where parents will not relinquish care voluntarily. The court here acts to give its authority to a change of custody. It is questionable whether this is necessary however. It would be possible to insert a provision in the governing legislation that the department may provide accommodation where a child is unable or unwilling to remain at home in the care of his or her family. More than this is not necessary unless there is some reason why the child welfare authority needs guardianship powers.
3. It is a 'catch all' ground for state intervention when the case cannot be fitted under any other heading, or as a reserve ground if the other cannot be proven. This appears to be the situation in the ACT where the 'serious incompatibility' ground is almost invariably brought alongside other grounds. Evidence from Victoria suggests this also. Between 1984 and 1988, nine admissions to wardship on the ground of irreconcilable differences involved children under ten years old. This may reflect Victoria's reluctance to use voluntary wardship agreements.
4. In Victoria, it is operating as the focal point for counselling services. Parents and young people may have their first contact with welfare services when they go to the court to ask for advice from court officials. The success of the Children's Court Advisory Service in Victoria is testament to this.
5. The threat of court proceedings is acting as a catalyst for action, and may lead parents in particular to face the need for outside assistance in dealing with the parent-adolescent conflict.

The danger remains however that as long as we see the problem of parent-child conflict as a legal issue, and as long as we think in terms of court proceedings even as a last resort, our attention and our resources will be diverted to courts and lawyers and away from counselling and mediation. We will think we have solved the problem of parent-child breakdowns because we have a procedure and a heading in our definitions of what it means for a child to be in need of care. Parent-child breakdowns reveal the limitations of legal ordering. Perhaps it is time that this was seen more clearly in other areas of family law as well.

Endnotes

1. A recent study in South Australia (Bailey-Harris and Naffine, 1988), indicates some success in dealing with this double standard.

2. In the USA the Federal Government initiated a programme in the Juvenile Justice and Delinquency Prevention Act 1974, by which federal funds were made dependent on the deinstitutionalisation of status offenders. See Sweet (1991), Bomar (1988).
3. In England, the Children and Young Persons Act 1969 (sl (2) (d)) made it a ground for care that the young person was beyond the control of his parents or guardian. By March 1984, 2,800 out of 78,900 children were in local authority care on this ground. However, there were some local authorities which did not use this ground at all and relied on voluntary care to deal with runaway problems (Parkinson, 1988). See now the Children Act 1989, s.31 (2).
4. Controversy erupted in 1986 when the use of the 'irreconcilable difference' procedure by a fifteen year old boy led to proceedings in the Supreme Court of Victoria. The parents succeeded in having the Children's Court order revoked on the grounds of a denial of natural justice to them (*J.B. and E.B. V. Director General of Community Welfare* S 22 Feb. 1988, unreported). The government ordered and enquiry chaired by a Family Court judge, which cleared the social workers concerned of any wrongdoing (*Fogarty Report, 1989*). This case is reviewed, and the Victorian legislation examined in detail in Parkinson (1990).
5. The criticisms made in Australia are reminiscent of the debate about the Washington State case of Cynthia Snyder (aged fifteen) who was allowed to declare herself 'incorrigible' and thereby to get away from restrictive parents. *In re Snyder* 85 Wash. 2d 182, 532 P 2d 278 (1975). See Hafen (1976), *BYU Law Review* (1976).
6. Del. Code Annot. 10-921(6), (Family Court has jurisdiction where 'a member of a family alleges that some other member of the family is by his conduct imperilling any family relationship') (Michie Supp. 1990); Iowa Code Annot. s232.122ff (West 1985) (court may make orders to assist family, including mandatory counselling, where there has been a breakdown in the parent-child relationship); Maine Rev. Stat. Annot. ch. 15 s.3501ff (1980 and West Supp. 1990) (provisions for interim care of runaway juveniles. Young person sixteen years and over may petition for emancipation).
7. Rev. Code Wash. Annot. 13.32A (West Supp. 1991).
8. Ibid 13.32A.170(1)(e).
9. Ibid 13.32A.190(3).
10. Ibid 13.32A.192-250.

Teamwork and Decision Making

The practice of child protection continues to rely on multi-disciplinary teams, often composed of staff from various agencies, who together bring a variety of approaches, disciplines and knowledge to the complex decisions that have to be made in order to protect children. This joining together of a disparate group of workers into teams is a complicated business in itself. The teams are then involved with families at critical moments in their life history. The families generate profound social and psychological issues, both for themselves and for all with whom they are in contact. Often the teams and their resultant decision making become dysfunctional. Conversely, considering the circumstances, it is impressive that so many effective decisions are able to be made with families.

The following chapters travel familiar ground — the struggle of working out how to make effective decisions. These are perennial issues that need to be constantly re-examined in order to better understand the processes involved. Our understanding can be deepened when responding to new challenges such as dealing with Munchausen by Proxy cases or in cases of group child sexual abuse. Or we can, with renewed vigilance, learn from our experiences in decision making through case conferences or in the tragedy of child death resulting from maltreatment.

The challenge of working together as an effective team remains paramount. The expectation that workers who often barely know each other, can come together, speak openly and honestly with the family and with each other, as well as respond to the obvious and subtle cries for help intermingled with messages of outright rejection by the family, is awesome. Yet remarkably, the commitment and professionalism of those involved usually ensure that the child and the family are heard and understood. This most delicate and demanding process provides a foundation on which effective decisions can be made with families.

All this is being done in the current Australian context of shrinking welfare resources which place additional demands on teams who are either short staffed or reliant on a disproportionate number of newly qualified staff with insufficient time for supervision and training. This group of chapters is one way of providing some fresh insights both into the 'well-known' and the 'recently recognised' which can lead to more effective team work and thoughtful decision making.

7
Case Conferences and Decision Making in Child Protection

Bruce Lord

The case conference method is one element in a general approach to child abuse work, which emphasises multidisciplinary responsibility for case assessment and management. The rationale for a multi-disciplinary approach is based on assumptions that child abuse is not the province of any one discipline and that a variety of professional skills and perspectives is required. The complexity and difficulty of the problem, it is argued, means that several professional fields are needed to understand and deal with it. This concept is summarised by Mouzakitis and Goldstein:

> The wide range of social, psychiatric and psychological problems involved in abuse and neglect requires that social workers, physicians, nurses, lawyers, judges, psychiatrists and many other professionals work together if the cycle of abuse and neglect is to be broken. These various disciplines make distinct contributions to a comprehensive diagnosis of the abusive family and the abused and neglected child as well as to the planning and treatment of such cases (1985, 218)

The concept of a multidisciplinary approach has received strong support from the time when child abuse first became a professionally and officially recognised problem. The early leaders in the field, such as Kempe and Helfer (1972) were strong proponents of a team approach, with a commitment to shared responsibility and joint decision making. The original concept was of a 'mini-team' comprised of a paediatrician and social worker, with back up psychiatric consultation. From this the team has grown to be multidisciplinary, with a number of other professionals having joined the group.

Proponents of the multidisciplinary approach frequently adopt a medical model, emphasising its benefits for both 'diagnostic' and 'treatment' purposes; that is, in ensuring comprehensive evaluation of the case and consideration of all avenues of intervention which may reduce the risk of abuse, or ameliorate its consequences. (Schmidt, 1978, Meddin and Grosz, 1986). Within this model, the problems of child abuse and neglect are conceptualised as a clinical syndrome that requires specialised intervention skills (Mouzakitis and Goldstein, 1985).

There are several strengths claimed for the multidisciplinary approach:

1. It has been demonstrated how access to a multidisciplinary team evaluation results in a greater uptake of services by families designated as at risk (Hochstadt and Harwick, 1985). It appears that the involvement of teams and holding of special conferences focus attention and effort on the particular case at hand, and serve as a catalyst to making additional resources available.
2. The multidisciplinary approach has been strongly advocated as the most appropriate way of making critical decisions, such as whether a child should be placed in alternative care (Kempe and Helfer, 1972) as an adjunct to decision making at all levels (Meddin and Gross, 1986).
3. The group involvement provides the advantage of greater creativity in producing ideas, and increases the possibilities for sharing tasks and responsibilities.

   This division of labour allows individuals to perform tasks for which they are most qualified; prevents or reduces overlapping activity; and allows decisions to be made more rapidly than would occur were one person responsible for gathering data from a variety of sources or specialisations. Protective service work lends itself to such task division (Bourne and Newberger, 1980, 139).

4. Group decision making alleviates some of the stress and strong sense of individual responsibility which may develop amongst staff. It may also provide an important level of support to staff in dealing with their own feelings and personal reactions to abuse

situations (Bourne and Newberger, 1980, Hallet and Stevenson, 1980). Stress is created also by the organisational and political context in which the work is carried out. Within hospitals, for example, the environment may become difficult or even hostile. Child abuse teams are frequently faced with an ambivalent or negative attitude by other staff and ambiguities about their role (Bourne and Newberger, 1980).

5. Through the multidisciplinary team approach, conflicts about the case which may arise can potentially be dealt with directly and openly. A team approach can also facilitate ongoing communication and cooperation amongst the parties involved.

The Role and Purpose of a Case Conference

The case conference is often seen as the particular mechanism through which the benefits of a multidisciplinary approach are expressed. It has been described as the most critical element in team functioning (Schmidt and Grosz, 1978). The case conference provides the setting for the pooling of information and sharing of different perspectives on the case at hand. It is an opportunity to clarify the needs, concerns and issues involved and the available options for intervention. It is also a forum in which planning of specific management procedures can be undertaken and the efforts of the various personnel involved be coordinated into a common direction.

This broad rationale is widely accepted and case conferences have become an established component of child protection services in most western countries, including the USA, the United Kingdom and Australia. In the USA, multidisciplinary child protection teams and case conferences operate within both hospital and community settings. The community teams, known as child protection panels, are supported by federal statute and have been adopted by many states (Meddin and Gross, 1985). The state of Colorado, for example, has developed an extensive network of panels covering almost the entire state. The panels review all child at risk cases referred by the statutory child protection service (Motz, 1984).

In the United Kingdom, the impetus for case conferencing developed in part through public enquiries into the tragic deaths of a number of child abuse victims (Jones, et al 1979). These enquiries were roundly critical of the organisation of social services, and in particular highlighted the lack of co-ordination and co-operation amongst agencies involved with families at risk (Browne, 1987). The concept of the case conference as a coordinating and decision making vehicle was advocated by reformers and became widely adopted. Moreover, the wave of public criticism created through the enquiries and consequent anxiety amongst professionals involved in the child abuse field, served as a further impetus to case conferences. The conferences appeared to provide a mechanism for sharing anxiety and responsibility and as a way of avoiding blame should things go wrong (Jones, 1987, Hallet and Stevenson, 1980).

Case conferences have remained a central element in the British and American child protection systems. However, their exact role and the limits of their authority and responsibility have remained a matter of debate particularly in the United Kingdom, (Hallet and Stevenson, 1980, Moore, 1985). In Australia, case conferences are now also a widely utilised method of case review and decision making. There has been strong support for the approach within paediatric hospitals, and state welfare departments have widely adopted the procedure within recent years.

Problems With the Multidisciplinary Approach

A number of writers have written on difficulties associated with interprofessional and interagency collaboration. One of the best known reviews of interdisciplinary work is by Hallet and Stevenson (1980) and is based on an observational study of a series of thirteen case conferences. In this descriptive study, Hallet and Stevenson graphically illustrate how attitudes of professional groups towards themselves and each other have a crucial impact on team functioning. Role perceptions were seen to determine significantly the degree of cooperation achieved. The stereotyping of roles frequently leads to conflict and frustration between professionals involved together in management of cases.

Case conferences may highlight these difficulties, given the varying backgrounds of experience, education and professional training of the participants. Indeed, some commentators on case conferences have argued that it is more likely a degree of ignorance and mistrust will prevail, especially where participants have not previously worked together.

The emotionally charged nature of the meeting may also influence its dynamics. Examples of the deleterious effects of anxiety have been recorded, including significant distortions of information and perceptions amongst participants (Dingwall, et al 1983, Monk, 1987). It appears there are potential problems at two extremes. Undue concern about an incident may be raised because of selective presentation or colouring of information, possibly leading to invasive and unwarranted action. On the other hand, a kind of inertia, or reluctance to intervene in apparently high risk situations, may develop out of the particular group dynamics. On the other hand, Moore

(1985) also refers to the phenomenon of 'risky shift' in which a group is prepared to take greater risks, than if the decision had been made by any one individual member.

In addition to these problems, issues of power, control and influence in the meetings have been seen as an important element in understanding the conference process. Hallet and Stevenson (1980) have traced the historical transition from a dominantly medical model of case conferences in the United Kingdom to the contemporary balance of power between medical and social welfare personnel. It is clear, however, that rivalries over the control of the meetings persist (Moore, 1985) which are often expressed in disputes over who should attend the conferences and over chairing arrangements.

Other specific problems were identified in a study by Castle (1977), involving a survey of case conferences conducted in the United Kingdom through the auspices of the National Society for the Prevention of Cruelty to Children (NSPCC). Questionnaires were administered to NSPCC case workers who attended a total of 777 case conferences during a three month period.

Castle's survey, which assessed professionals' concerns, uncovered numerous practical problems in the organisation and running of conferences. Specifically, there were frequent concerns regarding time wastage due to unprepared participants, failure of key personnel to attend, deficiencies in chairing arrangements and role conflicts with the meetings. Participants expressed frustrations associated with the refusal of courts to implement conference recommendations and with some situations where conferences were unable to reach agreement. Castle also commented on the high expectations of professionals towards conferences, in finding solutions to difficult and complex problems. Some of the disappointment and frustration identified may have resulted from unrealistic views of what conferences might achieve.

A more recent paper by Corby and Mills (1986) reported on an observational study of a series of 55 case conferences in Liverpool, United Kingdom. They reported a tendency for participants to be chiefly concerned to justify their own actions. They also noted different viewpoints on what constitutes abuse. Further they related instances in which the conference process was manipulated to deal with staff problems. For example, a particular conference chairman was noted to press for formal registration of a case, in order to ensure regular reviews because of his doubts regarding the competence of the worker involved. This occurred despite the views of others that the case involved a low level of risk. In other instances apparently higher risk cases were steered away from conferences because of a wish by some staff to protect the family from what was seen as intrusive intervention. In addition to these idiosyncratic problems Corby and Mills (1986) emphasised two general features of the meetings:

1. A lack of explicit discussion of the degree of risk involved in particular cases.
2. A lack of explicit and careful consideration of the type and amount of resources needed to ensure protection of the child.

An interesting dynamic was suggested which related to the anxiety and stress of child abuse work. On the one hand it appeared that anxiety about making mistakes drove people together; that there is a sense of safety in group decision making. On the other hand, the anxiety appeared to limit participants' ability to think through and directly discuss some of the difficulties and risks inherent in the case.

Whilst this study was mainly impressionistic (in that no systematic methodology was utilised), its findings bear a familiar ring to those involved in child protection work. It might be debated however, whether the identified 'deficiencies' of the conferences actually limited their usefulness as a procedure. The authors acknowledged for example, that at least 75 per cent of their sample conferences appear to have reached a satisfactory outcome in that the family did not represent with further abuse.

Bourne and Newberger (1980) have highlighted some of the particular issues relevant to established teams, that is, where the same group meets frequently to discuss cases. Their findings are based on participatory observation of team collaboration and case conferences in an American hospital setting. The problems emphasised include:

1. Experts maintaining influence outside their own domains. This, for example, was relevant in the case of high status groups such as physicians.
2. Conformity within the group for the sake of social approval.
3. Failure by group members to accept individual responsibility in areas where this was more applicable.

It seems that the key question for established teams is whether they can maintain sufficient cohesion and at the same time allow expression of individual differences which reflect the potential contributions of the disciplines involved. This also involves maintaining morale, and avoiding routinised or stereotypic approaches to cases discussed. 'It is an unending challenge to think each case through anew, instead of responding automatically once certain information is communicated.' (Bourne and Newberger, 1980, 140).

It would seem there are many potential pitfalls in case conferencing as a procedure in child protection work. Both newly constituted inter-professional groups and established teams are likely to encounter problems in achieving cohesive action. It is difficult to know the overall effectiveness of case conferences, given that available studies are descriptive or exploratory and mostly problem focused. These studies however, create a strong impression of controversy and conflict within the meetings, with outcomes determined by interpersonal dynamics, organisational and political factors. There is little that seems certain, predictable or rational about the process.

Perceptions of Abuse and Risk
One of the crucial factors underlying case conferences is the perception amongst participants of the seriousness of the problem under review, and of the degree of potential harm or risk to the child. Many of the practical difficulties in conferencing may well reflect discordant views on these issues. In this regard, it is important to remember that the process of defining and diagnosing child abuse is essentially value laden. 'Implicit in this process . . . are judgements about circumstances harmful to children, minimal requirements for adequate child development, and aspects of a child or person that are most important for society to protect' (Snyder and Newberger, 1986, 126).

The difficulty, of course, is that these judgements may be quite variable, and problems in achieving consensus have already been noted. Moreover, the whole process is open to inconsistency, bias and discrimination. Several studies have documented, for example, how social class and race are significant factors in labelling particular cases as child maltreatment and in affecting the dispositional outcome of cases entering the child protection system (Giovannoni and Becerra, 1979, Hampton and Newberger, 1985, Katz, et al. 1986) These factors were seen to influence particularly the perception of an event in ambiguous circumstances, where the intent of the parent figure and consequences for the child were not clear.

A number of writers have attempted to study systematically the varying perceptions of abuse amongst professional groups. Giovannoni and Becerra (1979) found marked differences amongst five professional groups (social workers, police, paediatricians, lawyers and a lay sample) in their ratings of a series of case vignettes. Whilst there was significant disagreement between the groups on the seriousness of the case, all groups tended to agree on the relative ranking of broad categories of abuse. Physical abuse, sexual abuse and fostering of delinquency were ranked most seriously and above problems of apparent neglect or emotional abuse.

Snyder & Newberger (1986) also found marked differences in the degree of risk or of seriousness attributed to cases amongst groups of hospital-based professionals. Nurses and social workers tended to rate cases as higher risk than physicians, psychologists and psychiatrists. In a similar finding to the previous study, the professional groups did discriminate between different forms of abuse and there was general agreement on the rank ordering of cases in broad categories. In a comparable study, Fox & Dingwall (1985) found no significant differences in the way social workers and health visitors in the United Kingdom evaluated cases of apparent abuse. Thus, while a degree of consensus was found regarding the significance of various types of abuse, in these studies the level of potential disagreement over individual cases was also underscored.

The significance of these variations in perceptions of risk within case conferences is a matter not well understood. Part of the rationale for the group approach to case decision making is to obtain a broader, more representative view and to counteract the problem of bias. Through the group process it is argued the participants can check each other's biases and there is a better chance of avoiding idiosyncratic decisions. It remains possible, of course, that the conference as a whole might embrace prejudicial views and discriminate against particular groups.

The way in which case meetings, in reality, deal with the varying perceptions of abuse is a matter which warrants further analysis and study. Whether the conference tends to even out participants' perceptions of risk in the case; or indeed whether the conference might serve to amplify concerns through the experience of pooling information, is a matter requiring clarification. In most instances participants have only a partial view of the case prior to the meeting, their view being limited either by the length of their involvement or professional domain. Additional information and opinions might have the effect of either increasing or allaying concerns. Given the problem focussed nature of the meetings and the tendency of participants to 'offload' their anxieties about the case, it is perhaps more likely that the overall level of concern will rise.

The group process itself and the need to work on an agreed plan of action may influence the members toward consensus. Indeed, this is one of the expressed purposes of case conferences. What is not clear from available evidence is the degree to which this is achieved and the implications of unresolved differences and conflicts.

Decision Making in Child at Risk Cases

Most writers on child abuse decision making and case conferences comment on the inherent difficulty of the task. The majority of cases in reality are ambiguous, and conferences are hampered by a lack of information, incomplete assessments and unclear or conflicting reports. In many situations teams are working without the co-operation of the parents and attempting to meet a dual commitment to both the needs and rights of the parents and of the children. Moreover, as child abuse is not a unitary phenomenon, a large range of situations may come within the gambit of the 'child at risk' conference, requiring the participants to deal with complex and varied problems.

As well as determining the nature of the current situation (was the injury non-accidental?), there are inherent difficulties in predicting future events with any accuracy (will it occur again?). There are some basic dilemmas, given our current state of knowledge, in attempting to evaluate abuse situations and whether intervention is likely to succeed. Parton highlighted this problem in 1986 following an extensive review of available literature on prediction and prevention of child abuse. He asserted that:

> Not only is there little agreement about the nature of child abuse and how it can be explained and defined, but there is little consistency concerning the characteristics of the perpetrators that have been identified so that it can be predicted and prevented in an individualised way. It is not just that research has failed to reveal any consistent patterns among violent parents that practitioners could take up, but that a clearcut psychological distinction between abusers and non-abusers does not exist (Parton, 1986).

Parton also strongly criticises the notion that high risk cases can be determined by identifying a cluster of key variables. In fact he claims there is little ground for confidence in the whole child at risk assessment process when he writes: 'Whatever is done prediction rates rise no higher than two wrong judgements for every right judgement' (Parton, 1986, 525).

More recent work appears to have improved the capacity to identify children at risk of physical abuse and neglect, and given rise to more optimism about prediction. Browne and Saqi (1988) have developed a short checklist (thirteen items) which when used with statistically determined weighting of different items on the scale, can correctly classify 86 per cent of cases. The checklist was developed on a population in Surrey, England and the results cannot be generalised beyond that area. Even with improved accuracy, the authors caution against the use of this type of scale as a single screening tool. A significant number of actual abuse cases were missed by the scale (eighteen per cent) and the number of non abusing families incorrectly identified as 'at risk' was twelve per cent.

In order to improve accuracy, Browne has argued that checklists of risk factors can be combined with other forms of clinical screening to provide a comprehensive assessment over several months. He believes that a systematic approach involving the checklist, observation of the parent/child relationship and attachment behaviour should provide a reasonably reliable way of identifying cases most in need of preventative help (Browne 1989). The feasibility and effectiveness of such a comprehensive approach however, have never been tested.

In a similar way, the literature concerning the recurrence of abuse following an initial reported incident, also gives rise to uncertainties. Rates of repeated acts of abuse against children have been variously reported and range from twenty per cent to fifty per cent (Browne, 1988).

Despite these contradictions and uncertainties, there have been ongoing efforts to identify factors which will predict recurrence and enhance reliability in case decision making. A study by Cohn (1979) for example, found only one factor, 'the seriousness of the initial incident', as predictive of subsequent abuse or neglect. The presence of 'stressful events' also appears related to the recurrence of abuse, but the inclusion of this factor in itself does lend to greater predictability (Browne, 1988).

Johnson and L'Esperence (1985) in a US study identified five variables as statistically related to subsequent incidents of abuse in cases already known to a child protection agency. The identified factors were:

1. the amount of time the abused child spends with the abusing adult;
2. the mother figure's parenting skill;
3. the reasonableness of the mother figure's expectation of the abused child;
4. the family's ability to use agency resources; and,
5. the presence of more than one child in the home.

The study data were collected through a review of agency records and a statistical model was developed to predict future instances of abuse based on the case characteristics. The authors reported an overall accuracy rate of 74 per cent which appears the most promising piece of research in this area. The authors however, also caution against use of this model in a definitive way because of the confounding 'treatment' effects. All cases in the study were receiving agency follow up at one level or another and it was not possible to control completely for the effect of this variable.

Coincidentally the study by Johnson and L'Esperence (1985) also found little correlation between the amount of time and effort put into cases by the caseworkers, and the actual degree of risk for further abuse. In fact, there was some evidence to suggest that 'cooperative clients, who are less likely to abuse their children, may receive better services from their workers' (Johnson & L'Esperence, 1985, 25).

In other words child protection personnel do not in practice discriminate between potential degrees of risk to the child; and other factors, such as the worker/family relationship, play a significant part in determining how time and other resources are allocated.

In a related line of research, several studies have attempted to identify factors which will predict a family's capacity to benefit from treatment. This work has been more helpful in establishing factors mitigating against a response to intervention, rather than positive indicators. For example, Yates et al, (1983) found three variables which strongly predicted against a positive response to treatment: the number of abused children in the family, the number of birth and bonding problems, and the number of prior family contacts with service agencies.

They were unable to find factors significantly predictive of a positive response to treatment, and indeed several variables ordinarily assumed to forecast a favourable outcome did not approach significance. Some other factors associated with poor outcome have included prior instances of abuse, refusal to acknowledge the maltreatment and failure to accept an active role in therapy (Cohn, 1979, Green, et al 1979).

The findings of studies such as these have only limited value as an aid to decision making in practice situations. Firstly, the findings are regarded as only tentative because of methodological weaknesses in the studies such as small sample sizes and lack of adequate controls (Yates, et al 1984). Secondly, what is lacking is a means of translating the findings into prospective case situations. It is difficult to see the practical application of some of the identified factors, particularly those related to motivation, which may only emerge through the process of attempting work with a family.

These studies thus raise serious doubts about the capacity of case conferences (or indeed any decision making body) to make reliable decisions in relation to the protection and safety of children. These doubts are reinforced by studies which focus on direct observation of parent-child interactions as a means of determining risk. Although there is some evidence that abusive parents can be distinguished from non-abusive parents by 'blind' observers in experimental situations, there is little support that this is an effective approach to identifying risks, in the normal practice context. Distinctions can be drawn between abusive and non-abusive parents only where observations are structured and systematic (Starr, 1987), which does not apply in 'normal' practice situations, for example, where caseworkers are visiting homes.

In this regard, an interesting study has found that experienced professionals in the child abuse field performed no better than at chance level when asked to distinguish 'abuse prone' from 'normal' parents through observation of a series of videotaped parent-child interactions (Starr 1987). This method is more likely to approximate the practice situation, as the participants were free to adopt whatever indicators of abuse and risk they usually employed. It is also noted that the performance did not vary between professional groups or differ significantly from a group of undergraduate students. In contrast, the positive findings associated with more structured observations of particular features of the interaction, leave open the possibility of the practical adaptation of these techniques in case decision making.

In addition to the difficulties of assessment and evaluation of risk, personnel in case conferences frequently face dilemmas regarding the alternatives to leaving a child within the family. Indeed, some reports suggest that concerns about the quality and durability of alternative care also have a bearing on case decisions not to remove a child, despite a perception of inadequate care in the natural family (Katz, et al 1986).

Decision making in child abuse work thus involves complex issues. These problems and complexities highlight the difficult tasks which inevitably confront the participants of case conferences and influence the processes which occur within the meeting.

Approaches to Improving Case Conferences and Decision Making

Several practitioners in the field have attempted to identify ways of improving case conferences. Jones et al (1979) described an approach to case conferencing in Nottinghamshire and specified several factors considered as prerequisites to effective meetings. These included a spirit of co-operation and commitment, theoretical and ethical agreement between the participants, understanding of the formal and informal relationships within the group and a 'facilitating structure' within the meeting. Attention was also given to practical details such as the preparation of participants, the amount of written material which can be reasonably digested in a meeting and the type of minutes to be kept.

Jones et al gave considerable attention to the role of chairperson, emphasising a need for clear policies for chairing arrangements and the degree of authority invested in the meeting. Training for prospective chairpersons was recommended and a number of procedural guidelines suggested. In particular these concerned the flow of information with the aim of ensuring that the relevant case material is presented in an orderly and logical way. The recommended meeting procedure involved the following sequence:

1. Introductions (roles of the participants identified).
2. Outline of the purpose of the meeting.
3. Identifying case details (the child and family).
4. The precipitating incident (the current problem).
5. Relevant background (life histories, personality profiles, etc).

The conference then moves on to the various decision issues. Similar prescriptions have been made elsewhere in the British commentaries on case conferencing (Hallet & Stevenson, 1980, Moore, 1985). In particular there is repeated emphasis on organisation and efficiency which no doubt reflects the degree of frustration and criticism over time spent in the meetings.

Whilst most of the above suggestions were aimed to help conferences overcome acknowledged deficiencies, it is not always clear how they may be operationalised. Some, in fact, remain at the level of general exhortations. For example, it is not clear what can be done when an absence of 'theoretical and ethical agreement' is apparent, or even how to check the level of such agreement amongst participants. Other suggestions, such as the procedural guidelines have a more immediate application.

There is also a strong emphasis on efficiency in the contemporary American approach as expressed, for example, in the Child Protection Team Handbook (Schmitt 1978). The 'Ground Rules for Effective Team Conferences' include the following:

- Each case conference should be limited to 30 minutes.
- Formal presentation time for each participant should not exceed three minutes.
- The case material should be presented in the format of a problem oriented record.
- All comments should be directed to a specific problem number (Schmitt & Grosz, 1978).

It is difficult to ascertain whether such 'efficiency' is ever achieved because of few evaluation reports. The question of efficiency is a matter requiring further careful evaluation.

Corby & Mills (1986) have argued that the process within case conferences needs to become more systematic and explicit. They suggest three areas in which more focused discussion and decision making should occur. First, an explicit cataloguing of concerns or risks would serve to centre the meeting on the task at hand:

> All too often the notion of risk is eschewed because practitioners, managers and society as a whole prefer not to think in terms of risk taking, particularly where the health and safety of children is concerned . . . it is far better to take a more realistic view of the risks involved in abused children remaining in their families (Corby & Mills, 1986, 540).

They suggest that conferences should aim to categorise the degree of risk based on the various factors presenting in the case. They outline a number of factors commonly and 'implicitly' used in decision making and argue for more explicit use of such factors.

In recognising the limitations in empirical evidence for predicting child abuse, Corby and Mills differentiate their concept of risk factors from actual 'predictors' of abuse. Indeed there is an argument that conferences need to make assessments and judgements about risk and plan action despite the lack of certainty in this area. And it would seem preferable to do this in an open and explicit way. 'The real problem lies in having a clear agreed upon set of criteria for all involved to use as an aid to decision making' Corby & Mills, 1986, 536).

It remains a moot point however, as to how the conference arrives at these criteria. At this point, Corby and Mills leave the argument, suggesting an individualised approach, with each agency drawing up its own risk categories. There would seem a case however, for utilising the best available empirical evidence and attempting to apply this in a systematic way. Moreover, an equitable child protection system requires there to be reasonable consistency in the way decisions are made and, on this basis, more general agreement about what constitutes 'risk factors' is desirable.

A second recommendation by Corby and Mills is to create an explicit hierarchy of strategies for intervention. The categories range from minimal intrusion into the family (eg monitoring through support services), through mandatory supervision, to removal of a child from the home. They point out the limited number of 'disposal options' and emphasise that the strategy selected by the conference should reflect the degree of risk defined.

The authors' third suggestion is to allocate resources more consciously in line with the degree of risk and complexity of the case. For example, the question of the level of experience and expertise of individual caseworkers is a matter rarely discussed. Certainly it would seem that this should be a legitimate matter for conferences to consider and it is obvious that the more difficult cases should be allocated to staff with experience and specialised skills.

Whilst these suggestions appear useful, the method of their implementation is again an area where further work is required. Several issues might need to be resolved including how the responsibility for raising key questions is to be assigned, what decision making method is to be adopted and what procedure will be followed in dealing with conflicts. In addition, a method is required for identifying participants' perception of risk factors, degree of risk and the preferred intervention. Such questions of procedure and method are important matters if suggestions about ways to improve the quality of decisions are to be incorporated.

Perhaps the greatest weakness in the case conference method is the dependence on the chairperson, in large part, for the quality and outcome of the meeting. Chairing case conferences is indeed a complex and demanding role. A large range of interpersonal skills is required to deal with the various ethical, theoretical and communication issues which have been noted above. One aspect which has not been developed in the literature has been the potential role of a consultant team rather than a single chairperson in running conferences. The use of teams in family therapy has been well established, and much has been written on team dynamics and approaches to team therapy. In a similar way a team concept can be applied to case conferences, with certain advantages. Such an approach has been developed within a paediatric setting at Westmead Hospital in Sydney, with paediatrician, social worker and psychiatrist as the consultant team. The most significant advantage reported in this has been the sharing of responsibility for managing the process of the case conferences.

It is interesting that efforts to improve case conferences have focused largely on the process of the meetings with less attention to structural considerations. The timing of case conferences is, for example, also likely to be significant. It is more likely that the meetings will be useful at an early stage when the professionals involved are forming their assessments and developing strategies. They are less likely to be useful after there has been long term involvement of the parties unless there is significant new information introduced into the system.

The composition of case conferences also wants more discussion. We have already noted that ethnic and minority groups are frequently discriminated against in child abuse assessments. There is a strong case for including members of ethnic or other minority groups in any decision making forums, affecting children of those communities.

Likewise, the issue of gender should be considered. It is notable that gender has been a neglected subject in case conference studies. Case conferences were first instituted to deal with problems of physical abuse and neglect and there was little discussion generally about gender issues. With development of sexual assault services, the question of the gender of the professionals involved in providing those services has become prominent. New insights on the role of gender in the perception and response to abuse, which have been gained through sexual assault services should be incorporated into the planning of case conferences.

A final structural variable is the level of resourcing and organisational support given to case conferences. Effective conferences are time consuming and this requires recognition within the organisations which sponsor them. Related to this is the status afforded to case conferences by professional leaders and administrators within those organisations. These external considerations are also likely to have a significant bearing on the performance of case conferences.

Decision Making Models

Other approaches to improving decision making in child abuse work have focused more on case criteria and 'action required' without specific reference to the mechanism or means through which decisions are made. These models, however, have relevance to the case conference approach. For example, Brown and Riley (1985) have produced a comprehensive set of procedures for child protection workers to follow through all stages of case investigation and management. Guidelines for case decision making by hospital based teams are also available (Schmitt & Loy, 1978). Another 'decision making model' developed by Meddin (1984) has been on trial in the field and some evaluation of its usefulness has been carried out.

Meddin's framework defines three types of decisions: initial decisions, investigation decisions and disposal decisions. Criteria are set out for the various decision options such as whether to place a child. The criteria were derived through a consultative process with agency personnel. In this respect, Meddin's ideas are similar to the approach advocated by Corby and Mills. The particular value of her work, however, has been the demonstration of how the consultative process and the adoption of a model produce greater consistency in decision making. In a field study Meddin was able to show how staff trained in the use of the model 'improved' their case decision making to be more consistent with an expert panel using the same criteria (Meddin, 1984).

The idea of an explicit decision making model has been taken a step further by a UK consortium which has produced a micro-computer program, known as Priority Decision System (Algie, 1986). The program utilises set criteria to check internal consistency of decisions made and can also assess the level of agreement between participants in a group decision making situation. Its main contribution would appear to be in identifying clearly the weight given by participants to various factors in formulating a decision. Computer technology may well become an additional aid to case conferences and the developers of this program have made wide claims regarding its application to child protection work. No systematic data are available as yet however, on its use in practice situations.

In an Australian study, Dalgleish and Drew (1989) have also worked on clarifying the elements of decision making in child protection cases. Through a field study involving child care officers in Queensland, they identified the weightings given to various risk factors (such as the severity of abuse, parenting problems, social isolation) in determining the overall perceived level of risk. They have also sought to define better the concept of risk and its components.

A model is presented in which case risk factors are related to four major components of risk assessment (Dalgleish, 1990).

- Magnitude of the current harm
- Strengths of the situation
- Chances of future harm
- Magnitude of future harm

Dalgleish has been able to demonstrate how different workers give varying weight to risk factors, and emphasise different components of risk in the overall judgements of risk, which may be of more than academic interest. To make use of these ideas however, it will be necessary for professionals to incorporate the model and become more proficient in analysing components of risk and the basis on which they are making decisions.

Innovations in Practice

Other recent developments in case decision making are based on the incorporation of new practice approaches. In particular the application of family therapy and systems concepts to assessment and decision making in child protection has produced some innovative approaches. For example, Dale et al (1986) have developed a system of 'network meetings' as an approach to dealing with families seen as difficult or having long term involvement with child protection agencies. Network meetings are convened when the management or helping process has become 'stuck', which usually signifies a build up of tension and conflict between the family and the professionals involved. The professionals have continuing concern about abuse or serious neglect and the family is resisting interventions.

The network meeting is convened and chaired by a neutral party. The unique feature is that it includes not only the child and family but all significant workers who have day-to-day contact and responsibility for the case. The 'ecosystem' therefore, may include child protection workers, foster parents and members of the extended family or community organisations. The purpose of the meeting is to clarify perceptions of problems from both the family's and professional's points of view. It also seeks to clarify what services are being offered and which aspects of services the family are willing to avail themselves of. For the process of the meeting, the family are 'put in charge' of their case and regarded as being the experts on themselves.

In this way the approach seeks to both re-empower families and require the family members and professionals to take responsibility for what they are prepared to offer and do. In the case of statutory personnel they must also state clearly to the family the legal requirements which are binding their action. The architects of this approach have described examples of significant changes flowing from the new perspectives developed in these meetings (Dale, et al 1986).

Bentovim and Tranter (1984) have described a similar approach within a child psychiatry setting at the Hospital for Sick Children, London. Bentovim and colleagues adopted network meetings as part of an assessment/consultative process by a team of mental health professionals. The purpose of the assessments is to make recommendations regarding the family's capacity to benefit from support or treatment interventions. As such, this consultative process has much in common with case conferences except in that the family are always included, and at the centre of the process. The other major difference is that the process is guided by the mental health team (who interview both the family and significant personnel). Moreover, a psychological and family systems assessment is conducted during the session. The recommendations arising out of the process, therefore, have a greater poignancy because of the immediate involvement with the child and family and the actual issues at hand.

The limitations of network meetings as a general approach to child protection decision making, are the amount of time and specialised skill required as well as the logistical problems of getting all parties together. As currently arranged in the United Kingdom they produce recommendations which the relevant authorities must decide whether or not to implement. A future development may be to include parties with the final decision making authority in the assessment process.

In New Zealand there has been a significant and recent innovation in the use of 'family group conferences' within the legal process of child protection. The family group conference has been given a prominent role in decision making and resolution of child protection problems and is recognised and supported by statute. The 'family', which is defined in wide terms, includes members of the extended family group, and is enshrined in legislation as carrying the fundamental decision making role in child protection cases. However, the power of the state to intervene and override the family's wishes in extreme circumstances remains in place. Nevertheless, a significant step has been taken, in rebalancing the power arrangement between family and kinship groups and the state.

The New Zealand situation has developed with significant influence from the Maori community and within a framework of severe restraints on the capacity of government agencies to provide alternative forms of care. The project remains in the early stages of development and evaluation is pending. Some anecdotal reports, however, are available indicating examples of effective and creative problem solving efforts by family groups within this new framework (Barbour, 1990, Caton, 1990).

The above approaches should be differentiated from the more traditional conference procedure in which parents are allowed to sit in and have their point of view expressed in the meeting. The issue of parental involvement in formal case conferences has been a controversial one and an area where there are marked inconsistencies in approach, particularly in the United Kingdom (Heptinstall, 1983). Some London boroughs encourage parental involvement in all stages of decision making and allow them an active role in case conferences. Others deny them this right.

In Australia there has been an apparent shift in practice over recent years toward parental participation. It is now common that parents are present during at least part of case conferences. Differences in philosophy have emerged with some community agencies, for example, agreeing to attend case conferences only where the parents are also invited for the full meeting. Paediatric hospitals, however, have generally maintained the conventional procedure of meeting with parents following the conference, whilst in the statutory agencies the practice is somewhat varied.

A review of the arguments for and against parental involvement has been provided elsewhere (McGloin & Turnbull, 1987). For the present purpose, it is noted that some have seen parental participation as a progressive step and a way of improving the quality of information and decision making in case conferences. (Atherton, 1986). Others have emphasised parental rights and focused on parental participation as an empowering procedure for the family (Waters, 1983, Monk, 1987).

Parental participation is a complex issue and a matter requiring further clarification and evaluation. The issues are the level and process of participation not only for the parents but (where possible) for the children also. Frequently agencies which claim to include parents actually meet in advance or organise the agenda and process of the case conference ahead of the event. These processes around the setting up of a case conference also need to be taken into account, in addressing ways to empower children and parents.

Power and control are always issues in child protection work. We need to move beyond simplistic notions of power being located either with the professionals or the family and develop a clearer understanding of power arrangements. When power is shifted away from professionals or agencies acting on behalf of children, we need to consider carefully whether this is truly empowering and resourcing families, and whether there are conflicting needs of parents and children. In times of economic constraints and contraction of resources, we also need to be wary of moves which switch responsibility to families. 'Empowering families' may simply be a means of the state's abdicating previously held responsibilities for provision of services and resources.

Summary

A multidisciplinary team approach has become the dominant model for the management of child abuse within Australia, the United Kingdom and the USA. Case conferences are the primary vehicle through which multidisciplinary teams operate, in making case management decisions and organising services. Several advantages are seen in this approach, including the utilisation of a diverse range of skills, and sharing of responsibility for crucial decisions regarding the safety and welfare of children.

However, a number of studies and commentaries have highlighted various problems and deficiencies in this method. Case conferences have been strongly criticised because of lack of efficiency and lack of rationality in their operation. In particular, problems of inadequate information, unresolved conflicts between participants and a lack of precision in case discussions have been identified. These observations have raised doubts about the validity of case conferences as an approach to decision making with regard to children at risk.

It is also apparent that decision making in child abuse cases is a highly complex and difficult task. Empirical studies on child abuse provide no certain method of predicting outcomes, so that case management and planning continues to require a process of judgement. The central task of case conferences lies in deciding the degree to which a child is at risk and what would be appropriate intervention. Other studies demonstrating the differences between professional groups, in evaluating the degree of risk, have also raised questions about the capacity of case conferences to reach consensus on problems and management.

Given these problems and limitations, a number of approaches have been suggested to improve the performance of case conferences. Various ways of enhancing the decision making process to make it more explicit, consistent and fair, have been discussed. The need for a more systematic approach in case conferences and decision making has been highlighted, along with the need for more careful evaluation of procedures and avoidance of simplistic solutions to complex human problems.

8
Practice Insights as Revealed by Child Death Inquiries in Victoria and Overseas

Penny Armytage and Carol Reeves

Practice wisdom in child protection work is the culmination of on the job experience, pre-service and in-service training and the guidance and direction of senior, experienced staff. The insights, understandings and skills individual workers build up over time then provide the basis for their case practice and also provide the basis for practice guidelines, standards and procedures.

Child death inquiries and critical incident reviews are an additional source of practice wisdom. They provide insights which are invaluable to the child protection system as a whole as well as to individual workers. Rarely do they reveal new findings or theories about how child welfare, and in particular child abuse and neglect cases, should be handled or how services to statutory clients should be provided. Instead they provide a powerful reminder of many of the basics which have long been recognised as fundamental to good child protection practice but which sadly can all too frequently be overlooked.

Examination of a sample of incidents in which statutory clients of Community Services Victoria (CSV) died, and consideration of overseas literature and review material has reinforced the notion that the failure to be mindful of some of the basic theories of effective management of child welfare cases can have dire consequences. Furthermore that the general picture of practice emerging 'is not of gross errors or failures of individuals on single occasions but of a confluence or succession of errors, minor inefficiencies and misjudgments by a number of agencies, together with adverse effects of circumstantial factors beyond the control of those involved' (Department of Health and Social Security (DHSS) 1982, 29).

This paper examines the findings and conclusions of ten child death inquiries and identifies some of the most commonly recurring errors, minor inefficiencies and misjudgments at both a practice and system level. It also proposes actions which individual practitioners and the protective services system as a whole can take to minimise the possibility of further recurrences of these tragic events.

Child Death Inquiries — Justified or Not?

Although the *Report of the Panel of Inquiry into the Circumstances of the Death of Jasmine Beckford* (Blom-Cooper 1985), suggests that the child protection system must respond to tragedies of this nature by refining its tools for predicting children at great risk, it appears that the very nature of child protection work and the children and families with whom it works makes it impossible either to predict all fatal child maltreatment or develop foolproof systems to prevent it (Korbin, 1989, Fontana and Alfaro, 1987). Critical incidents and child deaths are therefore likely to continue to occur despite efforts to improve case practice systems and procedures. What we must strive for therefore is that when these incidents occur, there is as little scope for 'if only' as possible.

Inquiries into things that go wrong are increasingly part of modern life. The difficulties that go along with these are not confined only to welfare workers. Public scrutiny is inevitable — inquiries are a form of this. Accountability in the child protection area, with its inherent power and responsibility is justly demanded. For the public not to be concerned would surely be worse — the welfare profession cannot on the one hand argue for a 'caring community' and then reject its less agreeable manifestations.

Inquiries of this nature, though undoubtedly necessary, are painful for the professionals involved. The incidents which precede them are the realisation of one of the major fears of child protection workers — the death of one of their clients. This fear, coupled with concern about potential physical assault, is frequently identified as a source of considerable anxiety for child protection workers, most especially during their first few months on the job. Further, although the purpose of inquiries of this nature is not to focus blame on individuals but rather to examine systems' failures, individuals involved often feel that they are victims of the inquiry even if this was not the intent.

This is particularly so when the media becomes involved and demonstrates a tendency as experienced in Victoria in 1988, and described by Greenland (1987), to transform concerns regarding the death of a child into public outrage.

> The result is a transfer of hostility from the assailant who struck the fatal blow to the social worker who failed to protect the victim from harm . . . In Canada, as well as in the UK, the public censure resulting from these deaths had an extremely damaging effect on the practice of social work. As with the practice of defensive medicine, defensive social work leads to unthinking adherence to procedures designed to protect the staff and their employer rather than promote the client's best interest (Greenland, 1987, xii).

On some occasions, child abuse inquiries have indeed been inquiries into social work itself, rather than the death of the child. To be effective, child death inquiries must address this danger and adopt processes which ensure that they achieve a balance so that the inquiry is neither a witchhunt nor a whitewash. Often the facts as determined by an inquiry are not essentially in dispute, yet there is considerable scepticism, particularly amongst workers, as to the inquiry's ability to inject working knowledge of the daily dilemmas of welfare workers and the pressures of day to day work into their deliberations. This is the difference between establishing the facts and understanding the truth.

This point was powerfully raised by Martin Ruddock (1988, 14), the team leader in the British tragedy involving the death of Kimberley Carlisle. Ruddock, conceding that his practice in this particular case was below standard, argued however that the inquiry report had failed to recognise sufficiently the context in which the tragedy occurred and, in particular, the context in which he was working at that time. At the time he worked on the assumption that if he could keep things ticking over until the team in which he worked acquired additional staff, a tragedy could be averted. With hindsight he acknowledged that this view was flawed. He went on to say that at the time he 'felt as if he was a professional juggler but someone kept adding additional balls'. In the end, he said, he reached the stage of not knowing which ball was which and to what it related. He said that it was in this context that he reached his lowest level of functioning.

Even when the public welfare organisations within which child protection workers are employed provide a less problematic environment than that described by Martin Ruddock, it has been questioned whether child death inquiries ever really grasp the essential nature of child protection work — the extraordinary delicacy of the decisions made daily. Barbara Garrett, the social worker assigned to the case of Wayne Brewer, a child who died in Britain as a result of non-natural causes, was emphatic that at the time she was 'not overburdened, not harassed, that the priority to be given to the family was well recognised' (Shearer, 1979a, 12). In her view, the inquiry which ensued was not able to pinpoint where things went wrong, as she hoped it would, precisely because of the inexact nature of the science of human behaviour. Thus, whilst it is certainly the case that most inquiries reveal system failures and miscalculations, it is equally true that children may die even when this is not the case and despite our best efforts.

To be a useful analysis of practice, child death inquiries must also come to terms with the problem of hindsight, an issue formally argued in the Beckford inquiry in Britain (Blom-Cooper, 1985). In this inquiry, counsel appearing for the health workers argued that in analysing the part played by the various persons providing services to the Beckford family, the panel of inquiry 'had the incalculable benefit of hindsight. Many things that now look like flashing amber lights might have seemed of little significance had Jasmine been alive and well today' (Blom-Cooper, 1985, 32). The Beckford Panel of Inquiry rejected the view that 'hindsight' can be used as a limiting factor in the proper judgement of past conduct. It asserted that

> in arriving at a sound judgement of past conduct we are helped rather than hindered by hindsight, so long as we remind ourselves of certain basic principles. In judging the actions of social workers or health visitors as at a particular time, we should ask ourselves what such a person did know, ought to have known, did foresee and ought to have foreseen at that time, bearing in mind all relevant circumstances. We are entitled to judge a person's actions by reference to what was and should reasonably have been in his or her mind at the relevant time. We are not entitled to blame him or her for not knowing, or not foreseeing what a reasonable person would neither have known or foreseen . . . hindsight is of assistance to us in our task being no more than reasonable foresight with the additional benefit of knowledge of what has actually occurred' (Blom-Cooper, 1985, 32).

The above dilemmas are recognised by many writers (DHSS 1982, Greenland 1987, Hallett and Stevenson 1980), all of whom concede the importance of the inquiry process. They nevertheless warn of their potential pitfalls and suggest that these pitfalls can only be avoided if there is a greater correlation between the recommendations which evolve from individual inquiries and corresponding action, and if they can be seen to play a constructive part in protecting the lives of vulnerable children.

Child Death Inquiries — History and Processes

A basic program design issue for any child protection system is how it deals with child fatalities of a non-accidental nature or situations in which a child dies in violent or accidental circumstances and where concerns about statutory supervision exist.

Although child death inquiries are part of the Australian, American and British child protection systems, to name a few, they have perhaps been most noteworthy in the British system. They have operated there since the first, and probably most well known, inquiry into the death of Maria Calwell, occurred in 1974. Since that time there have been over 35 inquiries into the deaths of children killed by their parents in Britain. The prominence of inquiries in the British system may best be explained by the fact that their inquiry reports are published and readily available to interested members of the community. Some of the best known are published in book form. A few of the most notable are: the Jasmine Beckford inquiry report entitled *Child in Trust* (1985) and *Child Abuse: Aspects of Inter-Professional Cooperation* by Christine Hallett and Olive Stevenson (1980), based on the minority report of the Maria Calwell inquiry on which Olive Stevenson, Professor of Social Work and Social Policy, sat.

British child death inquiries have basically taken three different forms:

- Full public inquiries
- Department of Health and Social Service inquiries
- Area Review Committee auspiced inquiries.

Not surprisingly, full public inquiries have been convened in response to the extent of public interest and outcry. The current British policy, regarding inter-agency co-operation, as enunciated in the Department of Health and Social Security 1988 guidelines establishes internal management case reviews under the auspice of the Area Child Protection Council (ACPC), (previously Area Review Committee), as the routine first level response to a child fatality. Agencies involved are required to appoint persons to act as the point of contact with the media in recognition of the need to keep the public informed via the media. This necessitates close cooperation between agencies on the release of statements. These case reviews are required to be completed within two or three weeks, and the report, with its recommendations for future action, presented to the appropriate authority by the ACPC within seven working days of its receiving all reports.

It is difficult to establish how systems apply to child deaths within America as states differ in their approach and, as revealed by an American Humane Association (AHA) national study on child abuse and neglect reporting in 1982, few states have systematic policies, procedures and established mechanisms to deal with child fatalities. AHA (1984) proposed therefore, that because of limited reporting, less was known about child fatalities than other child maltreatment. Attempts however have been taken to correct this, and in 1984 the National Centre on Child Abuse and Neglect (NCCAN) funded three demonstration projects to test procedures for inquiring into child fatalities caused by child abuse and neglect. The projects were based in New York City, St. Louis and Illinois and Louisiana.

Child death inquiries have not had the same public prominence in the Australian context as in the British system and, of course, state approaches differ, reflecting our federal system of government. In fact recent attempts to clarify current processes revealed that at this time some Australian states are only now developing guidelines for incidents of this nature and a few do not accept the need to establish discrete processes for this purpose.

Perhaps the best known Australian child death inquiry is that concerning the death of Paul Montcalm in New South Wales in 1982 which led in effect to the reorganisation of the then Department of Youth and Community Services (Lawrence, 1982). The first child death inquiry conducted in Victoria was an internal departmental inquiry conducted in 1984, into the death of a 16 month old female child who died as the result of non-accidental injury. This had occured whilst she was the subject of a protective service notification being investigated by the Children's Protection Society, a voluntary organisation which at that time was an authorised child protection agency.

In Victoria departmental policy regarding child death inquiries was first clearly enunciated in 1985. At that time Community Services Victoria (CSV) was preparing program documentation to facilitate its incorporation of the protective services' investigative and intervention functions which had been transferred from the Children's Protection Society. The policy was further refined in 1990 after a review of Victoria's child protection system (Fogarty and Sergeant, 1989) acknowledged the need to develop a quality control system which would ensure that the public, and workers in the field, had complete confidence in the system. A system of ministerial inquiries into the circumstances of deaths of client children was subsequently developed and endorsed.

As it stands now a child death inquiry will be held in Victoria whenever a child or young person who is on an order of the children's court, or regarding whom a protective notification has been received, dies as a result of non-natural means. The purpose of the inquiry is to investigate the circumstances of the client's death from the perspective of departmental policies, procedures or practice. The primary functions are to:

(a) as far as possible, establish the facts
(b) assess whether decisions and actions taken in the case were reasonable and responsible
(c) check whether established procedures were followed
(d) consider whether the services were adequate in relation to the circumstances of the client and family concerned
(e) recommend appropriate action in the light of inquiry findings.

An inquiry is therefore intended to identify any aspects of practice or policy which calls for modification or reconsideration in the light of experience in a particular case. It is intended to be a thorough examination of how the department and its officers have carried out their responsibilities in a particular case and is therefore in the nature of a quality control exercise.

When a child or young person dies in Victoria, who is either the subject of a protective services notification to CSV or a children's court (family division) order, the following process now occurs: —

- The minister for community services is advised — through the provision of an incident report — regarding the child's death within 24 hours.
- The responsible regional director provides through the general manager, supplementary advice to the director-general of community services within ten days, in the form of a regional director's report.
- Advice is prepared for the minister on the departmental position as to whether to hold an inquiry. The decision rests with the minister as to whether an inquiry will be convened.
- All inquiry panels consist of three members — the chairperson of the Family and Children's Services Council (or nominee), a departmental representative and a non-departmental member.
- Inquiries are established with formal terms of reference including a reference to timing. Currently all inquiries are to commence within four weeks of the death, and report within twelve weeks.

Unfortunately these time limits are not currently always being observed.
- The inquiry reports directly to the minister.
- The minister decides upon acceptance of all or some of the recommendations, following receipt of departmental advice.
- The minister notifies the director-general of decisions.
- Where recommendations regarding the internal operation of the department are made, relevant senior officers are informed and monitor implementation of recommendations.
- Recommendations regarding matters external to the department are referred to the appropriate minister.

The Victorian Sample

Annual Incidents

It is a tragic reality that children who are involved with child protection services are not always able to be safely protected. Victoria's experience in this regard is not unique, as confirmed by like incidents in other Australian states and overseas, and research such as that conducted in Texas and Illinois (Greenland, 1987), and other parts of the world (Korbin, 1989, Anderson, et al., 1983, Daro & Mitchell, 1990), which indicates that 25 per cent of child maltreatment fatalities occur among families previously known to, or under the supervision of, social service agencies. Even so, it is still suggested that '. . . the incidence of serious, that is, life threatening child abuse and child abuse and neglect fatalities, is under-reported by official statistics . . .' Greenland, 1987, 6).

The National Committee on Violence Report (1990) states that:

- the Australian Bureau of Statistics figures in 1987 indicate a homicide rate of 4.2 per 100,000 of the 0-1 year population
- approximately ten per cent of homicide victims were children under ten years of age
- infants up to one year old is the age group at greatest risk of homicide
- the overwhelming majority of these child victims are killed by their parents or other relatives.

Unfortunately, relatively little is currently known on a national level about the incidence of child fatalities involving children and young people who at the time of their death are current clients of statutory child protection services. Some Australian states currently have no reliable means of collecting and collating data on this issue, though a number are presently examining their data collecting systems to obtain such information in the future. Hence at this time there is no reliable means of comparing the events which occur in Victoria with similar events in other Australian states.

Likewise there is currently no way of knowing the incidence of non-natural child fatalities where the child is known to professionals within the non-statutory sector. Regrettably what we do know however is that as CSV's protective services client population has increased, so too has the incidence of child deaths within this population.

Sample Profile

Between 1984 and 1989, 28 children/young people under the care, control, or custody of the director-general of CSV died. For the purpose of this analysis an additional client has also been included upon whose death CSV conducted an inquiry but who at the time of death was under the investigation of the then authorised protective agency — the Children's Protection Society.

Analysis of the profile of the children and young people involved in these incidents revealed:

- The majority (72 per cent) of deaths occurred whilst the child or young person was under a court order. In 57 per cent of these cases maximum legal protection had been afforded to the child in the form of wardship.
- Eighteen (64 per cent) of the children and young people who died were male, and ten (36 per cent) female.
- In eleven (39 per cent) cases, the death of the child/young person was considered to be due to natural causes and no inquiry was recommended.
- In a further two (7 per cent) cases, inquiries were conducted. Their findings revealed however that the cause of death was consistent with natural causes and no substantial concerns existed about the management of the cases.
- Of the remaining sixteen cases there were:
  - Six cases in which at the time of writing either the cause of death was uncertain and/or a decision had not been made as to whether an inquiry would be conducted or an inquiry was currently under way.
  - Four cases in which the child/young person died in violent or accidental circumstances in which prima facie case management concerns appear to exist.
  - Six cases in which the death of the child/young person was considered to be due to intra-familial abuse or deprivation of necessities.

Factors of Special Note
1. *Age of child*
In five of the six cases in the Victorian sample in which the child died as a result of intra-familial abuse or deprivation of necessities, the deceased child was under the age of three and a half. The exception involved a seventeen year old youth. Further the male/female ratio of the children who died in these circumstances was equal.

These factors are consistent with overseas research. For example a study of cases of children who died of intra-familial abuse (Korbin, 1989) found that five of the children were female and four male. The age range of the children at the time of their deaths was five months to six years. Examination of a study of 267 child deaths in Texas (Anderson, et al., 1983), found the median age of the child death victims was 1.8 years, 55.1 per cent were male, and 44.9 per cent female. Analysis of 100 child abuse and neglect fatalities in Ontario found that there were slightly more deaths of boys than girls and that 'the majority of victims of life threatening child abuse and neglect are very young children, usually under five or six' (Greenland, 1987, 8). A study by the American Humane Association (1984) found that the average age of children who died from child abuse or neglect was 3.3 years. Hence the risk of death from child abuse or neglect declines with age.

Of the four cases in which the child/young person died in violent or accidental circumstances in which prima facie case management concerns appear to exist three were aged between fourteen and sixteen years of age and one was aged ten. All were male. In half of these cases the young persons involved committed suicide, albeit possibly unintentionally.

2. *Identity of perpetrator/s*
In five of the six cases in the Victorian sample in which the child died as a result of intra-familial abuse or deprivation of necessities, manslaughter or homicide charges were laid by the police against the perpetrator(s). The exception was a case of child homicide/parent suicide. In all of the incidents of fatal non-accidental injury the charged perpetrator was not a natural parent of the child but the natural mother's de facto husband.

The numbers in the Victorian sample are too small to permit useful tests of significance on this data and further research is required to develop a clearer understanding of this phenomenon. Overseas research on the profile of perpetrators of fatal child abuse or neglect reveals some data which may be useful.

- between 20-40 per cent of perpetrators are young, single mothers

- the parents, especially abusive mothers, tend to be younger than average, with many of them starting child bearing as teenagers. Most male and female perpetrators are under 30 years of age
- single parent families, low incomes, poor housing, and social isolation combine to cause significant stress which is frequently reported in the literature on child abuse and neglect deaths
- most perpetrators of fatal child abuse and neglect are unskilled or unemployed and poorly educated
- the majority of male perpetrators have criminal records, many of them for family violence

In a study of 100 child abuse and neglect deaths in Ontario (Greenland, 1987), natural parents were the perpetrators in 63 per cent of the cases (mothers 38 per cent, fathers 13 per cent, both parents 12 per cent); mothers and their common law partners or boyfriends were responsible for seven deaths; common law partners or boyfriends acting alone were responsible for eighteen deaths. In the latter cases the attacks by male common-law partners on unrelated infants tended to be more indiscriminate and violent.

In Scott's (1973) study of the death of 29 'fatal battered baby cases', the average age of the male perpetrator was 24.3 years. Fewer than half (48.3 per cent) of the male perpetrators were biological fathers of the deceased child.

Anderson et al. (1983), found 41.2 per cent of the incidents involved victims who were the only child in the family. No father was present in approximately 40 per cent of the child death victims' homes at the time of the child deaths. For those cases in which a father figure was present, 84 per cent of the victims were reported to be living with the natural father, as compared to stepfather (15 per cent) or adoptive father (1 per cent). For 65 per cent of the victims the natural or adoptive stepfather was alleged as the perpetrator.

Practice Insights

Whilst there is much that is different between individual cases and between those cases in which a child or young person, under the care, custody, or control of the Director-General of Community Services Victoria, dies as a result of intra-familial abuse or deprivation of necessities and those in which a child or young person dies in violent or accidental circumstances in which prima facie case management concerns appear to exist, there are amazing similarities in the ways in which the 'succession of errors, minor inefficiencies and misjudgments combine with adverse effects of circumstantial factors to contribute to the death of the child/young person' (DHSS, 1982, 29).

A similar trend was confirmed by Korbin (1989), in a study of nine women incarcerated for the death of their children. Korbin (1989, 481) noted that, although the cases were not homogeneous and the specifics of each case varied, the circumstances leading to the fatalities followed a similar progression they were characterised by a recurrent pattern of abuse culminating in the fatalities.

There are a number of significant issues raised by the Victorian sample of ten cases in which the child or young person died as a result of intra-familial abuse or deprivation of necessities, or in violent or accidental circumstances in which prima facie case management concerns appeared to exist.

Importance of Risk Assessment

The significance of individual factors or clusters of factors has not always been fully appreciated in the process of identifying risk in cases of physical abuse. For example even though we know in theory of the importance of focussing on the child, the critical indicator of the child's extreme wariness and avoidance of the mother's de facto husband in three cases in the Victorian sample was not noted as a substantial feature in the interpretation of risk for the child. Previous to this, less severe facial and body bruising and adult bite marks were not recognised as signalling an escalating pattern of physical abuse in three of the four Victorian cases of non-accidental injury. Thus the critical path of premonitory warning or help seeking behaviour (Greenland, 1987), leading to the tragedy was not identified.

In several incidents in the Victorian sample undue emphasis was given to perceived strengths in the family, in particular the attachment of mother and child. Insufficient weight was given to risk assessment — incorporating the role of the suspected perpetrator and the family's denial and resistance to intervention. These problems have been identified by other writers. For example Greenland (1987) noted that in many cases of fatal child abuse and neglect, recurrent patterns of abuse were maintained by the perpetrator's ability to explain, rationalise, and minimise the abuse to him/herself and his/her network. Similarly Korbin (1899) found that women minimised or denied the seriousness of their behaviour, particularly if supported by their networks in doing so.

This is seen to fit the profile — in the literature — of abusive parents denying the seriousness of their actions and their consequence for the child. A critical component in this denial is the rationalisation that the behaviour had occurred rarely or was an isolated incident. Thus those involved in the cases under examination either did not comprehend the potential danger to the child as indicated by previous incidents of abuse, or did not know how to respond effectively. The DHSS study (1982) revealed that in a number of cases workers had overidentified with the child's mother, or 'accepted one party's account of the child's circumstances too readily' (DHSS, 1982, 30).

Greenland (1987, 163) detailed a study by Oliver (1977) identifying the 'false love' phenomenon in which some maltreated young children appear to adapt happily to controlled happy social groups, and appear to relate well to (and lie on behalf of) abusive parents. This, he said, is particularly significant as it deceives professionals who consequently fail to persevere in initiating firm action to protect the child, or who relax supervision, or who make unjustified claims for successful casework treatment of abusive or neglectful patterns of behaviour.

Repeated denial of access to the child was not recognised as a critical danger signal in two cases. Greenland (1987), and DHSS (1982) suggest such incidents in a case of previously known child abuse or neglect should be recognized as a means by which parents delay or avoid discovery of the child's condition or health and should indicate an emergency situation which requires an immediate and effective response.

The vulnerability of a previously abused child during the period of reunification with his/her parents was not sufficiently recognized in two cases, and sufficiently intensive support and surveillance systems were not established. In one sample Fontana and Alfaro (1987), and Korbin (1989), found that a previously court-ordered placement was among the few factors that differentiated fatal from non-fatal abuse with the reunification period being particularly dangerous for the child. In Korbin's study several of the child fatalities occurred within weeks or months of the child's return to his/her parent(s).

Significance of Past Events

In a number of cases in the Victorian sample the significance of past events was not fully appreciated or communicated to fellow workers, with the result that effective warning systems were not established to manage identified risk and avoid potentially dangerous, or even lethal recurrences of threatening events. This issue is perhaps most powerfully demonstrated by example. One week before the death of an epileptic due to drowning, an incident occurred in which the young person had a seizure in a pool and had to be rescued. This vital information was not communicated to the residential facility in which the young person lived and their system was not on full alert when the next week they undertook a similar water activity. In another case past suicide threats and attempts were not fully appreciated or communicated, so that the staff of a residential facility were not alerted to the need to be particularly vigilant in the management of a young person in their care when he presented as depressed and aggrieved.

Importance of Risk Management and Case Planning
Priority in some instances in the Victorian sample was given to secondary maintenance and crisis management issues and attention was subsequently diverted away from the critical issue of risk management. Frequently, placement and accommodation options dominated workers' considerations and diverted attention away from resolving the issues which led to the child being made a statutory client. As a result, workers became so involved in the minutiae of family or day to day life that they did not note the significance of particular events or family processes. For example, in one case an adolescent in crisis required considerable assistance with accommodation and daily living tasks, with the consequence that the full extent of his family circumstances were not known when he visited his mother and was subsequently shot in the back by her de facto husband following an argument.

This factor was addressed in the *Report of the Inquiry into the Death of Jasmine Beckford* (Blom-Cooper, 1985) in which it was argued that the social workers involved in the case were prone to address the family's needs rather than those of the abused child. It was also addressed in Greenland's (1987) study in which fatal child abuse cases were frequently seen to reveal child protection workers' preference for crisis intervention, a strategy which, Greenland argued, often fails in high risk cases because it transforms complex and chronic family situations into technical problems requiring various forms of intervention on an ad hoc basis.

Frequently, there were no clear plans or management systems established, and those that were established were strategies rarely based on a comprehensive, up-to-date psychosocial assessment. Accordingly, on occasions case management lacked direction and purpose. In some instances in the Victorian sample, cases were allowed to drift and intervention became 'routine or "token" intervention without a clear follow through from plan to implementation' (DHSS, 1982, 43). At times this meant that there was no clear understanding of the purpose of a worker's visit to a client family nor of the goals of intervention.

The significance of the lack of adequate protective assessments was identified by Lawrence (1982), in the review of the Paul Montcalm case, by Greenland (1987) and DHSS (1982). Lawrence (1982) noted that the Montcalm case never received a full psychosocial assessment on which an adequate treatment plan could have been built. Greenland (1987) noted that assessments, the subject of many excellent text books on child abuse, were absent in many of the high risk cases which ended in tragedy; and the DHSS (1982) observed that repeated inquiry reports devote a great deal of attention to this topic stressing the need for complete and accurate assessment and re-assessment. The same report emphasised that the clear lesson from one particular case was that 'planning has no value if goals are not clearly defined, since the success or failure of the plan cannot otherwise be measured' (DHSS, 1982, 41).

Communication
Poor communication between staff involved in case management at the intra- and inter-agency level meant that in a number of instances vital information was not known to the workers or facility with primary case management responsibility. Plans were consequently made on the basis of incomplete, uncoordinated and unrecorded information and sufficient recognition was not given to the fact that 'effective communication is integral to good practice' (DHSS, 1982, 69).

For example, in one case CSV and the police had sufficient information if pooled together to identify clear risk factors, but there was an over-reliance on informal communication. The current basis for concern for the child's well-being was misunderstood and action was based on assumptions, not current facts. In another case no formal mechanism was established to ensure that essential information obtained from medical monitoring was promptly and effectively communicated to the case manager.

The importance of communication is emphasised in DHSS (1982) in which it stated that analysis of Maria Calwell's case showed a failure of the 'system compounded by several factors of which the greatest and most obvious [was] the lack of or ineffectiveness of, communication and liaison' (DHSS, 1982, 48). Furthermore the most common picture to emerge from the reports studied is one of information scattered between a number of agencies and never systematically collated to form a more complete view than that which the individual workers could achieve separately.

Clear Roles and Responsibilities
The roles and responsibilities which workers in different settings had for aspects of decision making were often not sufficiently clarified nor

agreement reached as to when, how and what information should be communicated between the professionals involved. Furthermore, case conferences were not used effectively and did not represent the core means of mobilising and co-ordinating the multidisciplinary team.

As noted in DHSS 'Problems can (and in these instances did) arise where there is lack of clarity about the different contributions of the various agencies and individuals involved' (DHSS, 1982, 5) and a clear understanding or commitment is not given to the principles of multi-professional work. Further, DHSS inquiry reports repeatedly note that critical occasions were missed when a case conference 'could have had a significant effect on the way a case was handled. They were either not held at all, or were ineffective' (DHSS, 1982, 21).

Recommendations
The overall purpose of conducting inquiries must be to use the conclusions and recommendations reached to develop initiatives which will strengthen and refine professional practice, the child protection procedures of individual agencies and inter-agency relationships. Given that an inquiry is primarily an exercise in learning rather than purely a matter of accountability, what then have we learnt from these experiences in Victoria?

At the Systems Level:
- Increased emphasis must be given to research in this area so that the dynamics leading to the death of children from abuse or neglect are better understood. In particular, further analysis must be done to establish whether the link between young, poor, and socially isolated minorities and child fatalities is valid in Australia. If so, its social and structural context must be recognised. More accessible support systems must be established for high risk groups in the community and social security provisions improved.
- A national data collection instrument on non-natural child fatalities must be established.
- Greater attention must be given to understanding and improving the processes of multidisciplinary work. Specifically, more effective cooperation and coordination between senior management of government departments and non-government agencies is required — which would in turn facilitate co-operation at the front line level.
- The value of practice standards and guidelines must be reaffirmed, and expectations of staff and their case practice clarified through the maintenance of up-to-date, comprehensive systems of procedures, guidelines and standards in the form of manuals which are readily available in the regions, in residential facilities, and at

head office. Such manuals should note the importance of specialised care and procedures for children with medical conditions or disabilities. It should not, however, be expected that the availability of procedures will of itself avoid child deaths. Most child death inquiries find that the problem is not due to lack of procedures, but rather that available procedures were not adhered to.
- Adequate provisions and standards must be established for the supervision of both child protection workers and direct care staff. It must also be recognized that supervision is an essential part of good practice which is able to meet the needs of client, worker, and organisation alike.
- Pre-service training of social workers and related professionals must give greater emphasis to public welfare and work with non-voluntary clients.
- Training must be provided for child protection staff in the core areas of their on-the-job responsibilities: in particular, chairing of case conferences, protective assessments, management of cases of physical abuse and 'in child development as this is the cornerstone of the workers' understanding of abuse and its outcomes' (Hansen, et al., 1989, 620).
- Systems must be established whereby senior workers formally ratify key case management decisions and the timing of their implementation. For example, senior workers should regularly read, discuss and initial workers' case notes and should not endorse decisions without reference to written records and a full knowledge and understanding of pertinent case issues (see DHSS, 1982, 52). Likewise senior workers must be prepared to reject a worker's recommendations for action if they believe that a distortion of judgement has occurred.
- Client record systems should be developed, which along with good writing skills, ensure that information in case files is recorded in a manner which preserves all relevant information in a clear and unambiguous form and incorporates periodic assessment statements and reviews. Such an approach will recognise, as noted by Lawrence (1982), that adequate case recording is essential for good, professional assessment and ongoing practice.
- Accessible and effective debriefing systems must be established to ensure that workers involved in incidents of this nature are able to reconcile the events.

At the practice level child protection workers must recognise that:
- They are 'agents of both care and control' (DHSS, 1982, 7) with a clear responsibility to exercise the authority inherent in their

mandate. They cannot delegate their mandate to others nor to case conferences. Recommendations can be sought from case conferences and other workers but it is only either individual protective workers or the contracted workers who can accept responsibility for decision making.
- When multiple agencies or workers are involved it must 'be very clear what each is expecting the other to do' (DHSS, 1982, 15). Formal documentation of this agreement should be retained on file and distributed to all concerned. Likewise workers should more often be prepared to put in writing to families their concerns and expectations for change. DHSS (1982, 41) emphasised this stating that 'where there is a need for both the workers in the case and the clients to be clear about objectives to be achieved, these should be put in writing and a copy given to the clients. . . .'
- Case conferences as noted in DHSS (1982, 20) should be used to their full potential and should be recognised as essential for effective multidisciplinary work by providing opportunities for structuring communication and collaboration and pooling crucial information. The child protection agency has responsibility for initiating and establishing interdisciplinary case conferences as necessary. To be effective, case conferences need to be scheduled at times which allow for maximum participation of all the relevant parties with the potential to contribute, including both 'allies' and 'protagonists'. They must be effectively chaired. A key caseworker is usually not able to be both chair and an effective contributor to a case conference. The chairing of a case conference should be seen as a distinct role.
- Case management and case planning must be based on a full protective assessment. This assessment must be re-assessed as the case develops to ensure original decisions and plans continue to be appropriate. Such assessment provides the basis for decision making and identifies the nature and level of risk for the child. It must therefore be based on accurate information which, wherever possible, should be corroborated. Case plans must spell out long and short term goals for the protection of the child and support of the family, time lines, methods for redefinition (if necessary) so that all parties are clear on what needs to be done and to what end.
- Case notes are an important instrument of case management and provide a valuable point of reference for case review and evaluation of change. To be effective they must in the first place be well-recorded and secondly read and used.
- Case files must be fully appraised by allocated caseworkers or responsible agencies so the full facts of the situation they are

dealing with are known, and blurring of fact, myth and rumour does not occur over time. Efficiency in case recording, transmitting, and storing information is an essential and integral part of case practice, 'yet we must remember that, information, even if seemingly comprehensive, is useless and possibly dangerous, if inaccurate' (DHSS, 1982, 35).

Conclusion
The debate concerning the utility of inquiry panels — in cases of child death — in assisting reform at the system and practice level will undoubtedly continue. Likewise lingering doubts of the, at best, unintentional tendency of inquiries to focus on the actions or inactions of individual workers, will ensure that child death inquiries remain controversial. However, it is important for child protection workers to remain objective enough to avoid the urge to simply rush to the defence of our often beleaguered profession. Certainly at times social workers make mistakes, but what child death inquiries illuminate in striking terms is the plethora of decisions, many being at the corporate rather than individual case level, made on a daily basis, which at times and in combination can culminate in such tragedies of this nature.

Child protection workers have to draw a sometimes impossibly fine line between protecting children and respecting the rights of families. At the same time they must recognise the differing risks associated with either not acting to safeguard a vulnerable child or precipitately removing a child from primary caregivers. Although risk taking is unavoidable in child protection practice, the findings of child death inquiries reinforce the need to be thorough and prudent when making decisions regarding high risk cases.

9
The Management of Polarisation in Munchausen by Proxy

Helen Freeland and Sue Foley

Working in the area of child protection, professionals encounter many forms of abuse suffered by children at the hands of their parents or other adults. One of the most serious forms is Munchausen Syndrome by Proxy. To date, the literature has focused on medical diagnosis of the syndrome (Meadow, 1982, 1984, 1985, Rosenberg, 1987); case studies (Pickford, 1988, Black, 1981, Masterton, 1988, Southall, 1987); treatment of families (Waller, 1983, Jones, 1987, Griffith, 1988, McGuire and Feldman, 1989); but little on the interplay of interdisciplinary/interagency intervention and case management.

Munchausen Syndrome by Proxy is a form of child abuse not often encountered by professionals, but when it is, the general effects of child abuse case management on workers escalate dramatically. The abuser, usually female, is frequently not like other abusers. She appears to be a caring, worried parent. She may relate capably with medical staff and social workers. As with other abusing parents, the personal history of the parent may evoke sympathy and a caring response from those with whom they interact. For example, one of our clients had a history of pregnancy resulting from sexual assault by her stepfather. This can be very confusing for workers when placed alongside the serious and insidious abuse that may have been suffered by the child. So it is difficult to describe accurately the extent of demands placed on workers in managing these cases. The stress, emotional turmoil and energy can exceed that required in almost any other kind of casework activity.

Meadow (1985), first described Munchausen by Proxy, which is also known as Meadow's Syndrome. He maintained that this syndrome has a lot in common with other forms of child abuse and that the parents' behaviour can be indistinguishable from that of parents with genuinely seriously ill children. Further, he wrote that 'even though the fabrication of signs and symptoms may persist for several years and be gross it can be most difficult to detect. Nevertheless, effective management for the child and the family is even more difficult' (Meadow, 1985, 385).

The more serious forms of the syndrome can involve some most bizarre behaviour on the part of the parents: 'the illnesses are fabricated by such methods as administering poison, adding substances to specimens of urine, blood or vomit; by inducing episodes of smothering or by deliberately giving the physicians misleading information so that the child appears to be suffering from an illness' (Rees, 1987, 268).

In addition, an even more troubling element of the syndrome may be unintended abusive behaviour by medical professionals. Prior to the diagnosis of Munchausen by Proxy, and acting in good faith on information from the parent, they may have subjected the child to treatment and invasive procedures which may, in retrospect, have constituted secondary abuse. Acknowledgement of their role in causing harm, and of their inability to see the deception to which they have been subjected, may limit or inhibit their capacity to shift their stance from that of a treating physician to that of protector of the child. In this, the seeds of polarisation can be sown.

Munchausen Syndrome by Proxy as a Form of Child Abuse

Proposition 1: Because of the potential danger of serious physical abuse to the children, the level of responsibility taken by the professional for protection of the child should be inversely related to the level of responsibility taken by the parents.

Even the most experienced practitioner is likely to be tested by serious Munchausen by Proxy cases. It is not a well understood form of child abuse, and the complexity of the dynamics which confront workers can restrain them from taking the action they need to take. In its more dangerous forms, the parent can exhibit obsessive behaviour patterns, rarely making full and detailed admissions.

- Ms D. admitted to only two instances of administering a poison to her child. Pathology subsequently revealed evidence of many other

instances and more than one substance. She maintained her denial in the face of this evidence, constructing elaborate explanations, none of which entailed any responsibility on her part.
- Ms M., mother of two children, both of whom were seriously injured, admitted to the detail but not the frequency of the abuse and subsequently retracted her statement in the course of the court hearing.

Where the denial in the parent is high and the abuse is serious, our proposition is that the professionals will need to be active and serious about the level of responsibility they take in investigating these matters. Paediatric and welfare staff all need to be aware that the innocent denial will impact on them, raising their own doubts, potentially immobilising them, especially as the role of investigator can be an unfamiliar one to paediatricians and hospital social workers.

It is important to note that the manifestations of Munchausen Syndrome by Proxy can range from misrepresentation or exaggeration of symptoms to more serious 'simulated or produced' illness. Some children die as a result. In three out of 66 cases described by Meadow in 1985 the child died. We are therefore dealing with a serious and potentially fatal form of abuse (Rees, 1987, 268).

Rosenberg (1987), an American researcher who analysed the features of 117 cases of Munchausen by Proxy described the range of presentations as including 'illness that was faked by the mother but did not directly, in or of itself cause harm . . . [as well as] . . . "produced illness" — illness that the mother actually inflicted upon the child' (Rosenberg, 1987, 551-552). She found that in 75 per cent of cases there was produced illness by the mother and in 70 per cent of these cases, abuse occurred in hospital (Rosenberg, 1987, 556).

The authors were closely involved with three families, and peripherally with others where Munchausen by Proxy was diagnosed and where many of the features described by Rosenberg were replicated.

- Ms J. travelled across three states in order to have her children seen by a medical specialist. The children were eventually admitted to intensive care because they were seriously failing to thrive. A diagnosis of Munchausen by Proxy was considered and the mother was allowed no contact with the children. Their weight gain was startling. Ms J. had insisted that only she feed the children in hospital. It later emerged that she had been interfering with the children's medical treatment in the hospital. She had been restricting the children's food intake and falsifying the records on the ward

so that the children were failing to thrive despite apparently adequate nutrition.
- Ms M.'s two children were treated at two hospitals for fits and a variety of other illnesses. She herself suffered from Munchausen Syndrome and had an extensive medical history. She had a detailed knowledge of hospital and medical procedures. Her husband worked in one of the hospitals. Both children were severely developmentally delayed and had suffered numerous investigative procedures and treatments including surgery. Ms M. presented the children with serious gastric reflux problems, apnoea, and one child bleeding from the ear. An example of Ms M.'s capacity for fabrication was her successful application for public housing in order to accommodate a third, non-existent child who was alleged to be confined to a wheelchair.
- Ms D., a mother of four children, also suffered with Munchausen Syndrome. Her lengthy medical history emerged after a long and painstaking investigation. The two older children presented with feeding difficulties shortly after birth. They subsequently suffered from identical, life threatening symptoms. Nurses described several instances in which apparent interference with treatment was strongly suspected but could not be proved. The eldest child died. The second child suffered severe illnesses leading to profound physical and intellectual disability. The youngest children have been fostered since birth because of the high risk of abuse.

Nine children were affected in these families. One child had died (cause unknown); two children were profoundly disabled as a direct result of abuse; two children were seriously developmentally delayed upon entry into foster care; two were removed just after birth, but are making good progress in foster care; two were living interstate with their birth father and were reported to be doing well. Of the eight surviving children, none was in the care of their mother and six were in foster care with guardianship vested in the state. In all three cases, the manifestations of the syndrome were serious in that they involved actual production of illness by the mothers by means of administration of poison (salt) and unprescribed medication (insulin and other substances), asphyxiation, interference with intravenous feeding lines, and obstruction of food intake. These were multiple incidents over years; and they also occurred serially through the sibling groups.

The multiplicity of abusive activity leads to the following proposition:

Proposition 2: When attempting to establish the existence of the syndrome, the vigour with which assessment information is sought needs to be greater than the apparent resistance of the parents to disclose.
The professional literature on Munchausen Syndrome by Proxy notes that a full understanding can only be obtained by piecing together the social and medical history (Rees, 1987, Rosenberg, 1987).

In these cases there was a great deal of hidden data, including false dates of birth, false medical history, and other false social history. For example, Ms D. gave four different dates of birth to different hospitals and described a variety of dramatic illnesses. The mother's own Munchausen diagnosis was a significant factor in amplifying the resistance to disclosure of the abuse. This also needs to be taken into account when assessing the seriousness of cases. The mothers' medical knowledge and familiarity with hospital routines, often gained through paramedical training or employment in hospitals or other medical settings, made it easier for them to present false information credibly.

If litigation is involved there is even less possibility of information being willingly given, and many means have to be found to search for important assessment data. This will include using material obtained by subpoena, and the results of police investigations. Since the family members have often been treated in many different hospitals, clinics and doctors' surgeries, the exercise of gathering and interpreting the medical histories is both painstaking and time consuming. It is one of the tasks which can best be accomplished within a cooperative, multidisciplinary team where a range of professional knowledge can be accessed. In some instances, the primary physicians can be initially highly sceptical and reluctant to take protective action on behalf of the children. This may be reflected in their inability to look for patterns in the past history and consider the possibility of a Munchausen by Proxy diagnosis. Their scepticism can be extended to expressions of hostility towards those workers who may pursue Munchausen by Proxy as a hypothesis and this can lead to the beginnings of a split team.

Issues of Polarity in Case Management
There is an apparent polarity between engagement and confrontation which can be seen as mutually exclusive. In any therapeutic situation it is extremely difficult to engage with a client and pursue problem resolution strategies when the existence of the problem is denied. When the central issues relate to the protection of children and are essentially of a social control nature, the question of engagement becomes even more problematic. Once a diagnosis of Munchausen by

Proxy is made, it can be difficult for the worker to believe that anything the parents do, will be good enough to ensure the physical and emotional safety of the child. The interaction between workers and the child's parents can tend, therefore, to focus on confrontation rather than engagement upon joint resolution of the problem.

From our experience, intervention in the more serious cases is likely to include adversarial litigation as well as the more conventional treatment approaches. There is an inherent paradox in this for both caseworkers and the family. The strong resistance by parents to take responsibility for the abuse, when added to the turmoil engendered in professionals by such apparently caring parents, may increase confusion and the need for early legal intervention in order to protect the child and obtain clarity about the evidence.

The processes and culture involved in investigative and adversarial court procedures mitigate against engagement with the family. Once in the legal arena, all parties are separated by a process which focuses on their separate rights and not purely on protection of the child. In any case of child abuse, entry into the world of litigation places a different meaning on disclosures about the abuse. The information becomes evidence for the legal proceedings and may act to separate the parties, rather than provide the potential for engagement in therapy. In two of the Munchausen by Proxy cases cited above it appeared that the abusing parent, previously engaged in a kind of competition with the medical profession, was enjoying being the focus of the courtroom drama.

- For example, Ms D. was overheard assessing the competence of her lawyer and expressing the view that she could have done a much better job of cross-examination than he did. This escalated the split between the family and the legal professionals.
- Ms M. had a succession of legal representatives, none of whom appeared able to satisfy her wishes in the course of representing her. A paediatrician recently gave one of the authors an account of a court hearing in which he was a witness for the child. The mother demonstrated great familiarity with the court situation, even to the extent of introducing him to the crown prosecutor by first names!

Proposition 3: Workers tend to deal with dependency in polarised ways.
The perpetrators in Munchausen by Proxy families share the feature of highly dependent behaviour. For example, in addition to the expected dependency on medical practitioners, Ms M. and Ms D. both had highly dependent peer relationships. Ms M. had used drugs of addiction over a long period of time. All three belonged to closed group religious groups.

In a hospital setting, nurturing and dependency are important dimensions of relationships between the professionals, patients and their relatives. Where the mother's dependency has already engaged the sympathies of workers, the polarisation of response can be extreme — from anger and rejection, to pity and enmeshment. These reactions will test the wisdom and insight of the best workers, and will also affect teamwork as members confront their own and their colleagues' responses in an attempt to arrive at a collective view about case management.

Proposition 4: Non-intrusive protective options become less viable with more serious abuse and the more entrenched abusive behaviour patterns in the perpetrator.

Whilst this proposition holds true for child abuse and neglect cases in general, the worker's role is usually to weigh up the strengths and risks in order to form a judgement about the degree of safety for the child in the family. A major aim is to shift the onus of responsibility onto the parents to demonstrate that their parenting is 'good enough' rather than for social services to make out a case that the parenting is 'bad enough' (Asen, et al 1987).

It can be difficult for workers to accept that in some serious Munchausen by Proxy cases, no treatment options will work. This can bring workers into conflict with their personal and professional principles about maintaining family integrity and assisting parents to solve the problems which led to abuse of their children. The fact is that Munchausen by Proxy does not appear to be situational abuse caused by the stress factors of poverty, isolation and so on. Rather, it is entrenched behaviour resembling drug abuse or alcoholism in which the abusive behaviour is symptomatic of more chronic issues. Its apparently compulsive nature also mitigates against optimism about the prognosis.

Making the diagnosis of Munchausen by Proxy almost seems to be the easy part. All three mothers made partial admissions thereby invoking the diagnosis. Deciding what to do next is the hard part. Assessment of the family's potential for change is made very difficult by splits in the team over perceptions about the extent of the abuse and its entrenched nature. The debate can lead workers to question their beliefs and assumptions about the capacity of families to change. In some cases the work of the team may be limited only to taking protective action through the legal system. Workers may need to struggle towards the realisation that where actual injury has been caused to the child over a period of time, the risk of ongoing abuse may be so serious that there is no point in considering the usual supportive services. Permanent removal of the child from its family becomes the goal.

The literature on Munchausen by Proxy offers remarkably little on the subject of successful treatment approaches. Jones (1987, 409) maintains:

> Severe forms of abuse are more likely to prove untreatable. Munchausen by Proxy, non-accidental poisoning and severe forms of non-organic failure to thrive are similarly resistant. An early recognition of untreatability may help to reduce burnout by diverting precious resources from the untreatable to the families for whom there is relatively more hope.

Apart from the risk of physical harm, Meadow (1990) in a personal communication, emphasised the additional emotional effects on the children in these families. The prevention and treatment of these effects is even more problematic. This issue can prove controversial and contentious in litigation where, in the light of very little research evidence, the determination that a family is untreatable becomes an issue of legal rights. Even the determination that a family will take two to three years to recover may conflict with consideration of the ongoing, present and future developmental needs of the child.

Proposition 5: The complexity of the system constructed by the workers for effective intervention, mirrors the complexity of the abuse.

Once the perpetrator has constructed a complicated story and the network of support has established itself, the intervention system becomes complex. For example, an initial case conference about Ms D.'s child attracted over twenty professional workers, all of whom presented themselves as involved in either investigation of abuse, or in the support and defense of the mother and her ailing child. The agencies were reluctant to invest time and energy despite the fact that the case generated intense curiosity about the diagnosis. The hospitals were content to be places of health and healing; the statutory welfare agency required clear evidence of abuse and validation for their intervention.

The involvement of powerful welfare, medical and legal systems creates its own dilemmas and potential for conflict between some agencies and workers which may mirror the conflict between the family and external systems. The convoluted dynamics within Munchausen by Proxy families have been well described by Griffith (1988), Waller (1983) and Masterton (1988).

Each professional group, although focusing on its own issues, must, as a priority, be concerned with the coordinated activities of intervention in order to ensure the protection of the children. In Munchausen by Proxy cases, the degree of coordination required is more complex and demanding, lying outside the experience of a number of professions and extending beyond the limits of some service functions. Meadow (1985, 390) noted that:

> all too often, the social worker designated to the case is rather young and inexperienced. (An important difference between medical practice and social services practice, is that in medicine, the most difficult case is dealt with by the most experienced clinician, whereas in the social services, the most experienced worker is involved only in administration and few do casework).

In all three of the above cases, a deliberate decision was taken by the statutory agency to ensure that this did not occur. The use of highly qualified, experienced workers was judged to be necessary to maintain the casework and undertake the preparation for litigation.

The degree of success in intervention may depend on the extent to which a group that is disparate in terms of status, experience and disciplinary background, can coalesce around the primary task of protection. Surprisingly, where the abuse is life threatening, protective activity is not necessarily promoted. Denial and retreat into the quest for the elusive rare syndrome can be the result. This impression is supported by Batten (1988, 14):

> Despite the high level of cooperation of the multidisciplinary hospital team, when a diagnosis of Munchausen Syndrome by Proxy was first mentioned doubt about the diagnosis was created by disbelieving team members. It appears there must be consensus amongst the team about the diagnosis or workers will unconsciously sabotage plans for integrated intervention.

For example in regard to Ms M. there was substantial conflict in conferences about management of the case despite suspicion that her child's fitting might be caused by deliberate asphyxiation. An incident occurred on one particular day when the police were the first agency to intervene. Their investigations, following the mother's confession, revealed that the child's symptoms were caused by the mother's attempt to smother the child.

Polarisation can flow into consideration of the case management options resulting in a debate between those who support protection of the child within the family system and those who argue to remove the child from parental care. The attractive personality of the abusing mother contrasts with the abhorrent effects of the abuse on the child and forms the issue around which the group polarises. There is a split between those professionals who feel attracted to the mother's personality and presentation and those whose focus is on the welfare of the child and the injuries or illness caused by the mother. The father might be absent either emotionally or physically, or blinded by his wife's superior intelligence, leading to his incapacity to accept anyone else's criticism of her, just as he cannot bring himself to criticise her.

Workers' responses tended to range from sympathy for the father kept in ignorance by the mother, to anger about the father's inability to act decisively in conjunction with workers to stop the abuse. All three fathers reacted with suspicion and anger towards the workers, laying blame for their increasingly fragmented family at the feet of the workers who, it was claimed, either refused to believe that abuse was occurring, or were themselves fabricating stories about the child's illness. Two of the fathers had early histories of life in state care, from which they appeared to have retained a negative view of welfare workers.

The husband of Ms D. was also suspected of having physically abused his child. The husband of Ms M. was possibly collusive in the abuse. He certainly was unable to protect the children; for example he gave her information to which she was not entitled. It is doubtful if either of these men, even now, believe that their wives caused the injuries and illnesses of their children.

Strategies and Structures

In casework and teamwork activity, structures and strategies are required to promote action to intervene in this complex system. The following ideas are proposed as procedures which may assist professionals to survive intact and ensure a high level of engagement in the case and interdisciplinary cooperation over a considerable period of time (sometimes years).

Proposition 6: The level of team work and cooperation is proportional to the permeability of the boundaries between different professional disciplines and within levels of bureaucracy.

It is important not to be thwarted by existing boundaries to cooperation. The authors engaged in consultation with overseas professors, with doctors in three main paediatric hospitals in Sydney, and with high status management within professional systems. We were surprised at the extent to which agency boundaries proved negotiable when it was clearly in the interests of the children. We learned the value of seeking advice and consultation from all available sources. This included obtaining advice from acknowledged experts overseas.

We have found it useful to create unusual structures outside the normal agency arrangements, involving more senior, experienced people in the agency to support the workers, to direct the management of the case and to ensure access to needed resources. In Munchausen by Proxy case management it is essential that there are no 'lone ranger' workers. It is our perception that workers on the ground must be strongly linked to and supported by line management for effective action to take place.

Whilst we maintained respect for agency and professional boundaries we were able to avoid adhering rigidly to roles by developing mutual trust, and through establishing accurate, open and frequent information sharing. It is essential that doctors, solicitors, social workers, nurses, foster parents and welfare staff all engage as colleagues in the task of protecting the children. There were of course some who were in opposition to the action taken to protect the children. In time, however, given access to further information, there were very few professionals who did not agree that the diagnosis was correct or at least possible, and that the action taken to protect the child was appropriate.

Supervision of workers in child abuse is not well practised. Most paediatricians do not get professional supervision other than in the medical aspects of diagnosis and treatment. Through the activities of child-at-risk interest groups within hospitals there is some focus on protection and risk assessment being introduced to medical training. In one of the cases described, this input was a critical factor in alerting a junior doctor to broaden the range of diagnostic possibilities. As a result, a new direction of investigation was initiated which revealed evidence of extensive abuse of the child.

Even for workers whose membership of a professional team includes access to supervision, the needs of workers who are involved in these complex cases can exceed what is available through their formal supervisory structures. For a number of workers in the cases described, extra consultation and supervision arrangements were established to allow them to deal with the personal dilemmas and professional issues which arose for them. Where the case is identified as contentious, special supervisory arrangements should be established very early in the case so that sufficient attention is given to the stressful impact of these cases on the workers involved.

After a time we developed specific strategies for support and supervision for all workers, which included regular, formal conferencing and debriefing processes. In two cases, a formal debriefing was conducted by independent facilitators. In the third case a formal case presentation to colleagues and peers seemed to serve the function of a debrief. In considering a debriefing process, we invited a facilitator with high credibility in the child protection field and specific group-work skills. In one case, maximum participation was promoted by circulating a questionnaire and agenda along with the invitation. It surprised us that some of those who could not attend, returned the completed survey and expressed a strong desire to be kept informed about the progress of the case. Perhaps completing the survey was a form of debrief for them in view of their inability to attend the meeting in person. Responses to the survey were collated and were beneficial in determining which were common experiences. For example, it was revealed that some feelings, opinions, hopes and doubts were shared by everyone. Others were unique to people in particular roles. Through the debriefing process, participants in the case felt that their contributions and their feelings were validated.

Proposition 7: The degree of cohesion and commitment of the team members is also related to the level of disclosure of information and self disclosure of doubts, issues and problems experienced by the team members.

When there is team trust, then support and caring follow. This can allow the team to relate laterally and not necessarily through a hierarchical, bureaucratic or professional structure or a leader. Team trust is built on recognition of the worth of the contribution from and the unique skills brought by each discipline, together with an acknowledgement that some tasks overlap professional boundaries and can be done cooperatively. The focus then, is on getting the job done rather than on reinforcing professional territory. We were convinced in the course of the work that acknowledgement of the importance of all professionals involved, including foster parents, is essential. The authors have experienced, in two of the cases, an unusual level of conflict and of threats expressed towards team members. The child protection focus of the team was maintained through cooperation and commitment between team members which provided a degree of safety for workers. The explicit focus on team-work included open acknowledgement of fears, doubts, anger, and conflict. Deliberate communication strategies embraced by the team included ensuring good access between all those involved — after hours contact numbers were exchanged; we came to value even brief written communications which kept us in touch with developments.

Proposition 8: In the final analysis, the commitment of the workers to team work and multidisciplinary intervention needs to be greater than the abusing parent's compulsion to abuse and avoid detection of that abuse.

Team work is hard work. In all child abuse case management, the team is an artificial one which crosses traditional boundaries and professional systems. In Munchausen by Proxy cases in particular, the perpetrator may actively try to split the team. Alternatively, the abusing parent may capitalise on team members' passive resistance to what they perceive to be a too 'hard line' approach being taken. In two cases children suffered further abuse as a result.

In summary then, these cases can be protracted and may consume an inordinate amount of energy and agency time. Professionals' experiences of these cases are outside their normal experiences of child abuse. They are drawn into ambivalence, anxiety and anger by the apparently bizarre and deliberate abuse of dependent children. They struggle at times to maintain professional distance and may experience serious self-doubts in the process of sifting through the facts. The importance of relief strategies should not be underestimated, nor should maintenance tasks for the team be overlooked, since much of the investigation and legal work is tedious and task focused. And in ways described above, the team can divide itself if adequate care is not taken. The keys to effective interdisciplinary case management are recognition of polarisation, a high level of commitment to the goal of protecting the child, mutual respect between team members, shared understanding of the dynamics within the team, and between the team and other systems (including the abusing family).

Acknowledgments

The authors would like to acknowledge the support and work of their colleagues, in particular, Dr Michael Cole, Richard Prunty, Pat Woods, Dr Susan Holliday, foster parents, field staff and medical staff and the many other workers from numerous disciplines involved with the management of these tragic and stressful cases.

10
The Abuse of Young Children in Day Care*

Suzette Booth and Andrew Horowitz

Child care is an important social and political issue. Societal and economic pressures such as the increased cost of home purchase, rises in the cost of living and the challenge by women of their traditional roles, have influenced the basic child care arrangements of Australian families by forcing both parents of young children to seek employment, increasing the demand and competition for child care places. In addition to the economic factors, there is also a recognised educational benefit in pre-school attendance in the three to five year age range, which contributes to the demand.

The types of child care arrangements in the community are varied and complex. They include long day care, preschools, after school care, vacation care, occasional care, family day care, baby sitters and nannies. In addition to these, schools should be included as a category of child care. Aside from these formal and mostly licensed care arrangements, there exists a variety of unlicensed voluntary arrangements where groups of children are entrusted to the care of adults for purposes aside from general care or education. These would include scouts, sports clubs, religious groups, youth groups, activity and interest groups and others. When the community entrusts

---

* This paper examines the epidemiological data of the Child Protection Unit of The Camperdown Children's Hospital in the abuse of young children in child care settings from July 1987 to April 1990. The following paper, 'Group Sexual Abuse of Children' (Lamb et al.) focuses on the effects on the worker, the therapeutic needs of children and families, and the response by systems to this type of abuse.

children to the care of other adults, there is an expectation that the standards of care will be professional and of benefit to the child. Many child care arrangements are licensed, supervised and funded by government authorities. The thought that children could be abused physically, sexually or emotionally by those to whom they are entrusted has been voiced only recently. When these concerns are raised, the community finds it very difficult to accept the possibility that some of those trained to provide professional care for children might also exploit and abuse them. These claims are often met with a great deal of disbelief and denial, based on the assumptions that children lie, are suggestible and cannot be trusted or that parents are being vindictive.

The abuse and exploitation of children has been noted since antiquity and dealt with in accordance with the prevailing morality. Ambrose Auguste Tardieu, professor of legal medicine at the University of Paris in 1860 in his paper 'A Medical Legal Study of Cruelty and Brutal Treatment inflicted on Children' wrote,

> Among the numerous and very diverse factors which make up the medico-legal history of blows and wounds, there is one that forms a group completely separate from the rest. These facts, which until now have remained in total obscurity, deserve for more than one reason to be brought to the light of day. I am speaking of the facts of cruelty and brutal treatment of which children are particularly the victims and which derive from their parents, their teachers, from those in a word, who exercise more or less direct authority over them (Masson, 1985).

In the 1990s in Sydney it is an atavistic sign that it is necessary to present material on the abuse of children in child care facilities. Over recent years the Child Protection Unit (CPU) of The Children's Hospital, Camperdown has had involvement with a significant number of cases of children who have been sexually, physically and emotionally abused in extra-familial care. The CPU's role has been to assess these children and their families, provide them with appropriate medical and psychological help, and work closely with the child welfare and criminal justice systems. The CPU's experiences seem to follow some trends described in the United States by Finkelhor (1988) who indicated that some 2,500 children were sexually victimised at more than 500 day care facilities over the three years 1983-1985 in the USA.

Epidemiological data from case notes and medical records is presented to illustrate the range of abuse seen by the Child Protection

Unit from July, 1987 to April, 1990. The CPU provides a service to a part of the Sydney metropolitan area with a population of approximately one million. In the period reviewed a total of 1,133 children were assessed at the CPU for all types of abuse and neglect. Of these children, 95 had been abused in extra-familial care.

Findings

Group A — 'Preschool A'
The 23 children from 'Preschool A' (twenty boys and three girls) were unusual in that boys predominated. The alleged offender was a male teacher. The children's allegations were of sexual abuse and maintenance of secrecy by threats of death of the children, close family members or pets if the secret was told. Eight children were examined medically with five having normal appearances. Abnormal anal findings were seen in two boys, and one girl had vulval inflammation.

These children had developed a range of behavioural changes, including nightmares, preoccupation with secrets, fear of death of self or relatives, aggression, regression (especially toileting), school refusal, sexualised behaviour (one boy would insert his fingers in his anus) and failure to progress at school. Even when they 'graduated' to primary school, they formed a recognisably distinct group by their behaviour.

Group B — 'Preschool B'
The 26 children from 'Preschool B' were predominantly female (17 girls and 9 boys). The alleged abusers were a female teacher and her husband. The descriptions of the abuse given by the children included emotional, sexual and ritual elements. Eighteen children were medically examined. Abnormalities were seen in five girls, four showing introital injuries and one anal abnormalities.

Emotional problems noted by the parents included sleep disturbances and nightmares, depression, self induced hypnotic state in one child, regression with soiling, compulsive behaviour, anxiety, aggression and school refusal. These problems continued for many months and again these children could be identified by their behaviours when they graduated to primary school.

Group C — Activity Care
Nine children were abused in various 'activity care' settings. All were boys with an age range of four to eleven years. The alleged offenders were also male and the allegations were of sexual abuse. One alleged offender was a sports coach/vacation care worker, one a church group

leader, one a gymnastics instructor and one an athletics coach. Anal abnormalities were detected in two of the five boys examined.

Parents noted behavioural changes including sleep disturbances with nightmares, anxiety, fear, detachment and aggression.

Group D — Family Day Care
This group of six children were abused in family day care settings. Four were girls, two were boys. The ages ranged from two to four years. All six alleged offenders were male and were the son or husband of the licensed family day carer. The allegation was of sexual abuse in five children and physical abuse in one child. All were examined medically, one having fractures, two having anal abnormalities and one having vulval injuries.

The parents had noticed a variety of behavioural changes in the children, ranging from crying in the physically abused child to sexually explicit behaviour, toileting refusal, separation anxiety, fearfulness and hyperactivity in the sexually abused children.

Group E — School Settings
The fifteen children abused in school settings ranged in age from five to fifteen years, including three intellectually handicapped adolescents. Eleven were girls and four were boys. The allegations were of sexual abuse in thirteen cases and physical abuse in two cases. The alleged offenders were all male and included strangers (four), peers (five), teachers (two), a cleaner, a teacher's aide, a trainee teacher and a bus driver. All the children were examined medically, with confirmatory findings in both the physically abused children and genital abnormalities in four of the cases of alleged sexual abuse.

The children showed a range of behavioural changes including fear of school, confusion and shock, school refusal, sleep disturbances with nightmares, sexually acting out and aggression.

Group F — Isolated Preschool Incidents
Ten children were abused in various preschool settings, three were female and seven were males. All allegations were of sexual abuse. Nine of the children were physically examined and abnormal findings consistent with the allegation were seen in two boys and one girl.

Of the alleged offenders, seven were male, one female and one unknown. One was a stranger (male), two were male peers, one was a child care worker (male), one a female teacher and one a male teacher's aide.

Group G — Nannies and Babysitters
Six children (four girls and two boys) were abused by baby sitters or nannies. The abuse was physical in four children, resulting in severe

bruising or fractures and sexual in two children, one of whom suffered vaginal and anal injuries.

The abusers were male in two cases, female in two cases and in the remaining two cases, could not be determined as several people were minding the children. Apart from the obvious effects of the physical injuries, emotional problems included depression, feeling frightened, being unsettled, not wanting parents to leave them alone and in the one baby, distress on nappy changing.

Discussion

In examining our data we expected to draw similar conclusions to those of Finkelhor (1988) who found that whilst the problem of child abuse in day care is a very serious, distressing and complex one, one should not lose sight of the fact that the most common arena of child abuse is the family. He cites that in 1985 in the USA nearly 100,000 children were sexually victimised by family members, whilst 1,637 were abused in day care, that is 1.6 per cent.

One might also speculate that were it not for child care facilities, more children would be in families at risk. This is because of the support and parenting models that child care centres provide to families. Child care facilities also play a major role in detecting and notifying abuse occurring in the home. However, as this data shows, there is sufficient risk of abuse in child care facilities to make it imperative that the community develop strategies and systems to detect, deter and prevent abuse.

Of the 1,133 children assessed by our unit from July, 1987 to April, 1990, 95 (8.4 per cent) were abused in a situation of child care outside the family. Sexual abuse in day care accounted for 17 per cent of our total sexual abuse figures.

Could this higher proportion reflect a sample bias? Certainly, this is a smaller sample than Finkelhor's. In addition, the assessment offered by our team included 'queried' cases where children were too young to make a definite statement of abuse. However, the data included only those cases where abuse was strongly suspected based on the child's disclosure, the physical findings, and/or because of concerning behaviours which resolved on removal of the child from the care situation. The effect on the figures of the two large preschool groups, which were exceptional occurrences both in our own experience and that of other child abuse investigators, may also have exaggerated the proportion of day care cases. However, exclusion of these cases still leaves a figure of 4.2 per cent of the total having been abused in day care. Of these day care cases, 91.6 per cent were cases where sexual abuse was thought likely to have occurred, whereas only 8.4 per cent showed signs of physical abuse. This differed from the overall Child Protection Unit case proportions where 70 per cent were sexually abused and 30 per cent physically abused. Children in whom sexual abuse in day care situations was confirmed, represented 17 per cent of all our cases of confirmed child sexual abuse, whereas children physically abused in day care represent only 1.8 per cent of the total for this form of abuse.

Medical examinations were carried out in 68.4 per cent of cases and were omitted if the child or parent refused or on the basis of the history. Anal or female genital findings were abnormal in 27.3 per cent of cases. These could not be compared with the total group because this data could not be accessed easily. However, figures from the NSW Department of Health (1988) found 57 per cent of children referred to the Department's services were medically examined and, of those examined, 52 per cent showed physical evidence of child sexual assault. The difference in incidence of medical findings reflects the preponderance of non-penetrating types of sexual assault in young children, that is, fondling or involving the children in masturbation.

Role and Sex of Alleged Abusers
Eighty-two per cent of alleged offenders were males, with 10 per cent females and 8 per cent sex unknown. This varies greatly from the preponderance of females involved in day care of children, and from Finkelhor's analysis, (1988) which showed one third of total abusers as female. It also has important implications in the selection of staff for the care of young children. These alleged offenders varied from professional teachers to relatives of the carers, strangers or ancillary staff, which reflects the calculated determination of paedophiles to take advantage of vulnerable children (see Budin & Johnson 1989, and Conte, et al 1989).

Further, Kelly (1988) drew some interesting comparisons within the American experience. In cases of ritual abuse, which she defined as 'the sexual abuse of children by adults who are satanists or devil worshippers, whose religious practices involve the sexual exploitation of children and bizarre religious rituals' (Kelly, 1988, 2), there tended to be multiple abusers, compared with cases of sexual abuse in a child care centre where there was usually only one offender. Also she reported a greater prevalence of significant medical findings in the ritual abuse group compared with the sexual abuse group. Kelly found a greater degree of psychological disturbance in the ritually abused group, because the ritual abuse was more extensive and included more severe types of sexual, physical and psychological abuse. Comparison of our preschool groups A and B tended to support these findings in that we observed a greater degree of psychological disturbances in Group B where ritual abuse had allegedly occurred; the victims reported multiple alleged offenders, and there was a greater number of medical findings consistent with more severe sexual abuse than in Group A.

Age
The age range seen at the Child Protection Unit reflected the care situation. Older children attend school activities and after school care, sports or club activities. Younger children are cared for in family day care, preschool, long day care or by nannies and so are seen in those subgroups. Before we can begin to protect children from abuse, we must look at factors which make them more vulnerable, to see if these can be overcome.

While some of the children were of school age and thus quite capable of differentiating normal from abnormal behaviour, disclosure of their abuse was often delayed, especially if the abuser was important to the child, for example, sports instructors, teachers, whereas abuse by a stranger usually led to the child reporting the incident promptly. The majority of the children, however, were younger than five years and thus very vulnerable, unable to physically protect themselves from an abuser. Young children accept guilt and responsibility for actions which an adult could see is not their responsibility. They have difficulty putting words to this perplexing behaviour, and, in addition, are aware of a continued disbelief of even ordinary reports they make. They have to trust adults and are expected to obey them. Thus, they are easily coerced and can be intimidated by threats which to an adult seem fanciful beyond belief, and yet seem very real to the child. For example, in one group, threats of the death of close family members or pets had been used to maintain secrecy and led eventually to detection of abuse when they produced nightmares and expression of concern about the imminent death of relatives.

Behavioural Problems
The range of behavioural problems described include many which are typical of young children, for example, separation anxiety with clinging behaviour, refusal to go to preschool, crying on separation; nightmares and difficulty going to sleep or sleeping alone all night; regression, especially with toileting, and aggressive behaviour.

Young children have many concerns and anxieties as they try to make sense of their world, and these may manifest themselves in these behaviours. How, then, does a parent or teacher differentiate the origin of behavioural changes if the child does not clearly disclose abuse? The delay in finding that sexual abuse was the cause of distressing behavioural changes, often despite counselling help, and in children of an age where disclosure should be a straightforward matter, produces great distress in parents. Obviously, the disclosure of abuse is very difficult even when the child is old enough to understand what actions are abusive. However, some children showed unusual behavioural changes which alerted the parents to the possibility of sexual abuse. These included sexually explicit 'acting out', involving themselves, brothers and sisters or friends, expressions of sexual knowledge not expected in that age group, compulsive cleaning behaviours and unusual fears, such as of bathing.

Outcome
Almost universally the child was removed from the day care, or the person held responsible was removed from the child. This sometimes required the intervention of the Department of Community Services and the local council bodies responsible for family day care. Abusers who were peers of the abused were recommended for counselling because of concerns regarding their age and the possibility of their behaviour being the result of previous abuse.

Use of the criminal justice system was dependent on the ability and willingness of the children to testify against the abuser. The legal system was thought not capable of accommodating the needs and abilities of young or handicapped children, including those who had been physically abused, unless other supporting evidence was available. The limitation upon the children's evidence was a source of great frustration and anger for many parents. Other parents deliberately chose not to bring charges, stating that their child was now protected and they just wanted the whole issue forgotten. Parents cited the delay in cases reaching the criminal court and the perceived stress to the child of appearing in court, facing the alleged abuser and being cross-examined, as reasons for not prosecuting.

Summary
This study has shown that of the 1,133 children seen at the Child Protection Unit from July, 1987 to April, 1990, 95 children or 8.4 per cent, were abused in a child care situation outside the family home, with the great majority being sexually abused. Most children were younger than six years of age, and had had behavioural changes which alerted the parents to the possibility of abuse, which was confirmed by disclosure to their parents, the Department of Community Services, police or to us, and in the cases of physical abuse, by the presence of

non-accidental injuries. Approximately two thirds of the children referred were medically examined, with findings supportive of the allegation found in about one third. If the number of places for child care outside the home is to increase in response to social and economic pressures, both those responsible for supervision of these services and parents must be mindful of the vulnerability of young children to abuse.

11

Group Sexual Abuse of Children

Robyn Lamb, Rhonda Mangan, Gay Pincus and Bev Turner

Cases of group sexual abuse of children by a person in a position of appointed responsibility in a child care setting present different issues for the professional workers involved from those in cases of individual sexual abuse. The Child Protection Unit of the Children's Hospital, Camperdown, has been referred an increasing number of cases of sexual abuse of children within group settings over recent years. In an eighteen month period beginning in August 1987, children from two separate preschools were referred to the unit. There were 23 children from one preschool and 26 children from another (see preceding paper by Booth and Horowitz). Many, but not all of the children from the former preschool had been seen or were being seen for ongoing counselling, support, and therapy, when some four months later, the first referral of children from the second preschool was made. The children were seen and assessed by a staff of twelve; six social workers and six doctors working together in pairs (as is usual practice) in varying combinations.

Understanding and dealing with cases of group abuse is in its early stages within the child protection system in Australia. Systems and procedures for improving the management of such cases in the future have been the subject of much discussion and consideration. Professional staff agree that the work is significantly different from the assessment and treatment of cases of individual abuse, and impacts differently on workers. In this paper we identify and explore these issues and suggest the key elements of a satisfactory response.

The Effect on Workers of Assessing Cases of Group Sexual Abuse of Children

There is an increasing body of knowledge in the area of child sexual abuse, as well as improved facilities and skills in the management of and therapeutic help for abused children and their families. However, what has too often been overlooked are the needs of the professionals working in this area. For a child protection unit to maintain a high quality service to children and their families, attention must be paid to retaining experienced staff and preserving expertise. For these workers to continue to function in a competent, adequate and healthy way, they must be supported, the value of their work affirmed, and their needs recognized and understood. If this does not occur, the resultant high staff turnover reduces the possibility of cases being handled by sufficiently experienced workers. Managing such cases in a specialised sexual assault unit also helps to preserve expertise. Professionals who specialize in a particular field acquire an ever increasing body of knowledge and experience in that field which leads to greater skill in assessment and management.

Fletcher (1982) noted emotional reactions that she had observed in professionals working in the field of child abuse. Certain reactions were striking in their consistency and intensity. They were pervasive feelings of anger, anxiety, stress, competitiveness, ownership, and mistrust. Workers often felt unsupported, undervalued, and these feelings could significantly inhibit their ability to function adequately. Rather than deal with these feelings themselves workers blamed others in an exaggerated manner for their feelings, resulting in scapegoating and 'colleague bashing'.

To understand further the experience of workers in group abuse cases, an open ended questionnaire was given to all staff involved in these cases. It looked at worker responses to the abuse of children in group situations. Most staff rated the assessment of group abuse as more stressful than single incidents of abuse. Differences identified by staff between single and group abuse were the sheer number of cases to be assessed, the loss of control in the intervention strategy, the different nature of the abuse and the difficulty in placing limits around the assessment of the abuse, often leading to highly emotional reactions among family members and to media involvement.

The age of the children presented particular difficulties in assessing them, as did the different evidentiary requirements for prosecution. The length of time the process took meant there was less time to focus on the needs of individual children. Coping with community reaction, the alarming and distressing feelings about the reality of abuse within such a group of children, and the fact the alleged abuser is in a position of responsibility for children also were factors identified by staff as particular to multiple abuse cases.

Workers also suggested that while dealing with these cases they felt disillusioned, overwhelmed, angry and drained. They wanted a more positive judicial outcome, more time to concentrate on the effects of the abuse, more time for each case, a coordinated response between agencies with clearly defined goals, expectations and guidelines, the taping of sessions, therapeutic group work for parents and children, extensive supervision and far greater opportunity for debriefing. Whilst we were confident that staff assessing these cases did a competent job, their own assessment of the outcome was that it was less than satisfactory. From the questionnaires five issues emerged which highlight the difference between group and individual cases of child sexual abuse:

(a) The Sheer Number of Cases
Group abuse produces a sudden influx of cases which can flood a unit, since workers still have their other ongoing caseloads and crisis referrals. Additional stress was placed on the unit during the three month period when staff were required to assess the two different situations of group abuse within the same time period. It was difficult to prioritise families for assessment as all were highly anxious and expressed the need for immediate help. The intra-group dynamics created by the group — abuse situations tended to make the needs of the families involved in these situations seem far more urgent and focused than in individual cases. Within the resources available, workers were unable to satisfy all their needs at once which exacerbated the families' demands for assistance. In consequence, these workers often felt overwhelmed. Management decisions about the allocation and sharing of case-loads were also very difficult because of the sudden and unexpected nature of case overloads that occurred, predictably the pre-existing system of allocating cases was buried by the avalanche of cases. The consequences reverberated in the team particularly in relation to role expectation and the need for supervision and debriefing.

(b) The Raw Nature of the Material
Conflicting information from different children and their families, and from other sources, usually emerged during assessment. That abuse is alleged to have occurred in public facilities, often with other workers around, leaves families with intense reactions ranging from denial to devastation and guilt. It is often difficult enough to contain these feelings in individual families, but when a number of families are involved, all living in the same community, often being close friends

and meeting regularly, the feelings and reactions are magnified. Families often cannot understand why other families do not react in the same way. These heightened levels of anxiety made workers more vulnerable to the families' grief, pain and distress.

Workers reported using a variety of defensive responses to reduce their identification and empathy with the children and families. These included a sense of protest about the extent and reality of the abuse, denial and disbelief, anger, rage and shock. Other workers reported believing they were the only ones capable of helping particular children and families. They worked beyond the optimal level of duty and refused to relinquish responsibility; for example, they were reluctant to refer families to others even when the need was obvious. Workers reported they felt the need to explore the issues raised for them by the families' constant demands and workers subsequent heightened vulnerability. Failure to do so led to feelings of stress and burnout.

(c) Unclear Roles

Workers frequently expressed frustration at the lack of clarity in their role. Given the seriousness of the allegations and the likelihood that the majority of cases would be reported to the police, the dilemma for staff was worsened by the disparity between the requirements of a therapeutic intervention and the precautions required by the legal process. Staff reported feeling unclear whether they had a primary role as preliminary investigators. Regardless of this, would the information gathered at assessment be considered part of the evidence, and if so how? Or, was the purpose of the assessment to understand the emotional and therapeutic needs of the family, regardless of future legal procedures?

These dilemmas, encountered in single case abuse, are further complicated in cases of group abuse when dealing with a community where information sharing is going to occur, regardless of the precautions staff take. Furthermore, this uncertainty of role expectation can inhibit productive engagement with families, and in itself creates stress for staff.

The roles of the three main agencies, the Police Service, the Department of Community Services, and the Department of Health changed with each case of group abuse. While responses and roles need to be flexible, a certain predictability in the inter-agency response strategy must also occur. Without this, staff experienced conflicting management plans. What was achieved in one domain was frequently destroyed in another. For a majority of children and families the staff in the Child Protection Unit were their first contact with the child protection system. However, a sense of powerlessness and frustration developed when families began to experience the negative impact of the legal investigatory process. This phenomenon, well known to all who work in the child protection system, became magnified by the experience of group abuse.

(d) Supervision
Supervision and management of these cases were identified as an issue by workers. They identified the need to provide more supervision than usual in times of 'flooding'; the need to use supervision time to attend to feelings of distress in staff, as well as for case discussion; and the need to be aware of, but not hindered by the requirements of the legal system. Concerns about contamination of evidence interfered with workers' identifying and obtaining sufficient supervision. Staff would inevitably inform others about case details in supervision. It was important therefore, for staff to be clear about what information came from the assessment interviews and what information was gained through supervision.

(e) Reaction of Fellow Workers to an Allegation of Child Sexual Abuse by a Person in a Trusted Position with Children
The reaction of workers to an allegation of abuse by a person who has chosen to work with children, and is appointed to a position of responsibility in relation to those children, is both complex and powerful. This may be because of an unspoken assumption that someone who chooses to work with children does so because they have the best interests of the child at heart. This supposition crosses many professional and non-professional boundaries. It is therefore quite affronting when another worker is accused of abusing children in their care. It can awaken primitive reactions about one's own caretakers and childhood experiences as well one's potential to abuse. It may lead to mistrust of colleagues, feelings of loss about the ideals of one's own professional calling, and questions of: 'who can you trust if you can't trust your own colleagues?'. It may also accentuate guilt feelings about being a working parent and leaving one's own children in professional care.

Single (1989) investigates the feelings of fellow workers and how these might impede subsequent intervention in such a situation. She found there may be 'disbelief', with workers finding it extremely difficult to believe that a colleague with whom they have worked could be capable of such abuse. This disbelief may continue for long periods but may change to belief after the child's story is validated. At this stage, there may be feelings of guilt, shame and despair about their previous disbelief. This shift in identification is often accompanied by rage, because of both the sexual exploitation and perceived deception of colleagues. This knowledge also may strike at the very core of professionals' self-worth and ideals because of identification with the alleged offender, and workers may feel despair, grief and depression. One of the most difficult situations is when a worker believes allegations, but the alleged offender is acquitted and returns to work, or the staff is split — with some believing and others denying.

Part of the distress experienced by staff may be related to the concept of the 'profile' of a child sexual offender. Usually this concept provides the individual with a clear demarcation between 'self' and 'offender'. When allegations arise that a professional in a position of trust with children has violated this relationship, staff can engage in a defensive response using displacement or projection to deal with the perceived assault on the reputation and trustworthiness of people working with children.

No matter how close or distant the association with the alleged offender is, it seems underlying tensions will remain, unless workers in both the site of the abuse and the agency appointed to assess the allegation have the opportunity to discuss their feelings. Failure to do so may have major implications for intervention and management of such cases and future cases. The importance of understanding the reactions of fellow workers and the need to provide support for them within the work situation must be recognised. Unfortunately, all too often, the crisis precipitated in the agency by such disclosures is so overwhelming that it results in staff splits, making it difficult to discuss the matter as a group. This inhibits the resolution of the issue for both the individual workers and the agency.

Therapeutic Needs of Children and their Families and The Difficulties in Providing Them

When children have been abused in a group situation, the therapeutic needs are a combination of the needs of the individual child as well as the need to address the wider issues which present themselves to the child in his/her social circle. An assessment of the family's competence in dealing with the trauma, in supporting the child, and the ability of the family members to provide sustained and consistent support for the child is important. Good relationships with other family members, particularly with the mother, the usual primary care-giver of the preschool child, are a strong positive determinant of how the child will react to the abuse and respond to intervention.

The individual needs are the same, whether abuse is isolated or experienced as a group. These are elicited during the assessment. Information about the actual abuse of the particular child is important in determining the medical components of the assessment, whether examination is performed, and/or sexually transmitted disease screening provided. It is also important to be clear about what actually happened to each individual child as the type of abuse may vary between different children in the same group. Their fears are usually related to the specific incidents experienced by them and, therefore, need to be dealt with appropriately in each case. This is when it is important to be aware of the source of information — from the child, as opposed to details revealed from other agencies or in supervision.

The sanctions against disclosure which the child adhered to for a variable length of time, have, in our experience, been one of the most damaging aspects of the abuse and can account for the pervasive anxiety which the child exhibits. When children are abused in a group situation, there is greater possibility of disclosure compared with the single child who is isolated by the experience. It is therefore usual for the offender to employ more powerful threats to ensure secrecy: examples include predicting the death of a loved one who is known by the offender to be ill. It is important to be aware of each child's individual 'list' of sanctions so that these can be processed with the child in therapy.

Information gained in the initial assessment will determine the direction of therapy and again this is where some difficulties can arise. Because of the number of cases presented in a short period of time, it is impossible for individual workers who offer a crisis assessment to take on more than a very limited number of children for longer term work. Many children and families are thus referred to other agencies. This can be difficult for the child and family who have formed a relationship with the professional who has helped them over the hurdle of this significant life event. Even under usual circumstances, a waiting period is anticipated and community services are limited. There is often a need to spread the referrals over a number of services in order not to overwhelm them.

It is desirable that all the children and their families are given the opportunity to receive help, since the crisis affects not only the child who was abused but the whole family. Many parents are reluctant to involve other family members because they feel uncomfortable about informing older or younger siblings or extended family. Their personal views need to be respected; however their fears of doing so should be explored. We believe they should be encouraged to involve the immediate family by telling them in broad terms what the disruption is about. Many visits to a child protection unit, sometimes at a distance from home, cannot be easily disguised or explained to others as 'just a check up'.

The therapeutic value of the initial assessment interview should not be underestimated. Some children show visible relief at having unburdened their fears after just twenty to thirty minutes. As mentioned above, ongoing individual work is desirable but not always achieved and if much is covered in the first contact, then the child, who is well supported, is on the way to regaining his/her 'former self'.

Group therapy offers some particular benefits for children who have been abused as a group. The advantages are that much can be achieved, more intensely over a shorter time frame. They have been abused together or by the same alleged offender, yet can experience healing together. However, many families do not want to be involved in any therapy and as in the case of other abuse, just want to put it all behind them.

Groups for parents are another therapeutic tool but may also present difficulties. The groups conducted are frequently limited in time and content and are only able to address this subject in broad terms; parental distress can be acknowledged and practical advice may help them deal with their children's distress. There can remain however, a feeling of disappointment for the parents that they are unable to have their specific needs met more clearly.

Issues for children attending the unit include chance meetings of the children in the canteen, playground and corridors. Some children are reassured by seeing friends whom they assume are there for the same reason. Others can be frightened by this experience and view it as a part of a trial because of their disclosure. Attention must be paid to the child if this occurs so that whatever fantasy they may have can be discussed and they can be reassured.

Amongst the biggest difficulties in providing therapeutic help are the constraints of the legal process if such action is taken. It is impossible for children in such a group not to discuss specific details of their experience. Group leaders' attempts to suppress this in a group therapy session may be seen by the children as the therapist not being available to the child's distress. Our unit has not offered such groups for various reasons, one of the most important of which is the threat of contamination of potential witnesses.

Systems Response
Agencies usually involved in responding include the Police Service, the Department of Community Services, various sectors of the Health Department, health professionals in private practice and the Office of the Director of Public Prosecutions. Specialised units have been set up in some departments to deal with sexual abuse cases. Personnel within these units frequently receive specific training into the nature of child abuse and the procedures for dealing with it. This is

in contrast to generalist units which can lack the expertise in this particular area.

Specific guidelines are needed for agencies and individuals to follow when working with these cases. The guidelines should take into consideration how resources in agencies are allocated, the caseload for each worker and the networking between agencies. Formulation of guidelines needs to include all agencies that may be involved during the lifetime of the case, not just those in the beginning stages. It is desirable, for example, that prosecutors be involved in meetings from the outset so those involved in the case understand the requirements of the legal system. Concomitantly the criminal proceedings should not override the assessment of the emotional and psychological needs of the child and family and the provision of appropriate follow up.

The services should be complementary rather than in competition and seen as part of an overall package. Time allocation for multi-disciplinary discussions about roles and procedures is essential. Agencies often cross paths in investigation and roles should be clear, to avoid a duplication of services in one area and lack of service in another. Unfortunately at times management by one agency may be inimical to the interests of another; it is essential that planning occur at the outset and agencies get together and reach agreement on defined roles and responsibilities for that particular case. Planning must consider how to deal with the media, how to deal with pressures and processes arising from the case and how resources should be allocated. Co-ordination and liaison between agencies will maximise the efficacy of the operation, reduce conflict and stress and promote a smooth and controlled operation.

Professionals working in this area and particularly in cases of multiple abuse, need to work within appropriately structured frameworks. Supervision can preserve workers positive feelings about themselves and the value of their work so they can adequately help the children and families they are serving. Supervision provides an opportunity to nurture the workers, to contain and understand their reactions and to recognize and process angry, competitive, and uncomfortable feelings. Workers unsupported, attacked or criticised by their colleagues are unable to work effectively.

There is a certain ignorance in the adult legal system about both child development and, specifically, the dynamics of child sexual assault particularly involving young children or group abuse (Stevens and Berliner, 1980). Many of society's myths about child sexual offenders pervade the court. The most common myths include: offenders are mentally ill, psychopathic or manifestly perverse. However, these myths are frequently not borne out in reality (Groth,

1978). A large number of child sexual offenders, in fact, appear respectable, are well educated, are employed and married with children. Thus, an offender who is also a professional, both in lifestyle and outward presentation, more closely resembles the court personnel than the majority of criminals involved in the adult court system. Such identification with the offender, combined with a general ignorance of child sexual assault in legal circles, may make it difficult for some court personnel to believe the offences could have occurred. The alleged offender may also have very high quality legal representation available to him. Although in many states attempts are made to provide children with equally high standards of service, the child victim, especially one of low status or one living in an isolated or country area, may not have access to high quality assessment services which could provide expert opinion and skilled advocacy for him or her in court. As far as we have been able to ascertain to date Australia wide, the number of convictions of alleged offenders charged with abusing a group of children remains very small.

In summary, the following points form the key elements of a satisfactory response to group abuse. They are:

- A recognition of the emotional effects of the case on the worker.
- Supervision of the staff group which should not only look at case material but personal and group feelings. It should be regular and all workers should attend.
- A co-ordinated response between agencies with someone designated with the overall responsibility. Regular meetings need to be held throughout the life of the case.
- Clearly defined roles for all staff from the various agencies involved.

Children's Rights, Adults' Responsibilities

A significant reorientating in the way we view children has occurred in recent years. We have been used to speaking of children's needs or welfare, or best interests. Now, increasingly, the talk is of children's rights. There are certain rights which children are accorded in law. With the advent of the United Nations Convention on the Rights of the Child, there are rights which children have been accorded in international law also. While many of these are stated at such a degree of generality that their application to specific circumstances is likely to be controversial, the United Nation's statement of children's rights is likely to have an on-going influence upon Australian law.

The language of rights may also be used outside of the legal context, in reference to people's moral claims upon other individuals or upon society generally. It is primarily in this sense that the language of rights is discussed in the following chapter. The author considers the way in which the perception that children have rights should affect the delivery of services by child welfare authorities. He goes on to consider the role that child welfare professionals can play in advocating children's rights within their own organisations.

The efficacy of child protection work depends to a large extent on the responsiveness of governments and departments within governments, to the rights of children. The expression of society's obligations to the next generation in terms of children's rights may focus attention upon the adequacy of state funding for children's services. Advocacy on behalf of specific children may ensure that the needs of individuals are not lost in the system.

12
Rights and Advocacy: A Framework for Child Protection Services

Greg Smith

In these days of economic rationalism, human service organisations are reviewed and modified almost exclusively on the criterion of minimised cost. Governments are either under pressure to, or have promoted policies that, reduce services to a minimal level. Public debate about the appropriate nature of human services and the rights of people receiving the service have been largely overtaken by these economic imperatives.

Yet it is at times of economic constraint that discussion of rights can help clarify and prioritise the role of human services in the community. An examination of the rights of consumers can ensure that services are responsive to client needs and therefore effective in their delivery. They provide a valuable framework enabling those concerned to prioritise competing demands for those services and clarify the complex and at times conflicting demands that can be placed on them. Child protection services provide an excellent example of this approach. If services are not responsive to the rights of parents or young people, the frequency and duration of intervention and hence inefficiencies of the service increase dramatically.

Child protection involves competing rights: protecting children from abuse or neglect whilst promoting the privacy and autonomy of families; protecting young people, whilst recognising their rights to retain a level of self determination. A rights framework assists in clarifying these competing demands and dilemmas. This assists the community in determining the priorities of competing interests, and helps child protection staff to design and implement services accordingly. With relevant presentation of the issues in public debate, this approach will also assist the community in prioritising funding for the service against the demands of other human services.

This paper proposes a definition of advocacy as the process of supporting the rights of citizens within the community. This approach emphasises that assertions of client rights have no impact unless a capacity to exercise those rights is achieved. Similarly, initiatives seeking to advocate on behalf of clients need to specify the rights and perspectives that they are seeking to support.

Part A: The Rights of Children

Why are Rights an Issue?
Rights issues are central to the question of child protection and have significant implications for the design and delivery of relevant services. It is argued that competing rights of the child, family and state authorities are integral to understanding the nature and role of child protection services. Recognising and responding to these conflicting interests is necessary not only in order to protect the differing interests of those involved, but to ensure that the service is viable in design and able to achieve its objectives. This can be seen in a number of aspects of child protection.

Child protection as coercive intervention
Child protection represents a prominent area in which government maintains formal authority to intervene in the lives of citizens. Legal powers relating to intervention are considerable, yet are exercised in the context of a high value placed by the community on the privacy of the family unit. Rights perspectives seek to clarify which rights of the child, young person and family are being supported or restricted by intervention.

Equity in service delivery
In circumstances where intervention has occurred, the respective rights of those involved need to be identified and addressed as intervention proceeds. Protective services need to be provided in such a way that other interests of the child and the parents are protected. Mearig (1982) noted that the 'children's rights' movement of the 1970s identified the need to ensure that children's services

- examine the value base of 'best interest' assessments,
- involve parents in defining problems and solutions,

- identify and respond to 'gaps' in services, and
- develop new services, including client advocacy.

Considerations of equity are also relevant on a broad social level. Disproportionate intervention in the lives of people with low income, in public housing or subject to related social indicators, has been well documented (Piper, 1989).

The factors involved in this interrelationship are complex. Although the family allowance initiatives of the federal government have sought to reduce the impact of poverty on children, there have been few attempts to address this pattern on a structural level or in the design and delivery of protective services.

Efficiency in service delivery
Family services that are not responsive to the rights of clients are rarely successful in achieving the change intended. Services that involve clients in problem definition and decision making are more likely to be responsive to their needs, and hence more effective in providing the required service.

Community expectations and public debate
Demands and concerns relating to the rights of various sections of the community arise in the media on a regular basis. Such demands are common within the field of child protection, where the rights of parents are subject to frequent comment. Whilst the child protection staff are generally sensitive to the rights of clients in service delivery, it is clear that in public debate they are often unsuccessful in clearly articulating the range of rights issues involved, particularly those of children subject to intervention.

What are Rights?
The literature and related definitions of rights are extensive. Martin Bibby suggests that rights may be defined within three categories (Bibby, 1989):

- *Legislative rights*, consisting of provisions established through legislation;
- *Institutional rights*, which, whilst not established in legislation, are formalised within the procedures of an organisation;
- *Moral rights*, including: *natural rights* relating to liberty and *human rights* relating to requirements.

Natural rights relate to freedoms, such as movement, association or speech. Civil and political rights may be considered within this category. Human rights relate to physical requirements and standards of living, such as food, accommodation, health care and education. Economic, social and cultural rights may be considered within this group. Human rights of children relate to the public expectations of adequate standards of care in relation to children and young people.

The National Inquiry into Youth Homelessness (Burdekin, 1989) has promoted debate specifically regarding the human rights of young people. The new United Nations Convention on the Rights of the Child examines these expectations in more detail than previous international agreements, and may prove to have significant implications for the field (Mason, 1990). Clarifying the nature of natural and human rights relevant to children, young people and families therefore has particular relevance to the continuing development and delivery of child protection services. It is important to note that natural and human rights may or may not be specifically supported in legislation or procedures of organisations. In these circumstances their capacity to be enforced is very limited. Consideration of these rights, however, remains relevant.

As the name suggests, moral rights relate to the morals or values maintained within a society. These therefore influence decision making and the nature of public services, irrespective of legal provisions or other formal requirements. For example, the new *Children and Young Persons Act 1989* currently being progressively proclaimed in Victoria increases the protection provided to families in regard to undue intervention, through a range of legal, procedural and practice requirements. These revisions derive from dominant community views about the desire to address the needs of children and young people in a manner that protects the liberty of members of the community from undue interference.

Limitations of 'Rights' Initiatives

Although the need to identify and protect the rights of clients is generally accepted within the field of child protection, incorporation of formal rights into practice requirements must address several limitations. On a general level, some commentators of both the political left and right argue that formalising rights initiatives in legislation restricts the potential exercise of the rights of those involved. Jacques Boulet (1988) argues that they formalise and hence legitimate existing relationships between elements of society. Boulet suggests that rights' provisions in child protection obscure the broad social issues contributing to the need for and nature of child protection. Francis (1990) represents a conservative view that civil legal process and other judicial and administrative processes have a more than adequate capacity to support and extend the rights of those involved. Francis argues in relation to the United Nations Convention on the Rights of the Child, that rights initiatives can be divisive and disruptive to the appropriate care and nurture of children.

In recognising the impact of social inequity on the incidence of protective intervention, it would appear particularly important to ensure that the rights of those involved are specified and protected. Similarly, recognising that rights perspectives have the potential for narrow and therefore unhelpful application provides a warning against restrictive implementation rather than bringing the rights themselves into question. It emphasises that rights legislation should clarify and formalise the values upon which practice is based.

In terms of specific practice considerations, the 'making sense of child protection' practice model, prepared by Community Services Victoria (CSV), suggests that responding to the rights of various members of a family in conflict may obscure the broad needs of the family as a whole for counselling or support (CSV, 1988). A related view is that advising parents or adolescents of rights in certain circumstances may distract them from confronting the issue at hand.

Family centred support and counselling are not in conflict with common 'rights' perspectives and legislative provisions require such services to be pursued in preference to intervention. Many cases also arise, however, where the opposing views of adolescents and parents must be confronted and addressed. Whilst at various times it is claimed that advising clients of their rights may be destructive to their interest, this amounts to restraining the exercise of rights by deceit. The relationship between competing rights of autonomy and protection of young people is defined within protective legislation and interpreted by the courts. The responsibility of protective staff does not extend to being selective in how these rights are communicated and put into practice.

Children's Rights
A brief examination of the development of children's rights provides insight into current issues in the field. Prior to the 1800s English law included no obligation on parents or government relating to the welfare of children. Religious and secular law presumed that the interests of children were exclusively the responsibility of parents. Children were viewed in law primarily as agents for the devolution of property. The development of child welfare law in England followed the Industrial Revolution, when reformers of the factory system established the Protection of Children Act in 1889. The emphasis in subsequent child welfare law remained essentially protective.

The civil rights movement in North America during the 1960s and 1970s sought to publicise the social inequality of disadvantaged groups in society, and the undue intervention of the state into the lives of those groups. This movement spawned a myriad of 'rights' movements, which have persisted and developed in many sections of society. One consequence of this movement was increasing interest in the rights of children. During the 1970s these primarily related to the freedoms (natural rights) attributed to children: a more libertarian perspective on children in society was being sought. Writers promoted the view that the capacity of children and young people to make decisions on their own behalf and take responsibility for their actions was unnecessarily restricted by society (Franklin, 1986).

The Child Welfare Practice and Legislation Review (1984) specifically promoted a 'rights' approach to child welfare in Victoria, including a proposed charter of children's rights. The *Children and Young Persons Act 1989* (Victoria) promotes principles consistent with the aims of the review. A major concern of the review was the disproportionate protective intervention into the lives of young people compared to other states, particularly in relation to young women. The review concluded that this practice saw inappropriate restrictions placed on the autonomy of young people, based on moral views of acceptable behaviours rather than specific harms. *The Children and Young Persons Act 1989* therefore precludes intervention on the basis of behaviourial concerns unless specific protective harms are identified. A family division of the Children's Court has been established to respond to protective concerns. Behaviour in other circumstances is only relevant in the context of offending, requiring specific criminal charges and disposition within the separate criminal division of the children's court. These initiatives reflect specific changes in the perceived rights of young people regarding intervention by the state.

The Human Rights of Children

Children have the same types of physical requirements for their existence and development as adults, such as food, clothing and accommodation. The range of developmental requirements relevant to various age groups represents additional needs within this category of rights. The important issue for child interveners is therefore the adequate level of response to a child's needs. The legislative mandate authorises intervention where there is reason to believe that adequate standards of care are not being provided. The major role of child protection services may therefore be described as intervening to protect the human rights of children in our society, in defined circumstances where these are not well protected by families.

During pre-court investigation and support, the mandate of child protection is to ensure that the needs of children are fulfilled to an adequate standard. It is difficult to argue successfully that this mandate extends beyond addressing the particular need identified as being inadequately addressed by the family. The responsibilities of child protection with respect to the human rights of children alter significantly, however, in the event of a statutory order being made by the Children's Court. The nature of these responsibilities will relate to the nature of the order.

Transfer of guardianship and placement of the child away from the family, for example, results in the Service being required to ensure that all the human rights of that child are satisfactorily addressed during that period. Whilst the aim would be to maximise the involvement of the family and the potential for return of guardianship, the legal responsibilities in addressing the needs of the child during the interim would remain with the child protection service.

A custody order supervised by Community Services Victoria (as included in the *Children and Young Persons Act*) would involve child protection staff addressing the day-to-day requirements of the child and planning direct care relevant to the duration of the order. A supervision order however, involves no legal responsibilities for actively promoting or addressing the needs of the child, other than by supervising the delivery of care by the parents or other care givers.

The significance of these responsibilities and of the demand on child protection services is particularly apparent in examining statistics for CSV's 'post-court' child protection clients. In 1988 approximately 75 per cent of guardianship clients lived away from home. It can be assumed that a major proportion of the 72 per cent of young people aged fifteen years or more placed away from their family would proceed directly to independent living, with the family unlikely to have a major direct role in addressing the practical human rights of these young people.

The Burdekin report (Burdekin, 1989) was critical of all state welfare departments for failing to address the needs of young people subject to state intervention. Burdekin concluded that the major problem with protective intervention was not that they intervened inappropriately, but that no satisfactory services were provided as a result of intervention. Burdekin, in fact, continues to argue that state guardianship of homeless young people may be required more often than it is provided. This suggests a view that the natural rights of young people to freedom from intervention have been used as an excuse for the state to avoid addressing the range of the other rights and needs of the young people (Burdekin, 1989).

The Natural Rights of Children

Natural rights involve freedom or liberties: the right to live without undue interference and the right to be able to undertake chosen activities without interference. Children's natural rights involve several differences from those of adults:

- children have a limited capacity to defend themselves from interference;
- children require limitations on their autonomy to protect them from harm; and
- the capacity of a child to exercise rights of liberty will increase as the child gets older.

The limited capacity of children to defend themselves from undue physical interference is central to the role of child protection in child abuse. It is the role of legislation and practice standards to identify the degree of intervention appropriate, considering — in the circumstances — the degree of risk of abuse.

The Development of Competence

The increasing autonomy that may be provided to children is an issue central to contemporary child protection. Young people of fifteen years or more represent the largest component (32 per cent) of clients subject to CSV guardianship. Judgements regarding the competence of young people to live independently are therefore critical in recommendations of the Children's Court regarding the role of statutory orders. This issue also points up the dilemma of child protection staff supervising those subject to the orders. To what degree should adolescents be permitted to engage in behaviour considered to represent risk to themselves? The capacity of many adolescents to pursue their chosen behaviour, irrespective of the judgements of protection staff, emphasises that all such decisions must include realistic consideration of the autonomy of the young people involved.

Bibby (1989) reviewed literature regarding the development of competence in decision making by children. He identifies two key issues to be considered in determining whether a child or young person has the natural right to make particular decisions. The first is *rationality*. Children are said to be generally capable of rational thought by the age of six. The second issue is *knowledge*. A six year old may be capable of rational decisions regarding familiar options. If a child does not have an understanding of particular consequences, owing perhaps to an incapacity to absorb relevant knowledge, then the particular decision cannot be considered rational. Bibby concludes that the natural right to autonomy therefore does not necessarily mean that freedom to pursue that decision will be provided.

Community views regarding such issues as sexual activity, drug abuse or suicide may preclude child protection staff from supporting the otherwise 'rational' choice of a young person. It is important, however, that in such cases child protection services identify that it is the implementation of the decision, rather than the rationality of the young person, that is at issue. It is therefore preferable that child protection programs identify unacceptable adolescent behaviour to facilitate debate and to ensure consistent application. The difficulty with such a process is that limited public debate may promote a more conservative approach to contentious issues than that preferred by those directly in the field.

The Rights of the 'Family'

A mission statement prepared by Community Services child protection staff in 1988 described the nature of child protection as 'child centred and family focused' (CSV, 1988). Although the statement has limitations, it accurately describes the high priority of the family within child protection. The importance of recognising the role of the family as the 'preferable' or 'normal' structure for rearing children has been recognised throughout the child protection field. Thus intervention into the autonomy of the family unit has been supported by legislation only in defined circumstances relating to risk of abuse or neglect. Irrespective of the principle of family autonomy, complaints regarding over-zealous intervention are common in the media and literature. Goldstein, Freud and Solnit (1980) claimed that the children's rights movement and the development of child protection services of the late 1960s contributed to excessive and unnecessary intervention into the lives of families. They claimed that neglect, abuse and 'best interest' provisions of legislation provide too subjective a basis for intervention, and that the state by nature is a poor substitute parent. These and other authors have concluded that the natural rights of families to be protected from undue intervention can only be ensured by inclusion of specific criteria and definitions for abuse and neglect in legislation (Besharov, 1985).

The *Children and Young Persons Act 1989*, rather than identifying specific criteria, prescribes a range of principles and procedural requirements to minimise intervention in families. These include:

- provision of alternative supports to the family in preference to intervention (s. 86);

- a range of dispositions to be specifically considered to minimise the degree of any necessary intervention (s. 87); and
- the involvement of parents in case planning decisions (s. 119).

Legislation, program guidelines and literature recognise the need to balance the rights of parents to *their* autonomy with the rights of children to be protected from abuse and neglect. The primary consideration in resolving any conflict in these circumstances is prescribed as the welfare and interests of the child (s. 119).

The Child Within the Family
One limitation of the 'family' versus 'state intervention' dichotomy is that the rights of the child in relation to those of parents are easily obscured. Until relatively recently, the assumption of legislation in England has been that, in circumstances other than child abuse or neglect, the rights and interests of children are consistent with those of their parents. That is, parents of minors retained the authority to make all decisions considered appropriate to the needs of their children.

In an appeal relating to the legality of prescribing contraceptives to adolescents against the wishes of their parents, the House of Lords determined that the authority of parents to determine the 'best interest' of their children was not absolute (*Gillick v West Norfolk and Wisbech AHA*, [1986] AC 112, Eekelaar 1986). It was determined that parents retain rights with respect to autonomy in child rearing to the extent required by the maturity of the child. Thus, according to this decision, the rights of parents vary according to the capacity of the child to make particular decisions on his/her own behalf, and progressively decline with the increasing age and maturity of the child. This decision has been endorsed by the High Court of Australia (*Secretary, Department of Health and Community Services v JMB*, [1992] 15 Fam LR 392).

Part B: Advocacy and Protective Services

The Nature of Advocacy
Advocacy is defined in dictionaries as the process of acting in the 'support' of (Oxford) or 'cause' (Webster) of another. This paper proposes that in the context of human services, a definition of advocacy is 'the process of supporting rights'. Such a definition promotes a higher degree of precision in analysing the various roles, responsibilities and perspectives employed under the general description of 'advocacy'.

The development of advocacy services for clients of protective or related human services has frequently occurred on an 'ad hoc' basis. This typically occurs when an agency describes itself as an 'advocacy service'. This was particularly common in North America in the late 1970s and early 1980s. The trend is currently apparent in Australia, particularly for non-government agencies. Government departments have also responded to community concerns regarding rights issues by developing an independent source of advocacy or review. The Ombudsman or the pro-active Children's Interest Bureau in South Australia are examples of this approach.

Both approaches in isolation have limitations as responses to the rights and advocacy requirements of clients. The former obscures the limitations of service delivery agencies in advocating on behalf of clients, and the latter may imply that providing a specialist source of advocacy is a sufficient response to the rights and needs of clients.

The history of advocacy services for clients of CSV intellectual disability services provides a valuable case example. Within the scope of a few years, CSV established:

- a citizens' advocacy program;
- a community visitors' program related to institutions and other residential facilities;
- an intellectual disabilities review panel with both dispute resolution and practice monitoring responsibilities; and
- access to the office of the public advocate.

As a result of the common roles involved, these services were recently 'rationalised', with the funding for the citizens' advocacy service discontinued in 1990.

By systematically examining the role of protective services in the context of the rights of members of the community, legislation and administrative procedures supporting the rights of clients can be established, the role of caseworkers as advocates can be clarified, and the relevant role of independent advocacy can be developed, in a way that ensures they have a specific and constructive role.

Protective Staff as Advocates

Clarifying the Mandate

The role of protective staff as advocates derives from their role in supporting the rights of children and young people described in Part A. As indicated in existing legislation and the new *Children and Young Persons Act 1989* (Victoria), these responsibilities may be summarised as giving primary importance to the welfare and best interests of the child. Thus protective staff have a legislative mandate to advocate actively on behalf of these interests. This frequently involves advocating within the family with the aim of ensuring that these interests are adequately protected.

The advocacy role of child protection staff, however, goes beyond the child in the family focus. The 'ecosystem model' promoted by CSV (1988) indicates that maximising the best interests of a child/young person will also frequently include the wider community and society. Protective staff therefore have an appropriate proactive advocacy role in supporting the rights of clients, in a range of contexts.

In addition to relevant rights located in legislation (*legislative rights*), or departmental process (*institutional rights*), these advocacy functions relate to *human rights* to secure support and services relevant to the standard of living and personal development of the child and *natural rights* to exercise the maximum degree of independence consistent with the maturity of the child, free from abuse or interference.

Implications for Management
The role of protective workers as advocates for their clients has a number of implications for management:

(i) *Staff advocating within the organisation:* Endorsing the role of protective staff in actively pursuing the interest of clients has consequences for the way those staff function within the organisation. It is unrealistic to limit the advocacy efforts of staff to the family context or maximising access to relevant community agencies. As the nature of protective service provision has significant implications for the circumstances of clients, it can be expected that protective workers will pursue an active interest in influencing the operation of the agency. The manner in which these interests are pursued by protective staff will depend on a range of factors, including their demonstrated potential to influence the nature of service delivery.

Depending on the attitude of management and the degree to which the expectations of staff are realistic, advocacy within the organisation can be perceived as a valuable resource for review and planning, or a source of irritation and misdirected expenditure of energy.

With the implementation of advocacy services for clients with intellectual disabilities (noted earlier), management of CSV became frustrated with the high rate of referrals of issues relating to these systems by the staff of Intellectual Disability Services. This required management to spend considerable energy in dealing with case-specific concerns, rather than with the limitations in service design which contributed to the complaints. Services were often provided to the client with the best advocate rather than on a rational planning basis. These difficulties primarily related to an incapacity to address the goals of the program owing to very limited funding, and the difficulties of redeveloping a service system depending on large and established institutions.

This example indicates how a co-ordinated approach is required in establishing advocacy services, and how the latter need to identify and pursue relevant issues in an effective manner. Diverse case-specific advocacy may otherwise do more harm than good.

Several principles are suggested to guide the approach of management to 'internal' advocacy by casework staff. First, the role of casework staff in internal advocacy should be acknowledged. Otherwise, staff will view the organisation as hypocritical and resistant to change. A positive approach to the involvement of service delivery staff in reviewing services and development is in the interests of the organisation. Second, staff should be familiarised with the political, financial and organisational influences on the agency. Relevant information and training initiatives will facilitate effective and realistic internal advocacy. Third, internal advocacy by staff is most active when staff view clients as powerless or disadvantaged by the service. If services are responsive to the rights and needs of clients, and clients have access to external sources of support and advocacy, staff do not feel compelled to agitate within the agency.

(ii) *Staff advocating with other agencies and departments:* As suggested above, the role of protective staff includes promoting access to services from other agencies relevant to the needs of their clients. When these efforts by caseworkers prove unsuccessful however, advocacy at the interagency management level is often not provided. Whilst this may result from a judgement regarding the likelihood of success, management is often reluctant to introduce or extend issues of disagreement with other agencies.

The nature of these agencies and their organisational relationship with the protective service will influence the strategies pursued and likelihood of success. An agency funded by protective services or a service delivered by the same department should be directly open to influence. Other state government or federal government services however, involve differing relationships and greater challenges to senior management.

The Limitations of Protective Staff as Advocates
The advocacy responsibilities of protective staff are insufficient for the needs of clients when a conflict of interest arises between the rights that are involved. These occur when assessments of requirements for relevant supports (human rights) or protection (particular natural

rights) conflict with those natural rights promoting independence and autonomy. These conflicts arise from:

- the authority of child protection staff: irrespective of formal decision making and appeal procedures, the nature of the protective worker/client relationship is such that the latter is not an equal partner in the decision making process.
- the assessment and supervision responsibility of protection staff: protective staff are not independent supports to clients. The assessment and related responsibilities of staff will frequently differ from the views of the clients.
- organisational constraints: organisation structures limit the autonomy and effectiveness of staff in pursuing advocacy issues.

Independent Advocacy

What Roles are Appropriate?
The potential conflict of interest between particular rights of children, young people and families primarily relate to the decision making process. It is the role of independent advocates to be available to support and advocate on behalf of clients within this process.

On the part of most welfare systems, major intervention and service planning decisions are made within forums at which clients, and if requested their independent advocates, should be present. Protective services departments typically use forums such as case conferences and case planning meetings for relevant decision making. Appeals and complaints procedures also involve explicit role conflict between the views of clients and the actions of a service, where access to independent advocates is necessary. The role of independent advocacy is also frequently combined with external review of the adequacy of protective or child welfare services.

What Organisational Location is Appropriate?
There are two main issues influencing the appropriate organisational location of independent advocates:

(i) *The degree of independence:* The 'rights' analysis above infers that 'independent' advocates would not exercise any authority to influence the autonomy of children, young people or the family. Independence, however, extends beyond the personal responsibilities of the individual advocate. Whilst an advocacy unit may be off line from protective intervention or supervision structures, common management at the senior level will still restrict autonomy.

The history of the liaison and advocacy unit within CSV reflects these limitations. The unit had responsibility to minimise placements of protective clients at statewide institutions, and in order to provide a level of independence was responsible to central CSV management. Although many issues of concern could be resolved by liaison and negotiation with protective workers, issues of disagreement between management at the unit and regional level were seldom resolved. Senior regional management appeared reluctant to overturn decisions of staff they supervised, and staff of the unit were often frustrated with the limited options available in pursuing contentious issues. At the same time, agencies external to CSV criticised the location of the unit as promoting a compromising or conciliatory approach to the rights of young people.

Responsibility direct to the relevant minister increases the degree of independence from the protective services administration. The Children's Interest Bureau in South Australia has this reporting arrangement, which presumably has contributed to the success and respect achieved by the Bureau in promoting the rights and interests of young people in South Australia. Castell McGregor (1989) has noted that common ministerial responsibility can be argued to limit the independence of the Bureau.

The citizen's advocacy program established for clients of CSV's intellectual disabilities services sought to promote independence by the use of volunteers. The program was funded, however, by CSV and it has been argued that it was limited in its independence by this arrangement. An alternative arrangement is for advocacy mechanisms to be responsible direct to parliament, as is typically the case for ombudsman's offices. The Office of the Public Advocate in Victoria, with responsibilities to promote the rights and interests of people with disabilities, reports directly to parliament. This has contributed to the high profile that the office has achieved.

Lawyers are being increasingly used in case planning meetings, a trend which will increase with proclamation of the new legislation. This role could be formalised and extended to other protective services procedures, perhaps by developing protocols with the Legal Aid Commission. The major restriction of this approach is the limitation of a legal framework in responding to the range of issues relevant to effective service delivery.

Citizen advocacy programs, such as established for clients of CSV intellectual disability services, may have relevance for child protection. Community visitor programs have also been established for many residential services for the disabled and the aged. Such programs provide access to consistent advocacy services, and a flexible non-professional approach. It seems likely, however, that statutory clients may be reluctant to involve unknown volunteer advocates from the community to assist them in interaction with CSV.

Service user support groups for clients of statutory services have been established in England for several years. In addition to providing general support to clients, these groups have a capacity to empower clients to participate effectively in service provision. These groups also advocate on a systems level to encourage improvements in services available to statutory clients.

Child ombudsman offices are well established in many European countries (Verhellen and Spiesschaert, 1989). 'Save the Children Fund' is planning to establish an ombudsman for children in Victoria in the near future. The role often undertaken by the ombudsman has some limitations in providing the advocacy functions discussed above. Ombudsmen generally provide a point of review and mediation regarding administrative process. In the Victorian context, this function will be undertaken in part by granting access on the part of protective services clients to the Administrative Appeals Tribunal.

The ombudsman role also tends to be reactive rather than proactive. An individual experiences a difficulty with service delivery and approaches the ombudsman to mediate. Unlike other advocacy models such as the Children's Interest Bureau, the ombudsman role does not normally include making themselves available to assist an unconfident client in case planning meetings, monitor casework practice, to intervene when considered appropriate, or to pursue general issues relevant to service delivery or community awareness.

An alternative in Victoria could involve the Office of the Public Advocate, which is independent of CSV and retains a capacity to be proactive in the support of individuals or in raising general issues regarding service delivery. The Office, however, would not normally be involved in particular cases unless a particular issue of concern could not be resolved by an individual.

(ii) *Access to service delivery process:* Being placed within the same organisation can have benefits both for the advocate and direct service providers. This arrangement minimises the degree of the formality of liaison, discussion and dispute resolution, and can assist the advocate to influence the general approach of service providers in addition to specific decisions. Thus typically advocacy staff are able to establish effective working relationships with caseworkers quickly, and be familiar with the range of influences on case practice. Files can be readily accessed without specific approvals necessarily being required.

Organisational independence therefore tends to be at the cost of a direct working relationship at the case practice level. Relationships with the State Ombudsman, for example, tend to be highly formalised. Communication is generally limited to letters via heads of department. Castell-McGregor (1989) argues, however, that it is possible to develop close working relationships, despite independence. Social workers recently recruited to CSV from the United Kingdom report that independent guardianship *ad litem* advocates in that country also manage to work closely with protective caseworkers.

Major Themes in Improving Advocacy Responses
CSV is pursuing a 'systems' approach to promote the rights of protective services clients and their access to relevant advocacy supports.

Legislation
The Children and Young Persons Act 1989 involves a major reform of relevant legislative provisions and administration relating to protective services, young offenders and related community support services. The Act was developed in response to the Child Welfare Practice and Legislation Review (1984) which sought to identify and support a range of rights of people in contact with relevant government and support services. Within protective services provisions, the Act:

- promotes responses to protective concerns by means of relevant community supports, and an alternative to intervention where possible;
- requires specific indications of abuse and neglect to justify formal intervention;
- within the court process, requires legal representation of the child or young person;
- establishes a range of intervention orders, with powers specific to the demonstrated needs of the child or young person;
- requires the case planning process to involve actively the views of children, young people and their parents; and
- provides access by clients within the case planning process to supports or advocates of their choice.

Administrative Procedures
The Children and Young Persons Act includes a range of principles promoting equity in decision making practices within protective services. Practice guidelines responsive to these principles are being developed. A major area of program development relates to appeal procedures. In addition to improved regional procedures, the Act will provide for

appeal to the Administrative Appeals Tribunal of case planning and management decisions.

Protective Services Casework
Program development is seeking to apply rights and advocacy principles within the delivery of protective and related services. This will include:

- maximising the awareness and responsiveness of staff to the range of rights issues involved in protective services;
- including advocacy functions in all job descriptions relevant to protective services specifying the nature of the advocacy involved;
- supporting the appropriate advocacy role of casework staff in advocating actively on behalf of children and young people, in the context of their families and relevant community resources; and
- encouraging managers to provide relevant supports to service delivery staff in pursuing rights and related advocacy issues.

This requires appropriate initiatives in program documentation, supported by staff development initiatives directed at relevant staff groups.

Independent Advocacy
A major principle will be promoting access to supports and advocates of the client's choice. Relatives, friends, youth workers and community agency staff can have a major role in assisting children, young people and parents to participate in decision making and the effective provision of services. Models of independent advocacy are also being examined with a view to establishing a relevant source of support to which clients may be referred.

The Salvation Army, in a review of responses to youth homelessness in Victoria, have proposed the establishment of a youth advocacy service (Waters, et al 1991). This would provide casework advocacy for young people subject to protective or corrective orders. The Salvation Army have proposed that such a service should report to the Family and Children's Services Council, which provides policy advice for the Minister of Community Services. It is argued that this arrangement would provide independence, whilst maximising the constructive use of the policy and program proposals generated by such a service.

In the context of the court process, the *Children and Young Persons Act* provides for the development of guardians *ad litem* as are used extensively in the United Kingdom (Caudrey, 1985). Care will be required in developing this program, however, as there is a significant potential for role confusions as guardians *ad litem*, protective services staff and lawyers each pursue their own interpretation of the interests, rights and views of the child or young person.

Bibliography

Algie, J. (1986). 'Weighing up Priorities,' *Community Care*, 11, September, 18-20.
Allinson R. (ed) (1978). *Status Offenders and The Juvenile Justice System: An Anthology*. New Jersey: National Council on Crime and Delinquency.
American Humane Association. (1984). 'Child Abuse and Neglect Related Fatalities-Implications for CPS,' *Protecting Children*, I, 2, Summer.
Anderson, R., Ambrosino, R., Valentine, D. & Lauderdale, M. (1983). 'Child Deaths Attributed to Abuse and Neglect — An Empirical Study,' *Children and Youth Services Review*, 5, 75-89.
Andrews R. & Cohn A. (1974). 'Ungovernability: The Unjustifiable Jurisdiction,' *Yale Law Journal*, 83, 1383-1409.
Arthur, L. (1977). 'Status Offenders Need a Court of Last Resort,' *Boston University Law Review*, 57, 631-644.
Asen, K., George, E., Piper, R. & Stevens, A. (1989). 'A Systems Approach to Child Abuse: Management and Treatment Issues,' *Child Abuse and Neglect*, 13, 45-47.
Asher, R. (1951). 'Munchausen's Syndrome,' *The Lancet*, February, 339-41.
Atherton, C. (1986). 'Let Parents Participate,' *Social Work Today*, 2, October, 25.
Atkin, W. (1990). 'The Courts and Child Protection — Aspects of the Children, Young Persons and their Families Act 1989,' *Victoria University of Wellington Law Review*, 20, 319-342.
Australian Law Reform Commission (1981). *Child Welfare, Report No 18*. Canberra: Australian Government Publishing Service.
Bailey-Harris, R. & Naffine, N. (1988). 'Gender, Justice and Welfare in South Australia: A Study of the Female Status Offender,' *International Journal of Law and the Family*, 2, 214-233.

Bandura, A. (1986). *Social Foundations of Thought and Action: A Social Cognitive Theory*. Englewood Cliffs, New Jersey: Prentice-Hall.

Bandura, A. (1991). 'Social Cognitive Theory of Moral Thought and Action' in *Moral Behavior and Development: Advances in Theory, Research and Applications*, W. M. Kurtines & J. L. Gewirtz (eds). Hillsdale, New Jersey: Erlbaum, 45-103.

Barbour, A. (1990). 'Family Group Conferences: Context and Consequences,' *Social Work Review*, III, 4, 16-21.

Batten, R. (1987). 'Munchausen Syndrome by Proxy: The Need for Service Integration,' *Australian Child and Family Welfare*, 12, 2, 13-14.

Bentovim, A. & Tranter, M. (1984). 'A Family Therapy Approach to Decision Making,' *Adoption and Fostering*, VIII, 1, 25-32.

Berkner, P. et al, (1988). 'Chronic Ipecac Poisoning in Infancy: A Case Report,' *Paediatrics*, 82, 3, September, 384-6.

Berliner, L. & Barbieri, M. K. (1984). 'The Testimony of the Child Victim of Sexual Assault,' *Journal of Social Issues*, 40, 125-137.

Besharov, D. J. (1985). 'Rights Versus Rights: The Dilemma for Child Protection,' *Child Welfare*, Spring, 19-27.

Bibby, M. (1989). *The Human Rights of Children: A Philosophical Analysis*. Paper presented to the Human Rights of Children Conference, University of New South Wales Human Rights Centre.

Binet, A. (1900). *La Suggestibilité*. Paris: Schleicher-Freres.

Black, D. (1981). 'The Extended Munchausen Syndrome: A Family Case,' *British Journal of Psychiatry*, 138, 446-469.

Blackwell, B. (1968). 'The Munchausen Syndrome,' *British Journal of Hospital Medicine*, October, 98-102.

Blom-Cooper, L. (1985). *A Child in Trust. The Report of the Panel of Inquiry into the Circumstances of the death of Jamie Beckford*. Middlesex: Kingsford Press.

Blumberg, M. L. (1978) 'Child Sexual Abuse: Ultimate in Maltreatment Syndrome,' *New York State Journal of Medicine*, 78, 1, 612-616.

Bomar, R. (1988). 'The Incarceration of the Status Offender,' *Memphis State University Law Review*, 18, 713-740.

Bottoms, B., Goodman, G.S., Schwartz-Kenney, B., Sachsenmaier, T., & Thomas, S. (1990). *Keeping Secrets: Implications for Children's Testimony*. Paper presented at the biennial meeting of the American Psychology and Law Society, Williamsburg, VA.

Boulet, J. (1988). 'Societal Descriptions of Child Abuse: Politics, the Media and Public Opinion,' in *International Perspectives on Psychiatry, Psychology, and the Law: Proceedings of the Ninth Annual Conference of the Australian and New Zealand Association of Psychology, Psychiatry and the Law*, D. Greig & I. Freckelton (eds). Melbourne.

Bourne, J. D. & Newberger, E. H. (1980). 'Interdisciplinary Process Group in the Hospital Management of Child Abuse and Neglect,' *Child Abuse and Neglect*, 4, 137-144.

British Columbia Royal Commission, (1975). *Children and the Law Part V, The Protection of Children*. British Columbia Government Printer, 58-63.

Brown, E. (1983). 'Maria Calwell Revisited: When Good Intentions are not Enough', *Australian Social Work*, 36, 4, December, 2-5.
Brown, L. & Riley, J. (1985). 'Agency Procedures with Abuse Reports,' *Juvenile and Family Court Journal*, XXXV, 4, 45-51.
Browne, D. H. (1988). 'The Role of Stress in the Commission of Subsequent Acts of Child Abuse and Neglect', *Early Child Development and Care*, 31, 27-33.
Browne, E. (1987). 'Social Work — What Went Wrong?,' *Australian Social Work*, XL, 2, 3-9.
Browne, K. D. (1989). 'The Health Visitor's Role in Screening for Child Abuse,' *Health Visitor*, LXII, 275-277.
Browne, K. D. & Saqi, S. (1988). 'Approaches to Screening Families at Risk for Child Abuse,' in *Early Prediction and Prevention of Child Abuse*, K. D. Browne, C. Davies & P. Stratton (eds). Chichester: John Wiley.
Budin, L. E. & Johnson, C. F. (1989). 'Sex Abuse Prevention Programs: Offenders' Attitudes about their Efficacy,' *Child Abuse and Neglect*, 13, 77-87.
Burdekin, B. (1989). *Our Homeless Children. The Report of the National Inquiry into Youth Homelessness*. Canberra: Australian Government Publishing Service.
Bussey, K. (1986). 'The First Socialization' in *Australian Women: New Feminist Perspectives*, N. Grieve & A. Burn (eds). Melbourne: Oxford University Press.
Bussey, K. (1988). *The Content and Purpose of Children's Lies*. Paper presented at the conference of the American Psychological Association, Atlanta, GA.
Bussey, K. (1989). *Children's Definitions and Evaluations of Lies and Truths involving a Misdeed*. Paper presented at the Meeting of the Society for Research in Child Development, Kansas City, MO.
Bussey, K. (1992) 'Lying and Truthfulness: Children's Definitions, Standards and Evaluative Reactions,' *Child Development*, 63, 129-137.
Bussey, K. (August, 1990). 'Adult Influence On Children's Eyewitness Reporting' in Ceci, S. (Chair), *'Do Children Lie? Narrowing the Uncertainties'*. Symposium conducted at the American Psychology and Law Society Biennial Meeting, Williamsburg, VA.
Bussey, K., & Lee, K. (1990). *The Effect of Coaching on Children's Eyewitness Reports*. (Manuscript in preparation).
Bussey, K., Lee, K., & Rickard, K. (1990). *Children's Reports of an Adult's Transgression*. (Manuscript in preparation).
Bussey, K. & Steward, M. S. (1985). 'Children's Preparation for and Participation in the Legal System: Considerations from a Social Cognitive Developmental Perspective' in *Age and Criminal Responsibility in Children*, R. A. Cummins & Z. M. Burgess (eds). Melbourne: The Australian Psychological Society.
BYU Law Review, Comment (1976). 'Status Offenses and the Status of Children's Rights: Do Children Have the Legal Right to Be Incorrigible?' *Brigham Young University Law Review*, 659-691.
Calvert, G. E. (1991) 'Getting Child Abuse onto the Political Agenda' in *Action Speaks: Strategies and Lessons*, E. Baldry and T. Vinson (eds). Melbourne: Longman Cheshire, 105-118.

Cashmore J., & Bussey, K. (1990). 'Children's Conceptions of the Witness Role' in *Children's Evidence in Legal Proceedings: An International Perspective*, Spencer, J. R., Nicholson G., Flin R. H. & Bull R. (eds). Cambridge: University of Cambridge Press.

Castell-McGregor, S. (1989). 'The South Australian Children's Interest Bureau' in *Ombudswork for Children*. Verhellen, E. & Spiesschaert. F. Acco (eds). Leuven/Amersfoort.

Castle, R. L. (1977). 'Case Conferences — Cause for Concern,' in *Child Abuse: Prediction, Prevention and Follow-up*, Franklin, A. W. (ed). London: Churchill Livingstone, 145-154.

Caton, A. (1990). *Legislation in New Zealand — A Radical Change*. Paper presented at the Australian Child Protection Conference, Sydney.

Caudrey, A. (1985). 'Speaking up for Children', *New Society*, November.

Ceci, S. J., Toglia, M. P. & Ross, D. F. (1987). *Children's Eyewitness Memory*. New York: Springer-Verlag.

Chandler, M., Fritz, A. S. & Hala, S. (1989). 'Small Scale Deceit: Deception as a Marker of Two, Three, and Four Year Olds' Early Theories of Mind,' *Child Development*, 60, 1263-1277.

Chassin, L., Presson, C. & Sherman, S. (1985). 'Stepping Backward in Order to Step Forward: An Acquisition Oriented Approach to Primary Prevention', *Journal of Consulting and Clinical Psychology*, LIII, 5, 612-622.

Cheng, L. & Hummel, L. (1978). 'The Munchausen Syndrome as Psychiatric Condition,' *British Journal of Psychiatry*, 133, 20-21.

Chesney-Lind, M. (1982). 'Guilty by Reason of Sex: Young Women and the Juvenile Justice System' in *The Criminal Justice System and Women*, B. Price and N. Sokoloff (eds). New York: Clark Boardman.

Child Welfare Practice and Legislation Review, Report, (1984). *Equity and Social Justice for Children, Families and Communities*. Melbourne: Government Printer.

Choo, C. (1990). *Aboriginal Child Poverty*. Melbourne: Longman Cheshire.

Cohn, A. H. (1977). *Evaluation of Child Abuse and Neglect Demonstration Project (1974-77), Final Report, X1*. Berkley Planning Associates.

Cohn, A. H. (1979). 'An Evaluation of Three Child Abuse and Neglect Treatment Programs,' *Journal of American Academy of Child Psychiatry*, XVII, 283-291.

Cohn, A. (1983). *An Approach to Preventing Child Abuse*. Chicago: National Centre for the Prevention of Child Abuse.

Community Services Victoria (1986). 'Irreconcilable Differences — When Parents and Children Just Can't Agree,' *CSV Links*, 12, 3.

Community Services Victoria (1988). *Making Sense of Child Protection: A Model Developed from Practice*. Melbourne: Government Printing Office.

Community Services Victoria (1990). *Supervision of CSV Protective Workers — Standards and Position Paper*. Melbourne: Government Printing Office.

Conte, J. R., Wolf, S., & Smith, J. (1989). 'What Sexual Offenders tell us about Prevention Strategies,' *Child Abuse and Neglect*, 13, 293-301.

Cooper, D. (1986). 'The Child Abuse Inquiry Force. Why Do Social Workers Always Get the Blame?,' *Social Work Today*, April, 14-15.

Corby, B. (1987). *Working with Abuse. Social Work Practice and the Child Abuse System*. Philadelphia: Open University Press.

Corby, B. & Mills, C. (1986). 'Child Abuse: Risks and Resources,' *British Journal of Social Work*, 16, 531-542.

Crittenden, P. (1988). 'Family and Dyadic Patterns of Functioning in Maltreating Families' in *Early Prediction and Prevention of Child Abuse*, Browne, K., Davis, C. & Stratton, P. (eds). Brisbane: John Wiley & Sons, 161-187.

Dale, P. & Davies, M. (1985). 'A Model of Intervention in Child-Abusing Families: A Wider Systems View,' *Child Abuse and Neglect*, 9, 449-455.

Dale, P., Davies, M., Morrison, T. & Watters, J. (1986). *Dangerous Families — Assessment and Treatment of Child Abuse*. London & New York: Tavistock Publication.

Dale, P., Waters, J., Davies, M., Roberts, W. & Morrison, T. (1986). 'The Towers of Silence: Creative and Destructive Issues for Therapeutic Teams Dealing with Child Sexual Abuse,' *Journal of Family Therapy*, 13, 1, 1-25.

Dalgleish, L. I. & Drew, E. C. (1989). 'The Relationship of Child Abuse Indicators to the Assessment of Perceived Risk and to the Courts Decision to Separate,' *Child Abuse and Neglect*, 13, 491-506.

Dalgleish, L. I. (1990). 'Assessment of Perceived Risk in Child Protection: A Model, some Data and Implications for Practice.' Paper presented at First International NSPCC Conference, Leicester, England.

Daro, D. & Mitchell, L. (1990). *'Current Trends in Child Abuse Reporting and Fatalities.' The Results of the 1989 Survey*. The National Committee for Prevention of Child Abuse, Working Paper No 808.

Davies, M. (1988). 'Making Children Safer — Effective Child Protection Work in Rochdale,' *Facing the Future: Proceedings of the First Victorian Conference on Child Abuse*. Victorian Society for the Prevention of Child Abuse and Neglect, Port Melbourne, 1-37.

De Paulo, B., & Jordan, A. (1982). 'Age Changes in Deceiving and Detecting Deceit,' in *Development of Nonverbal Behavior in Children*, R. S. Feldman (ed), New York: Springer.

Department of Health and Social Security (1982). *Child Abuse — A Study of Inquiry Reports 1973-1981*. London.

Dingwall, R., Eekelaar, J. & Murray, T. (1983). *The Protection of Children*. Oxford: Blackwell.

Eekelaar, J. (1986). 'The Emergence of Children's Rights,' *Oxford Journal of Legal Studies*, 6, 161-182.

Elliot & Shanahan (1986). *Benchmark Study for Child Sexual Assault Campaign*. Unpublished.

Elliot & Shanahan (1986). *Post Launch Study I*. Unpublished.

Elliot & Shanahan (1987). *Post Launch Study II*. Unpublished.

Ferdinand T. (1991). 'History Overtakes the Juvenile Justice System,' *Crime and Delinquency*, 37, 204-224.

Fine, S. (1981). *The Marketing of Ideas and Social Issues*. New York: Praeger Publishers.

Finkelhor, D. (1982). 'Sexual abuse: a sociological perspective,' *Child Abuse and Neglect*, 6, 95-102.
Finkelhor, D. (1986). *A Sourcebook on Child Sexual Assault*. London: Sage Publications.
Finkelhor, D. (1988). *Nursery Crimes*. Newbury Park: Sage Publications.
Flandreau-West, P. (1989). *The Basic Essentials: Protective Behaviours, Anti-Victimisation and Empowerment Process*. Burnside, South Australia: Essence Publications.
Fleisher, D. & Ament, M. E. (1988). 'Diarrhoea, Red Diapers and Child Abuse,' *Clinical Paediatrics*, 82, 3, September, 820-824.
Fletcher, L. (1982). 'The Battered Professional' in *Child Abuse: A Community Concern*, R. K. Oates (ed). Sydney: Butterworths.
Fogarty, J. & Sergeant, D. (1989). *Protective Services for Children in Victoria*. Melbourne: Government Printing Office.
Fogarty, J., (1989). *Report of the Review of the Case of "Damien" and Section 104 of the Community Welfare Services Act 1970*. Melbourne: Government Printing Office.
Fontana, V. & Alfaro, J. (1987). *High Risk Factors Associated with Child Maltreatment Fatalities: New York Mayor's Taskforce on Child Abuse and Neglect*.
Fox, S. and Dingwall, R. (1985). 'An Exploratory Study of Variations in Social Workers' and Health Visitors' Definitions of Child Mistreatment,' *British Journal of Social Work*, 15, 467-477.
Fraenkel, J. R. (1980). *Helping Students Think and Value: Strategies for Teaching the Social Studies*, 2nd ed. New Jersey: Prentice Hall.
Francis, C. (1990). 'The Legal Consequences of the United Nations Convention on the Rights of the Child,' *The Australian Family*, 11, December, 23-30.
Franklin, B. (ed), (1986). *The Rights of Children*. Oxford: Blackwell.
Gamble H. (1985). 'The Status Offender' in *Juvenile Delinquency in Australia*, A. Borowski & J. Murray (eds). Sydney: Methuen.
Garlock P. (1979). ' "Wayward" Children and the Law, 1820-1900: The Genesis of the Status Offense Jurisdiction of the Juvenile Court,' *Georgia Law Review*, 13, 341-447.
Geismer, J. (1988). *Family and Community Functioning*. New Jersey: Scarecrow Press.
Giovannoni, J. M. & Becerra, R. M. (1979). *Defining Child Abuse*. London: Collier Macmillan.
Globe Newspaper Co. v. Superior Court (1982). 102 S. Ct. 2613.
Goddard, C. & Carew, B. (1988). 'Protecting the Child: Hostages to Fortune,' *Social Work Today*, 12-13.
Goldman, R. and Goldman, J. (1986). 'Australian Children's Sexual Experiences within the Family'. Paper presented at the 6th International Congress of Child Abuse and Neglect, Sydney.
Goldstein, J., Freud, A. & Solnit, A. J. (1980). *Before the Best Interests of the Child*. New York: Free Press.
Goodlin, R. C. (1985). 'Pregnant Women with Munchausen Syndrome,' *American Journal of Obstetrics and Gynaecology*, 153, September, 207-210.

Goodman, G. S., Hirschman, J., & Rudy, L. (1987). 'Children's Testimony: Research and Policy Implications,' in *Children as Witnesses: Research and Social Policy Implications*. S. Ceci (Chair). Symposium presented at the Society for Research in Child Development, Baltimore.

Goodman, G. S., Jones, D. P. H., Pyle, E. A., Prado-Estrada, L., Port, L. K., England, P., Mason, R., & Rudy, L. (1988). 'The Emotional Effects of Criminal Court Testimony on Child Sexual Assault Victims: A Preliminary Report' in *The Child Witness — Do the Courts Abuse Children?*, G. Davies & J. Drinkwater (eds). British Psychological Society.

Gopnik, A., & Astington, J. W. (1988). 'Children's understanding of representational change and its relation to the understanding of false belief and the appearance-reality distinction,' *Child Development*, 59, 26-37.

Green, A. H., Power, E., Gaines, R. W. & Steinbook, B. (1979). *Factors Associated with Successful and Unsuccessful Intervention with Child Abusing Families*. Annual Meeting of American Academy of Child Psychiatry.

Greenland, C. (1987). *Preventing Child Abuse and Neglect Deaths : An International Study of Deaths Due to Child Abuse and Neglect*. London: Tavistock Publications.

Gregory J. (1978). 'Juvenile Court Jurisdiction Over Noncriminal Misbehaviour: The Argument Against Abolition,' *Ohio State Law Journal*, 39, 242-272.

Griffith, J. (1988). 'The Family Systems of Munchausen Syndrome by Proxy,' *Family Process*, 27, 423-437.

Groth, A. N. (1978). 'Patterns of Sexual Assault Against Children and Adolescents' in *Sexual Assault of Children and Adolescents*, A. W. Burgess, L. L. Holmstrom & S. M.

Hafen B., 'Children's Liberation and the New Egalitarianism: Some Reservations about Abandoning Youth to Their "Rights",' *Brigham Young University Law Review*, 605-658.

Hallett, C. & Stevenson, O. (1980). *Child Abuse — Aspects of Inter-professional Co-operation*. London: Allen and Unwin.

Hampton, R. L. & Newberger, E. H. (1985). 'Child Abuse Incidence and Reporting by Hospitals: Significance of Severity, Class and Race,' *American Journal of Public Health*, 75, 56-60.

Hancock L. & Chesney-Lind M. (1985). 'Juvenile Justice Legislation and Gender Discrimination' in *Juvenile Delinquency in Australia*, Borowski, A. and Murray (eds). Sydney: Methuen.

Handler J. & Zatz J. (eds) (1982). *Neither Angels Nor Thieves: Studies in the Deinstitutionalisation Of Status Offenders*. Washington DC: National Academy Press.

Hansen, C., Diamond, P. & Ludwig, S. (1989). 'Can We Protect Children from Abuse? A Review of Three Cases,' *Child Welfare*, 68, 6, 615-621.

Haugaard, J., & Crosby, C. (1989). *Children's definitions of the truth and their competency as witnesses in legal proceedings*. Paper presented at the Southeastern Psychological Association Conference.

Hausfater, G. & Blaffer Hardy, S. (1984). *Infanticide — Comparative and Evolutionary Perspectives*. New York: Aldine Publishing Co.

Heptinstall, D. (1983). 'Are Comparisons Invidious?,' *Community Care*, May, 41.
Hickey W. (1977). 'Status Offenses and the Juvenile Court,' *Criminal Justice Abstracts*, 9, 1, 91-122.
Hochstadt, N. J. & Harwicke, N. J. (1985). 'How Effective is the Multi-disciplinary Approach? A Follow-up Study,' *Child Abuse and Neglect*, 9, 365-372.
Hogwood & Gunn, L. (1984). *Policy Analysis for the Real World.* Melbourne: Oxford University Press.
Institute of Judical Administration/American Bar Assocation Joint Commission Juvenile Justice Standards Project (1982). *Standards Relating to Noncriminal Misbehavior.* Cambridge, Mass: Ballinger.
Johnson, W. and L'Esperance, J. (1985). 'Predicting the Recurrence of Child Abuse,' *Social Work Research and Abstracts*, February, 21-26.
Jones, D. (1987). 'The Untreatable Family,' *Child Abuse and Neglect*, 11, 409-420.
Jones, D. N., McClean, R. & Vobe, R. (1979). 'Case Conferences on Child Abuse: The Nottinghamshire Approach,' *Child Abuse and Neglect*, 3, 583-590.
Jones, D. P. H. & Alexander, H. (1987).'Treating the Abusive Family with the Family Care System' in *The Battered Child*, 4th edition, Helfer, R. & Kempe, R. (eds). Chicago: The University of Chicago Press, 339-360.
Jones, J. G. et al, (1986). 'Munchausen Syndrome by Proxy,' *Child Abuse and Neglect* 10, 33-40.
Katz A. and Teitelbaum L. (1977). 'PINS Jurisdiction, the Vagueness Doctrine and the Rule of Law,' *Indiana Law Journal*, 53, 1-34.
Katz, M. H., Hampton, R. L., Newberger, E. H., Bowles, R. T. & Snyder, J. C. (1986). 'Returning Children Home: Clinical Decision Making in Cases of Child Abuse and Neglect,' *American Journal of Orthopsychiatry*, LVI, 2, 253-262.
Kelly, S. J. (1988). *Responses of Children to Sexual Abuse and Satanic Ritualistic Abuse in Day Care Centres.* Paper presented at National Symposium of Child Victimisation, Anaheim, California.
Kempe, C. H. & Helfer, R. E. (eds) (1972). *Helping the Battered Child and His Family.* Philadelphia: J. B. Lippincott Co.
Korbin, J. (1989). 'Fatal Maltreatment by Mothers: A Proposed Framework', *Child Abuse and Neglect*, 13, 481-489.
Kotler, P. & Roberto, E. (1989). *Social Marketing.* New York: Macmillan.
Kovitz, K. E., Dougan, P., Riese, R. & Brummitt, J. R. (1984). 'Multidisciplinary Team Functioning,' *Child Abuse and Neglect*, 8, 353-360.
Lamond, D. (1989). 'The impact of mandatory reporting legislation on reporting behaviour,' *Child Abuse and Neglect*, 13, 471-480.
Lawrence, J. (1982). *Responsibility for Service in Child Abuse and Child Protection.* Unpublished paper.
Leaper P. (1974). *Children in Need of Care and Protection.* University of Melbourne Criminology Department.
LePoole, F. (1977). 'Law and Practice Concerning the Counterparts of "Persons in Need of Supervision" in Some European Countries with a

Particular Emphasis on the Netherlands' in *Beyond Control: Status Offenders in the Juvenile Court*, Teitelbaum L. & Gough A (eds). Cambridge Mass: Ballinger, Chapter 3.

Lewis, M., Stanger, C., & Sullivan, M. W. (1989). 'Deception in 3-year-olds,' *Developmental Psychology*, 25, 430-438.

Libai, D. (1969). 'The protection of the child victim of a sexual offense in the criminal justice system,' *Wayne Law Review*, 15, 977-1032.

Light, M. J. & Sheridan, M. S. (1990). 'Munchausen Syndrome by Proxy and Apnea,' *Clinical Paediatrics*, 29, 3, 162-168.

Mahoney A. (1977). 'PINS and Parents', in *Beyond Control: Status Offenders in the Juvenile Court*, Teitelbaum L. & Gough A. (eds). Cambridge, Mass: Ballinger, Chapter 4.

Makar, A. F. and Squier, P. J. (1990). 'Munchausen Syndrome by Proxy: Father as Perpetrator,' *Paediatrics*, 85, 370-373.

Martin, J. & Pitman, S. (1986). *A New Family Support Service: A Formative Research Study for the Children's Protection Society*. Melbourne: Research Unit, Family Care Organisation.

Martin, L. & Snyder P. (1976). 'Jurisdiction Over Status Offences Should Not be Removed from the Juvenile Court,' *Crime and Delinquency*, 22, 1, 44-47.

Maryland v. Craig (1990). *US Law Week*, 58, 5044.

Mason, D., (1990). 'The Rights of Australia's Children in a Global Context,' *Children Australia*, 15, 2, 6-7.

Masson, J. M. (1985). *The Assault on Truth*. London: Penguin Books.

Masterton, J. et al, (1988). 'Extreme Illness Exaggeration in Paediatric Patients: A Variant of Munchausen by Proxy?,' *American Journal of Orthopsychiatry*, 58, 2, 188-195.

McGloin, P. & Turnbull, A. (1987). 'Strengthening Good Practice by Bringing in the Parents,' *Social Work Today*, 20, July , 14-15.

McGuire, T. and Feldman, K. W. (1989). 'Psychological Morbidity of Children Subjected to Munchausen Syndrome by Proxy,' *Paediatrics*, 83, 2, 289-292.

McIntosh, J. (1986). *Alys Key Family Care: Evaluation Design Document*. West Heidelberg: Children's Protection Society.

McIntosh, J. (1987). *The First Year of Service: Alys Key Family Care: A Demonstration Project of the Children's Protection Society*. West Heidelberg: Children's Protection Society.

McIntosh, J. (1988). *Alys Key Family Care — A Demonstration Project of the Children's Protection Society — The Second Year of Service: New Growth*. West Heidelberg: Children's Protection Society.

McIntosh, J. (1989). *Alys Key Family Care — A Study of Growth and Change — Final Research and Evaluation Report*. West Heidelberg: Children's Protection Society.

Meadows, S. R. (1977). 'Munchausen Syndrome by Proxy, The Hinterland of Child Abuse,' *Lancet*, 2, 343-345.

Meadow, S. R. (1982). 'Munchausen Syndrome by Proxy,' *Archives of Disease in Childhood*, 57, 92-98.

Meadow, W. R. (1984). 'Fictitious Epilepsy,' *Lancet*, 2, 25-28.

Meadow, S. R. (1985). 'Management of Munchausen Syndrome by Proxy,' *Archives of Disease in Childhood*, 60, 385-393.

Mearig, S. J. (1982). 'Ethical Implications of Children's Rights,' *American Journal of Orthopsychiatry*, 52.

Meddin, B. J. (1984). 'The Future of Decision Making in Child Welfare Practice: The Development of an Explicit Criteria Model for Decision Making,' *Australian Child and Family Welfare*, IX, 4, 3-6.

Meddin, B. J. & Gross, C. J. (1985). 'The Multi-disciplinary Child Protection Panel: Critical Factors for Viable Functioning,' *Australian Social Work*, XXXVIII, 3, 11-16.

Melton, G. B. (1981). 'Children's competency to testify,' *Law and Human Behavior*, 5, 73-85.

Melton, G. B. (1984). 'Developmental psychology and the law: The state of the Art,' *Journal of Family Law*, 22, 445-482.

Melton, G. B. (1985). 'Sexually abused children and the legal system: Some policy recommendations,' *The American Journal of Family Therapy*, 13, 61-76.

Melton, G. B. (1987). 'Children's testimony in cases of alleged sexual abuse' in *Advances in Developmental and Behavioral Paediatrics*, M. Wolraich & D. K. Routh (eds). Greenwich, CT: JAI Press, 179-203.

Molin, R. & Herskowitz, S. (1986). 'Clinicians and Caseworkers: Issues in Consultation and Collaboration Regarding Protective Service Clients,' *Child Abuse and Neglect*, 10, 201-210.

Monk, D. (1987). 'Participation not Persecution,' *Community Care*, 13, April, 22-23.

Moore, J. G. (1985). *The ABC of Child Abuse Work*. Hants, England: Gower Publishing. 83-89.

Morris, A., Giller H., Szwed E. & Geach H. (1980). *Justice for Children*. London: Macmillan.

Motz, J. (1984). *Colorado's Community Based Child Protection Team*. Colorado Department Social Services.

Mouzakitis, C. M. & Goldstein, S. C. (1985). 'A Multi-disciplinary Approach to Treating Child Neglect,' *Social Casework*, April, 218-224.

National Committee on Violence. (1990). *'Violence: Directions for Australia.'* Canberra: Australian Institute of Criminology.

Nichol, A. R. & Eccles, M. (1985). 'Psychotherapy for Munchausen Syndrome by Proxy,' *Archives of Disease in Childhood*, 60, 344-348.

Norgard Report (1976). *Report of the Enquiry into Child Care Services in Victoria*. Melbourne: Government Printing Office.

Note (1953). 'The competency of children as witnesses.' *Virginia Law Review*, 39, 358-370.

NSW Child Protection Council (1986). *Child Sexual Assault: How to Talk to Children*. Sydney: Government Printer.

NSW Child Protection Council (1987). *Child Sexual Assault: No Excuses Never Ever*. Sydney: Government Printer.

NSW Child Protection Council (1988). *Child Sexual Assault: It's Often Closer to Home Than You Think*. Sydney: Government Printer.

NSW Child Protection Council (1988a). *Child Sexual Assault, Where to Get Help*. Sydney: Government Printer.
NSW Child Protection Council (1989). *Annual Report 1986-88*. Sydney: Government Printer.
NSW Department of Health (1988). 'Child Sexual Assault Centres, 1987 — Statistics.' *NSW Health Services Information Bulletin No 10*. Sydney.
NSW Department of Health (1988). 'Child Sexual Assault Centres, 1987 — Statistics.' *NSW Health Services Information Bulletin No 10*. Sydney.
NSW Department of School Education (1989). *Child Protection: Preventing Child Sexual Assault, Kindergarten to Year 6*. Sydney.
NSW Department of School Education (1989). *Child Protection: Preventing Child Sexual Assault, Years 7 to 12*. Sydney.
NSW Department of School Education (1989). *Child Protection: Preventing Child Sexual Assault, Students with an Intellectual Disability*. Sydney.
NSW Department of School Education (1989). *Child Protection: Preventing Child Sexual Assault, Early Childhood Curriculum Ideas*. Sydney.
NSW Department of School Education (1989). *Child Protection: Staff Development Package*. Sydney.
NSW Department of School Education (1989). *Child Protection: Parents and Community Information Manual*. Sydney.
NSW Government (1985). *Report of the NSW Child Sexual Assault Task Force*. Sydney: Government Printer.
Orten, J. D. & Soll S. K. (1980). 'Runaway Children and Their Families: A Treatment Typology,' *Journal of Family Issues*, 1, 2, 249-261.
Palenski, J. & Launer H. (1987). 'The Process of Running Away: A Redefinition,' *Adolescence*, 22, 347-362.
Palmer, A. J. & Yoshimura, J. (1984).'Munchausen Syndrome by Proxy,' *Journal of American Academy of Child Psychiatry*, 23, 503-508.
Parkinson, P. (1988). 'Leaving Home,' *Family Law*, 18, 480-485.
Parkinson, P. (1990). ' "Boy, Fifteen, Divorces Parents": Irreconcilable Difference Applications in Victoria,' *Australian Journal of Social Issues*, 25, 4, 301-317.
Parton, N. (1986). 'The Beckford Report: A Critical Appraisal,' *British Journal of Social Work*, 16, 511-530.
Parton, C. (1990). 'Women, Gender Oppression and Child Abuse,' in *Taking Child Abuse Seriously*. The Violence Against Children Study Group, London: Unwin Hyman.
Perry, D. G. & Bussey, K. (1984). *Social Development*. Englewood Cliffs, N.J: Prentice-Hall.
Peterson, C. C., Peterson, J. L. & Seeto, D. (1983). 'Developmental changes in ideas about lying,' *Child Development*, 54, 1529-1535.
Piaget, J. (1965). *The Moral Judgment of the Child*. Harmondsworth, England: Penguin Books, (Original work published 1932).
Pickford, E. et al, (1988). 'Munchausen Syndrome by Proxy: a Family Anthology,' *The Medical Journal of Australia*, 148, June, 646-650.
Piper, K. (1989). *Child Protection and Social Inequality*. Paper presented to the

Victorian Society for the Prevention of Child Abuse and Neglect, Annual Conference.

Platt, A. (1969). *The Child Savers: The Invention of Delinquency*. Chicago: University of Chicago Press.

Read, P. (1982). *The Stolen Generations: The Removal of Aboriginal Children in NSW 1883-1969*. Occasional Paper No 1, NSW Aboriginal Affairs, Sydney: Government Printer.

Rees, S. V. (1987). 'Munchausen Syndrome by Proxy: Another Form of Child Abuse,' *Practice*, 3, 267-282.

Repucci, N. D. (1990). *Developmental research can inform legal decision making*. Paper presented at the American Psychology and Law Society Biennial Meeting, Williamsburg, Va.

Rogers, C. M. (1982). 'Child sexual abuse and the courts: Preliminary findings' in *Social work and Child Sexual Abuse*, J. Conte and D. A. Shore (eds). New York: Haworth Press, 45-153.

Rogers, D. et al, (1976). 'Non-accidental poisoning: an Extended Syndrome of Child Abuse,' *British Medical Journal*, April, 793-796.

Rolf, J. (1985). 'Evolving Adaptive Theories and Methods of Prevention Research With Children', *Journal of Consulting and Clinical Psychology*, LIII, 5, 631-646.

Rosenberg, D. (1987). 'Web of Deceit, a Literature Review of Munchausen Syndrome by Proxy,' *Child Abuse and Neglect*, 11, 547-563.

Rosenberg, M., Reppucci, N. (1985). 'Primary Prevention of Child Abuse', *Journal of Consulting and Clinical Psychology*, LIII, 5, 576-585.

Ruddock, M. (1988). 'A Child in Mind, A Lost Opportunity,' *Social Work Today*, January, 14-15.

Rumack, B. H. & Temple, A. R. (1974). 'Lomotil Poisoning,' *Paediatrics*, 53, 4, April, 495-500.

Sacks H. S & Sacks H. L. (1980). 'Status Offenders: Emerging Issues and New Approaches' in *Child Psychiatry and The Law*, D. Schetky & E. Benedek (eds). New York: Brunner/Mazel.

Saywitz, K., Goodman, G. S., Nicholas, E., & Moan, S. (1989). 'Children's memories of genital examinations: Implications for cases of child sexual assault' in *Can children provide accurate eyewitness testimony?* G. S. Goodman (Chair). Symposium presented at the biennial meetings of the Society for Research in Child Development, Kansas City, Mo.

Scarlett, J. A. et al, (1977). 'Factitious Hypoglycaemia,' *The New England Journal of Medicine*, 297, 1029-1032.

Schiefelbusch, R. L. (1981). *Language Intervention Strategies 2*, Maryland: University Park Press, USA.

Schmitt, B. D. (ed) (1978). *The Child Protection Team Handbook*. New York: Garland STPM Press.

Schmitt, B. D. & Grosz, C. A. (1978). 'Ground Rules for Effective Team Conferences' in *The Child Protection Team Handbook*, B. D. Schmidt (ed). New York: Garland STPM Press, 169-174.

Schmidt, B. D. & Loy, L. L. (1978). 'Team Decisions on Case Management' in

The Child Protection Team Handbook, B. D. Schmidt (ed). New York: Garland STPM Press, 187-203.

Scott, P. D. (1973). 'Parents Who Kill Their Children' in *Medicine, Science and the Law*, XIII, 2, 120-126.

Sgroi, S. (1982). *Handbook of Clinical Intervention in Child Sexual Abuse*. Massachusetts: Lexington Books.

Shane, P. (1989). 'Changing Patterns Among Homeless and Runaway Youth,' *American Journal of Orthopsychiatry*, 59, 2, 208-214.

Shearer, A. (1979). 'Tragedies Revisited 2,' *Social Work Today*, 10, 20, 9-16.

Shearer, A. (1979a). 'Tragedies Revisited 3,' *Social Work Today*, 10, 21, 11-21.

Sigal, M., Gelkopf, M. & Meadow, R. (1989). 'Munchausen by Proxy Syndrome: The Triad of Abuse, Self-Abuse and Deception,' *Comprehensive Psychiatry*, 30, 527-533.

Single, T. (1989). 'Child Sexual Assault in which the Alleged Offender is a Child Care Professional,' *Australian Social Work*, 42, 4, 21-28.

Snyder, J. C. & Newberger, E. H. (1986). 'Consensus and Difference Among Hospital Professionals in Evaluating Child Maltreatment,' *Violence and Victims*, I, 2, 125-139.

Sodian, B. (1989). *The development of deception in young children*. Paper presented at the biennial meeting of the Society for Research in Child Development, Kansas City, Mo.

Southall, D. P. et al, (1987). 'Apnoeic Episodes Induced by Smothering: Two Cases Identified by Covert Video Surveillance,' *British Medical Journal*, 294, 1637-1641.

Starr, R. H. (1987). 'Clinical Judgement of Abuse-proneness Based on Parent-Child Interactions,' *Child Abuse and Neglect*, 11, 87-92.

Steinhauer, P. D. (1983). 'Assessing for Parent Capacity,' *American Journal of Orthopsychiatry*, LIII, 3, 468-481.

Stevens, D. and Berliner, L. (1980). 'Special Techniques for Child Witnesses' in *The Sexual Victimology of Youth*, Schultz, L. G. (ed). Charles C. Thomas III.

Steward, M. S. (1989). 'The development of a model interview for young child victims of sexual abuse: Comparing the effectiveness of anatomical dolls, drawings and video graphics.' *Final Report of grant © 90CA1332 for the National Center on Child Abuse and Neglect*, Washington D.C.: U.S. Office of Health and Human Services.

Steward, M. S., Bussey, K., Goodman, G. & Saywitz, K. (1992). 'Implications of developmental research for interviewing children,' *Child Abuse and Neglect*. (In press.)

Stiller, S. & Elder, C. (1975). 'PINS — A Concept in Need of Supervision' *American Criminal Law Review*, 12, 33-60.

Stone, F. B. (1989). 'A Case Study, Munchausen by Proxy Syndrome, an Unusual Form of Child Abuse,' *Social Casework, The Journal of Contemporary Social Work Family Service of America*, April, 243-246.

Stouthamer-Loeber, M. (1987). *Mothers' perceptions of children's lying and its relationship to behavior problems*. Presented at the annual meeting of the Society for Research on Child Development, Baltimore, Md.

Sweet, R. (1991). 'Deinstitutionalisation of Status Offenders: In Perspective,' *Pepperdine Law Review*, 18, 389-415.

Teitelbaum, L. and Gough, A. (eds) (1977). *Beyond Control: Status Offenders in the Juvenile Court*. Cambridge, Mass: Ballinger.

Vasek, M. E. (1986). 'Lying as a skill: The development of deception in children' in *Deception: Perspectives on human and non-human deceit*, R. W. Mitchell & N. S. Thompson (eds). Albany: State University of New York Press, 271-292.

Verhellen, E. & Spiesschaert, F. (1989). *Ombudswork for Children*. Acco, Leuven/Amersfoort.

Waller, D. (1983). 'Obstacles to the Treatment of Munchausen by Proxy Syndrome,' *Journal of American Academy of Psychiatry*, 22, 80-85.

Waller, D. (1990). Unpublished correspondence with the authors.

Warner, J. & Hathaway, M. J. (1984). 'Allergic Form of Meadow's Syndrome (Munchausen by Proxy),' *Archives of Disease in Childhood*, 59, 151-156.

Wasserman, S. & Rosenfeld, A. (1986). 'Decision Making in Child Abuse and Neglect,' *Child Welfare*, LXV, 6, 515-529.

Waters, J. (1983). 'Giving the Family Credit for Being Experts About Themselves,' *Community Care*, 10, 36-39.

Waters, K., Sheehan, G. & Eldridge, D. (1991). *Unfinished Business*. Melbourne: Salvation Army.

Wigmore, J. H. (1940). *On Evidence*. 3rd ed. Boston: Little, Brown & Co.

Williams, C. (1986). 'Munchausen Syndrome by Proxy, A Bizarre Form of Child Abuse,' *Family Law*, 16, 32-34.

Wimmer, H., Gruber, S., & Perner, J. (1984). 'Young children's conception of lying: Lexical realism — moral subjectivism,' *Journal of Experimental Child Psychology*, 37, 1-30.

Wimmer, H., Gruber, S., & Perner, J. (1985). 'Young children's conception of lying: Moral intuition and the denotation and connotation of "to lie",' *Developmental Psychology*, 21, 993-995.

Wimmer, H., Hogrefe, J. G. & Sodian, B. (1988). 'A second stage in children's conception of mental life: Understanding sources of information,' in *Developing Theories of Mind*, J. W. Astington, P. L. Harris, & D. R. Olson (eds). New York: Cambridge University Press, 173-192.

Yates, A., Hull, J. W. & Heubner, R. B. (1984). 'Predicting the Abused Parent's Response to Intervention,' *Child Abuse and Neglect*, 7, 37-44.

Young, C. (1987). *Young People Leaving Home in Australia*. ANU & AIFS, Canberra.

Young R., Mathews G. & Adams G. (1983). 'Runaways: A Review of Negative Consequences and Diminishing Choices,' *Family Relations*, 32, 275-281.

Index

Aboriginal and Islander Child Care Agencies (AICCA) 17, 19
Aboriginal and Islander Child Care Agency (Townsville) 18
Aboriginal Child Poverty 14, 16, 19
Aboriginal Medical Service 39
Aboriginals 14-19, 39
   adoption of children 16
   agencies 16, 17-19
   see also specific agencies eg Aboriginal and Islander Child Care Agency (Townsville)
   alcoholism 16
   assimiliation 15
   Australia's debt owed to 15
   counselling services 39
   culture 15, 16, 18
   dispossessed 17
   education 14, 15, 17, 18
   employment 17
   enslaved 15
   environment and 14
   essential services 16
   extended families 15, 18, 91
   genocide 15
   health 14, 17
   homelessness 16, 17
   identity 16, 17, 18
   income 17
   indigenous foods 14-15
   institutions and 17
   kinship 15
   land guardianship 15
   languages 15
   oppression 16
   ownership concept 15
   poverty 16, 17, 18
   pre-European occupation 14-15
   prisons and 17
   psychiatric disorders 19
   racism and 17
   religion 15
   removal of children 15, 16, 18, 19
   rights 19
   self-esteem of 17
   sexually transmitted diseases 17
   socialisation 14
   spiritually linked with the land 15, 16
   State promotes abuses against 16
abuse 86, 91, 93, 94, 174, 182, 183, 185, 190
   drug 146, 147, 182
   emotional 36, 108, 155, 159, 160
   incidence 110
   intra-familial 130, 131, 132, 133
   perceptions 107-8
   physical 36, 108, 109, 123, 133, 155, 157, 159, 161
   recurrence 110
   ritual 156, 159-60
   secondary 142
   sexual *see* sexual assault

substance 65
verbal 36
access
  denial of 134
accommodation 94, 97, 135
  funding 93
ad litem guardianship 190, 191
Administrative Appeals Tribunal 189, 190
adolescents 87, 134, 157, 137, 178, 181-2
  behaviour 182
  contraceptives and 183
  rights 187, 188
adults 80
  educating 24
  fear of 43
  relationships with children 24, 41, 42, 43, 44, 57, 76, 82, 168
  responsibilities 173-91
  rights 67
advocacy 174-91
  citizen's 184, 188
  definition 183
  family involvement 185
  improving responses 190-1
  independent 187-90, 191
  internal 186
  protective services 183-91
  staff 186-7
  youth 191
after-school groups 60
age
  as factor in deaths 131
  range of abused children 160, 164
aged 188
agencies
  guidelines 17
  networking 171
  see also specific agencies
aggression 156, 157, 160
alcoholism
  Aboriginals and 16
Alice Springs (NT) 18
Alys Key Family Care Demonstration
  Project 53-65
  aims 57
  family groups 56
  group programs 60
  operating principles 54
  research 61-2
  service design 54
  service model 57

specific roles 59-60
target populations 55-6
American Bar Association 95
American Humane Association 127, 131
analogue studies 72
analysis (strategy) 48
ancillary staff
  as offenders 159
anger 64
anxiety 156, 157, 169
  separation 157, 160
Area Child Protection Council 126, 127
Area Review Committee 126
asphyxiation 149
  see also smothering
assault, sexual 23-40, 41-52, 67, 69, 85, 93, 141, 155, 157, 158, 159, 161
  roup 99, 163-72
  mistrust of colleagues 167-8
  numbers of cases 165
  raw nature of material 165-6
  supervision 167, 171, 172
  unclear roles of staff in 166-7, 172
assertiveness 48, 60
'at risk' 42, 103, 109, 111, 181
  assessment 133-4
  determining 109-11, 123
  factors 117
  families 102
  perceptions of 107-8
  youth 96
at risk cases
  decision making in 109
attachment behaviour 110
attitudes, society's 25, 26, 27, 36, 39, 48
Australian Bureau of Statistics 129
Australian Capital Territory 86, 88
  'serious incompatability' 90, 97
Australian Law Reform Commission 90
autonomy 182, 187
  family 182
awareness, public 24, 26, 36, 50, 51, 67
  see also campaigns

babysitters 157-8
'band-aid' protection 40
  Aboriginals 17
Beckford, Jasmine 123, 125, 126, 135
behaviour 48, 50, 158
  adolescent 182
  attachment 110
  changes in 156-61
  clinging 160

Index

compulsive 156, 161
dependent 146, 147
parental 142
problems 60, 160-1
  see also specific behaviour eg aggression
sexualised 156, 157, 161
sexually exploitative 47
behaviour-rehearsals 49
beliefs 45, 48, 52
  false 75, 81
'best interest' 175, 182, 183, 184
billboards 25, 36
blame 26, 44, 92, 123
booklets 25, 26, 36, 37, 38, 39
brainstorming 49
Brewer, Wayne 124
bribery 71, 82
Brotherhood of St Laurence 14, 19
Burdekin Report *see* National Inquiry into Youth Homelessness
bus drivers 157

Calwell, Maria 126, 136
campaigns 24-40
  booklets 25, 26, 36, 37, 38, 39
  educational 41-52
  funding 40
  government involvement 32, 37, 40
  languages 37, 38
  limitations 38-9
  mass media 22-40, 43, 51
  multilingual wall posters 25
  national identity of 21
  posters 25, 26, 36, 37, 38, 39
  radio 25, 36
  stickers 25, 26
  success 35
  television use 25, 26, 28, 34-5, 36, 37
Canada 89, 124
capital punishment 31, 32, 35
Carlisle, Kimberley 124
case by case determinations 79
case conferences 99, 101-21, 187
  communication in 136
  composition 116
  improving 112-16
  parental involvement 120
  resourcing 116
  role and purpose of 103-4
case files 139-40
case management 21, 166, 168
  group sexual asssault 163, 164

Munchausen Syndrome by Proxy 145-51
supervision 166
case notes 139
case planning meetings 187, 188
case planning process 190
case vignettes 107
Catholic Education Commission 24
Central Australian Aboriginal Child Care Agency (Alice Springs) 18
Child Abuse: Aspects of Inter-Professional Cooperation 126
child-at-risk interest groups 151
child care 54, 60
  extra-familial 155-62
  see also day care
child care workers as offenders 157
child-courtrooms 83
Child in Trust 126
child protection panels 103
Child Protection: Early Childhood Curriculum Ideas 50
Child Protection: Parent and Community Participation Manual 45
Child Protection: Staff Development Package 50
Child Protection Unit (The Children's Hospital, Camperdown) 155-62, 163, 166
Child Sexual Assault, How to Talk to Children (booklet) 25
'Child Sexual Assault, It's Often Closer to Home Than You Think' 25
'Child Sexual Assault Offenders. No Excuses Never Ever' campaign 25, 35
Child Sexual Assault Program (CSAP) 23-24, 35, 36, 37, 42
child welfare 67, 68
  legislation 16, 19, 179, 190
Child Welfare Practice and Legislation Review (1984) 179, 190
children
  developmental stages 44, 45
  empowering 43
Children and Young Persons Act 1989 (Vic) 90, 177, 179, 180, 182, 184,1 90, 191
Children (Care and Protection) Act 1987 (NSW) 90
Children, Young Persons and Their Families Act 1989 (NZ) 91
children, pre-school 60, 154-62, 163
Children's Court (Vic) 179, 180

Children's Court Advisory Service (Vic) 89, 92, 97
Children's Court Rules 1988 (NSW) 90
'children's divorce' 92
children's homes 93
Children's Hospital, Camperdown (NSW)
　Child Protection Unit 155-62, 163, 166
Children's Interest Bureau (SA) 184, 188, 189
Children's Protection Society 53, 55, 127, 130
children's rights 44, 46, 47, 52, 67, 109, 173-91
　human 179-80
　natural 181
Children's Services Ordinance 1986 (ACT) 90
children's services workers 57, 59-60
Christianity 15
citizen's advocacy program 184, 188
　funding 184
civil rights 176, 179
cleaners 157
cleaning, compulsive 161
client record systems 138
closed circuit television 82, 83
cognitive theory
　social 71, 73, 78
colleague bashing 164
Colorado (USA) 103
commercials
　radio 25, 26, 36, 37
　television 25, 26, 28, 34-5, 36, 37
communication 136, 190
　skills 44, 47, 49
community based groups 24
community justice centres 90
Community Services Victoria 53, 91, 92, 93, 122, 127, 128, 130, 132, 136, 178, 180, 181, 182, 187-8, 190
　Aboriginals and 18
　ecosystem model 185
　intellectual disability service 184
community visitors program 184, 188
Community Welfare Services Act 1978 (Vic) 88-9
competence
　development of 181-2
　testing 82
computer assisted interviewing 84
confrontation 145, 146
confusion 157

contraceptives 183
contracts, working 59, 62, 63
counselling 39, 52, 90, 91, 92, 97, 161, 163, 178
　family 54, 86, 92, 93, 94, 95
　telephone 92
counsellors 73
court hearings 146
court orders 96, 130
courtrooms
　modification for child witnesses 82-4
courts
　children's 93-4, 128
　juvenile 86, 87
criminal offences 33
crisis intervention 59, 135
critical incident reviews 122, 123
cross examinations 84
crying 157, 160
CSAP *see* Child Sexual Assault Program (CSAP)
cultural diversity 21
cultural rights 177
curriculum
　child protective 22, 24, 35, 43, 45, 46
　materials 46-51
custody 97
　orders 180
　parental 95
　police 95

day care 154-62
de facto husbands 131, 132, 133, 135
death 99, 103, 144
　gender 130
　incidences 129
　inquiries 122-40
　of loved ones 169
　perpetrators' identities 131
　threat of 156
　see also homicides
debriefing 151-2, 165
　systems 138
deceit 81
decision making 99-172, 179, 181, 190
　children's 48
　improving 112-16
　joint 101-2
　models 116-17
　parents in 191
　team 99-172
defendants 83
delinquency 107

Department of Community Services
    (NSW) 161, 166, 170
Department of Education (NSW) 24
Department of Health and Social Service
    (UK)
    inquiries 126, 133, 136, 137
Department of Health (NSW) 159, 166,
    170
Department of School Education (NSW)
    41, 42, 46-52
Department of Youth and Community
    Services (NSW) 127
depression 156, 158
deprivation of necessities 130, 131, 132
    see also neglect
detachment 157
detection 21
detention centres
    juvenile 40
determinations
    case by case 79
developmental psychologists 70, 71
Diamond Valley (Vic) 55
disabled 138, 188
    intellectually 49, 144, 157, 184, 185,
        188
    physically 144
disclosure 24, 36, 40, 42, 51, 52, 70, 71,
    73, 75, 77-8, 146, 152, 158, 160, 161,
    168, 169, 170
discrimination 116
diseases
    sexually transmitted 17, 169
disengagement 81
disobedience 45
'disposal options' 114-15
dispute resolution 184
    alternative 91
doctors 42, 108, 163
domestic violence 65
drug abuse 146, 147, 182
    see also substance abuse

early childhood
    curriculum materials 50
economic rights 177
ecosystem model 185
education
    Aboriginal 14, 15, 17, 18
    non-Aboriginal 17
    protection 41-52
    school 31, 32, 35
    sequential 44

Eltham (Vic) 55
emotional abuse 36, 108, 155, 159, 160
emotional pressures 44
employment
    Aboriginal 17
empowerment 189
    children 43, 47, 63
    families 118, 120
engagement 145, 146, 160
equity 176
essential services
    Aboriginal access to 16
Europe 189
European occupation of Australia 14-15,
    17
evidence 166
    children's 161
    contamination of 167
    uncorroborated 80
expectations 73
exploitation 155, 159, 167
extended families 15, 18, 91, 118, 119, 169
    Aboriginal 15, 18, 91
eyewitnesses
    capabilities 72

facilitators 151-2
failure to thrive 148
false beliefs 75, 81
'false love' phenomenon 134
families 68, 99, 118, 139, 174
    abusive 101, 158
    advocacy in 185
    aide work 54, 59
    at risk 102
    capacity to change 147
    counselling 54, 86, 92, 93, 94, 95, 178
    empowering 118, 120
    extended 15, 18, 91, 118, 119, 169
    functioning of 56, 62, 64, 65
    high risk 55-6, 61, 63, 64, 65, 135,
        136, 137, 140
    low risk 56
    medium risk 56
    powerlessness 166-7
    privacy 174, 175
    removal from 148
    rights 140, 175, 178, 187
    services 53-65
    single parent 65, 132
    socio-economic profiles 55-6, 132
    support 26
family allowances 176

Family and Children's Services Council (Vic) 128, 191
family counsellors 57, 59, 63
family group conferences 119
Family Reconciliation Act (USA) 96
family support workers 57, 59
family team meetings 57
family therapy 57, 115, 117, 168-70
fantasies 170
fathers 55-6, 132, 144, 150
    biological 132
    step 132, 141
fault 44
fear 64, 157
    of adults 43
    of disclosure 73
Federal Rule of Evidence 601 (USA) 79
feelings 44, 46, 47
females
    as offenders 156, 159
Fogarty Report (1989) 96
fondling 159
foster care 93, 94, 144
foster parents 92, 118, 152
friends 25
funding 188
    prioritising 175

Garrett, Barbara 124-5
gender bias 87, 116, 130, 156
genitalia
    examination of 72
    injuries to 157, 158, 159
    names for 45-6
government
    see the State
group therapy 170
guardianship 180, 181
    ad litem 190, 191
    independent 190
    permanent 89
    state 144
    temporary 89
guidelines
    for agencies 171
    practice 190
guilt 82, 83, 160
    protection workers and 167

Hallett, Christine 126
Happiness, Understanding, Giving and Sharing (HUGS) *see* HUGS
Heidelberg (Vic) 55

high risk families 55-6, 60, 63, 64, 65, 135, 136, 137, 140, 144
home placements 92, 93
homelessness 68, 86, 93, 177, 180, 191
    Aboriginals and 16
homicides 131
    rate 129
hope 64
Hospital for Sick Children, London 118
hospitals 103, 143, 144, 145, 147, 148
    paediatric 119-20, 150, 155-62, 163, 166
House of Lords (UK) 183
HUGS 60, 62
human rights 176, 177, 179-80, 185, 186
    children 179-80
husbands
    de facto 131, 132, 133, 135
hyperactivity 157
hypnotic states
    self-induced 156

'I Know That Now' (puppet show) 24
Illinois (USA) 127, 129
illnesses 141-53
inadequate supervision 90
income
    Aboriginals 17
independence 187
independent guardianship 190
Indian Child Welfare Act (North America) 19
Industrial Revolution 178
industrial rights 185
injuries
    non-accidental 162
    physical 156-58
inquiries
    death 122-40
    ministerial 127
    panels 140
    reports 126
Institute of Judicial Administration/American Bar Association Joint Commission on Juvenile Justice Standards 95, 96
institutional rights 176
institutions
    Aboriginals in 17
intellectually disabled 49, 144, 184, 185, 188
Intellectual Disability Services (Vic) 185, 188

interactions
    parent-child 54, 55, 112
interference
    physical 181, 185
intervention 36, 40, 42, 52, 54, 67, 89, 90, 102, 109, 118, 127, 133, 167, 168, 174, 175, 176, 178, 179, 181, 182, 187
    crisis 59, 135
    interdisciplinary 141-53
    state 87, 91, 94, 97, 179, 180, 182, 183, 190
    strategies 93, 114, 164
    therapeutic 167
    token 135
interviews 169-70
    computer assisted 84
    face-to-face 92
intra-familial abuse 130, 131, 132, 133
investigations 21, 52
I.O.D.E. (Intake, Organisation, Demonstrate, Expression) model 48
'irreconcilable differences' 88-90, 96
isolation
    social 54, 60, 137
It's Often Closer to Home Than You Think (booklet) 26

judges 71, 80, 82, 84
juries 71, 79, 80, 82, 84
Juvenile Justice Standards 95, 96

kinship groups 119
knowledge, in decision making 181

land
    Aboriginal guardianship of 15
language
    appropriate 45
lawyers 67-8, 107, 188, 191
learning styles 44
Legal Aid Commission 188
legal processes 166, 170, 171
legal reforms 24, 35, 40
legal rights 148
legal system 52, 67-97
legislation 16, 19, 41-2, 70, 82, 177, 178, 181, 182, 183, 185, 188, 190
    ACT 90
    NSW 90-1
    New Zealand 91, 119
    Vic 88-90
legislative rights 176, 185
Little Learners 60, 62

Liverpool (UK) 105-6
Louisiana (USA) 127
low risk families 56
lying 155
    actual 74-8
    adults' influence 76
    children's understanding of 73-4

'making sense of child protection' practice model 178
males 26, 48, 76, 77, 159, 160
    as offenders 156, 157
    see also de facto husbands; fathers
manslaughter 131
Maori community 119
market research 26-7
marriage breakdown 65
mass media 80, 81, 92, 123, 126, 164, 171, 176, 182
    campaigns 22-40, 43, 51
    monitoring 26
    masturbation 159
Meadow's Syndrome *see* Munchausen Syndrome by Proxy
media *see* mass media
mediation 189
    parent-child 86, 97
medical evidence 70
    see also doctors
medical examinations 157, 159, 162, 168-9
medium risk families 56
meetings
    case planning 187, 188
Melbourne 55, 90, 91
mental health system 40
Minister of Community Services (Vic) 191
Ministry of Housing (Vic) 56
minority groups 137
mistrust of colleagues 167
Monday Mums on Thursday 60
Montcalm, Paul 127, 135-6
moral danger 86, 87
moral rights 176, 177
mothers 55, 60, 62, 110, 132, 133, 135, 147, 150, 168
    behaviour 146
    single 131
multicultural aspects 91
multilingual wall 25
Munchausen Syndrome by Proxy 99, 141-53

case management 145-50
  manifestations 143
  perpetrators 146-7
  strategies and structures 150-3
myths 25, 171-2

nannies 157-8
National Centre on Child Abuse and Neglect (NCCAN) 127
National Committee on Violence Report (1990) 129
National Inquiry into Youth Homelessness 93, 177, 180
National Society for the Prevention of Cruelty to Children (NSPCC) 64, 105
natural rights 176, 179, 180, 181, 185, 186-7
neglect 27, 36, 86, 91, 93, 94, 101, 102, 108, 109, 174, 182, 183, 190
  see also deprivation of necessities
network meetings 118-19
networking 171
New South Wales 23-4, 41, 52, 86, 88, 127
  Aboriginal children removed 19
  'irretrievable breakdown' 90-1
New York (USA) 127
New Zealand 86, 87, 88, 91, 92, 95
  family group conferences 119
  Maori influences 119
  'serious differences' 91
newspaper articles 28
nightmares 156, 157, 160
no fault divorce (child welfare law) 86-97
non-accidental injuries 162
non-natural child fatalities 130, 132
notification 45, 52
  protective 128
  statistics 51
notifiers
  teachers as 41-2, 50
Nottinghamshire (UK) 112
NSW Child Protection Council 41, 42, 43, 51
  Aboriginals and 39
  campaign 24-40
  corporate image 37
  funding 27
NSW Child Sexual Assault Taskforce — Report 37, 41, 70
NSW Teachers' Federation 41
nurses 107
nutrition 143-4

offenders 25-6, 32-3, 35, 49, 67, 83, 156-8, 161, 164-5, 170
  convictions 172
  multiple 159, 160
  power over children 24
  profiles 168, 171-2
  role and sex of 159-60
  self esteem 48
  talking to 34
  workers identify with 168
  young criminal 88
Office of the Director of Public Prosecutions 170
Office of the Public Advocate (Vic) 188, 189
ombudsman 184
  children's 189
  state 190
Ontario (Canada) 131
oppression
  Aboriginal and 16
orders
  custody 180
  statutory 180
  supervision 61, 180
ownership
  Aboriginal concept of 15

paediatricians 67, 102, 107, 115, 146, 151
paedophiles 159
parent-child mediation 86
parent-child relationships 42, 54, 55, 60, 68, 110, 112
parent organisations 45
Parental Guidance Recommendation ratings 25
parenting
  family patterns 57
parents 129, 155, 175, 178
  abusive 133
  behaviour 142
  case decision making 183
  de facto 131
  distress 161
  foster 92, 152
  group therapy 170
  included in decision making 191
  involvement in protection education 45
  natural 131
  rights 45, 93, 95, 109, 120, 174, 176
  single 65, 131, 132

training 54
violent 109
past events
  significance of 134-5
peers
  as offenders 157, 161
penalties 32
  see also capital punishment
perpetrators
  identity of 131, 133
Personal Understanding and Self Help (PUSH) *see* PUSH
physical abuse 36, 108, 109, 123, 133, 155, 157, 159, 161
  see also sexual assault
physical injuries 156-8
physically disabled 144
Piaget, J. 73-4, 81
placements 134, 135, 180
play 59
poisons 142, 144, 148
polarisation 142, 149, 153
police 33, 52, 91, 95, 107, 136, 145, 149, 166
Police Service 166, 170
political rights 176
politicians 32, 37
posters 25, 26, 36, 37, 38, 39
poverty 176
  Aboriginal 16, 17, 18
power 36, 120
  see also relationships
powerlessness 49
practice insights 122-40
practice monitoring 184
pre-school children 60, 154-62, 163
prediction 109, 110, 114, 123
Preston TAFE College (Vic) 61
prevention 21-65
  levels 23
  programs 22-40, 42
  strategies 24-40
Priority Decision System 117
prisons 40
  Aboriginals in 17
problem solving skills 60
procedures 24
programs 22-40, 182
  advocacy 184-91
  Alys Key Family Care Demonstration Project 53-65
  centre based 54
  community visitors 184, 188
  development 190
  documentation 191
  funding 52
  group 53-65
  guidelines 183
  home based 54
  prevention 41
  training 24, 35, 39
  treatment 22
  see also campaigns
promotion 23
prosecution 83, 85
prosecutors 171
Protection of Children Act 1889 (UK) 178
'Protective Behaviours Program' 24, 37
protective staff
  as advocates 184-7
  limitations as advocates 186-7
psychiatrists 108, 115
psychiatry 102, 118
psychologists 84, 108
  developmental 70, 71
public awareness 24
punishment 75, 81, 83
  see also capital punishment
PUSH 60

Queensland 24, 117
Queensland Centre for the Prevention of Child Abuse 24
questioning (strategy) 49
questionnaires 105, 152, 164, 165
  telephone 26-7

racism
  Aboriginals and 17
radio commercials 25, 26, 36, 37, 38
rationality 181
Read, Peter
  The Stolen Generation 19
record systems
  client 138
reforms
  legal 24
regression 156, 160
rejection
  by families 99
relationships
  adult-child 24, 41, 42, 43, 44, 57, 76, 82, 168
  men and women 24
  parent-child 42, 60, 68, 110
relatives 25, 129, 159, 160

Report of the NSW Child Sexual Assault Task-force 37, 41, 70
Report of the Panel of Inquiry into the Circumstances of the Death of Jasmine Beckford 123, 125, 135
reporting of offences 34-5, 71, 72, 73, 77
   see also disclosure
rescue model 53
research 21-2, 23, 24, 42, 51, 69, 70, 71, 109, 137
   psychological 68
resistance 64
respite care 60
responsibilities
   adult 173-91
   children's 46
retaliation 76
rights 190, 191
   Aboriginals 19
   adolescents 187, 188
   adults 67
   children's 44, 46, 47, 52, 67, 109, 146, 173-91
   civil 176, 179
   cultural 177
   definition 176
   economic 177
   families 140, 178, 182-3, 187
   human 176, 177, 179-80, 185, 186
   industrial 185
   institutional 176
   legal 148
   legislative 176, 185
   limitations 177
   moral 176, 177
   natural 176, 179, 180, 181, 185, 186-7
   of others 48
   parent's 45, 93, 94, 109, 120, 146, 174, 176
   political 176
   social 177
   victims 67
risky shift 105
ritual abuse 156, 159-60
Rochdale NSPCC (UK) 64
roleplays 49
roles
   conflict in 187
   expectations 165
   workers' 166-7, 172
Royal Commission on Family and Child Law in British Columbia 89

Ruddock, Martin 124
running away 87

St Louis (USA) 127
salt
   as a poison 144
Salvation Army 191
Save the Children Fund 189
school refusal 156, 160
schools 154
   as settings for abuse 157
   education in 31, 32, 35
   see also curriculum
screening
   checklist 109-10
Secretariat for National Aboriginal and Islander Child Care (SNAICC) 14
secrets 156
self determination 174
self esteem 44, 47, 48, 60
   Aboriginal 17
   offenders 48
   parents' 60
self-help 54, 60
sentences 35
'serious differences' (NZ) 91
'serious incompatability' (ACT) 90, 97
service models 61, 62
service user support groups 189
services 24, 35, 40
   counselling 39, 52, 90, 91, 92
sexual activity 182
sexual assault 23-40, 41-52, 67, 69, 85, 93, 108, 141, 155, 157, 158, 159, 161
   community knowledge 30-5
   group 99, 163-72
   incidence 35
   mistrust of colleagues 167-8
   numbers of cases 165
   raw nature of material 165-6
   supervision 167, 171, 172
   unclear roles of staff 166-7, 172
sexuality 48
sexually transmitted diseases 169
   Aboriginals 17
shock 157
siblings 60, 144, 161, 169
single mothers 131
single parents 65, 131, 132
Sixth International Congress on Child Abuse and Neglect (Sydney: 1986) 27
sleep
   alone 161

difficulty with 161
disturbances 156, 157, 160
smothering 142, 144
see also asphyxiation
SNAICC *see* Secretariat for National Aboriginal and Islander Child Care (SNAICC)
social cognitive theory 71, 73, 78
social rights 177
Social Welfare Act 1970 (Vic) 88-9
social workers 33, 54, 67, 91, 92, 93, 102, 107, 115, 125, 135, 138, 140, 143, 149, 163, 190
South Australia 184, 188
Standards Relating to Non-criminal Misbehaviour 95
the State 24, 32, 35, 36, 39, 40, 85, 91, 119, 120, 175
   guardianship 144
   intervention 87, 91, 94, 97, 179, 180, 182, 183
   programs 17, 18
   recognition of Aboriginal work 18
state wards 61, 88, 92, 94, 97
statistics
   notification 51
status
   offences 87-8
   statutory 61
statutory orders 180
statutory status 61
statutory supervision 126
stepfathers 132, 141
Stevenson, Olive 126
stickers 25, 26
stories
   unfinished 48
stranger danger 25, 32
strangers 157, 159, 160
strategies 41-52
   effectiveness 51-2
   intervention 164
   see also campaigns
street kids 93
stress 54, 103, 106
student welfare 45, 50
students' groups 61
substance abuse 65
suggestibility 72
suicides 131, 135, 182
supervision
   in case management 167, 171, 172
   inadequate 90

orders 61, 180
statutory 126
Supreme Court of the USA 83
Surrey (UK) 109
surveys 31
Suspected Child Abuse and Neglect (SCAN) Team 18
Sydney 26-7, 156-62
systems
   client record 138
   concepts 117
   debriefing 138

taboos 37
TALK 60, 62
Talk and Action for Living with Kids (TALK) *see* TALK
Tardieu, Ambrose Auguste 155
teachers 48, 49, 50, 80, 155
   as notifiers of sexual abuse 41, 43, 50
   as offenders 156, 159
   trainee 157
   training 50-1, 52
   see also education
teacher's aides 157
team meetings
   family 57
team-work 57-65, 99-172
   chairperson 113, 115
   communications 136, 139, 152
   decision making 99-172
   group sexual assault effects workers 164-8
   intra-group dynamics 165
   morale 106
   multidisciplinary 99, 102-3, 139
   problems 104-7, 145, 149, 171
   roles and responsibilities 136-7
   training 100
   trust 152
telephone questionnaires 26-7
television
   closed circuit 82, 83
television commercials 25, 26, 28, 34-5, 36, 37
   award 38
   believability 29
   comprehension 29-30
   recall 28-9
testifying 161
   children's competency to 70-3
testimonies 71

testing
    competence 82
Texas (USA) 129, 131
therapy 163, 168-70
toileting regression 156, 157, 160
token intervention 135
Townsville (Qld) 18
training 52, 100, 122, 138, 186
    parents 54
    programs 24, 35, 39, 40
    teachers 50-1, 52
    workers' 170
trauma 84
treatment programs 22
truancy 87
trust 44
trustworthiness 69, 155
truthfulness
    actual 74-8
    children's understanding of 73-4

uncontrollable children 86, 87, 88, 89
uncorroborated evidence 80
unfinished stories 48
United Kingdom 103-4, 105, 108, 117, 118, 119, 120, 124-5, 178, 183, 189, 190, 191
United Nations Convention on the Rights of the Child 173, 177, 178
United States of America 53-4, 80, 83, 84, 87, 95, 103, 110, 120, 127, 155, 159, 179, 184
    Federal Rule of Evidence 601
    Supreme Court 83
    team work 106-7

values 44, 45, 48-9, 52
values inquiry 48

values judging 49
verbal abuse 36
victimization 83, 84
Victoria 18, 53-65, 86, 88, 91-2, 97, 127, 140, 177
    Alys Key Family Care Demonstration Project 53-65
    deaths 122-40
    irreconcilable differences 88-90
    see also Community Services Victoria
Victorian Aboriginal Child Care Agency 18
videos 24, 45, 82
violence
    domestic 65
voir dire 79-80
volunteer advocates 188, 189
volunteers 54, 57, 60

wards
    state 61, 88, 92, 94
wardship
    voluntary 97
Washington State (USA) 96
Westmead Hospital (Sydney) 115
Where to Get Help (booklet) 26
witnesses 146
    children as 67, 68, 69-85
    contamination of 170
    sole 81
working contracts 59, 62, 63

youth
    at risk 96
Youth Advocate 90
Youth Advocacy Service (Vic) 191
youth refuges 93
youth workers 93